Project Life Cycle Economics

Project Life Cycle Economics

Cost Estimation, Management and Effectiveness in Construction Projects

Edited by

MASSIMO PICA

Foreword by

RUSSELL D. ARCHIBALD

Routledge
Taylor & Francis Group

LONDON AND NEW YORK

First published in paperback 2024

First published 2015 by Gower Publishing

Published 2016 by Routledge
4 Park Square, Milton Park, Abingdon, Oxon OX14 4RN

and by Routledge
605 Third Avenue, New York, NY 10158

Routledge is an imprint of the Taylor & Francis Group, an informa business

Publisher's Note
The publisher has gone to great lengths to ensure the quality of this reprint but points out that some imperfections in the original copies may be apparent.

British Library Cataloguing in Publication Data
A catalogue record for this book is available from the British Library

Library of Congress Cataloging-in-Publication Data
Pica, Massimo.
  Project life cycle economics : cost estimation, management and effectiveness in construction projects / by Massimo Pica.
    pages cm
  Includes bibliographical references and index.
  ISBN 978-1-4724-1964-4 (hbk) -- ISBN 978-1-4724-1965-1 (ebook) -- ISBN 978-1-4724-1966-8 (epub) 1. Construction industry. 2. Project management. 3. Product life cycle. I. Title.
  HD9715.A2P477 2015
  624.068′4--dc23
                    2014041194

ISBN: 978-1-4724-1964-4 (hbk)
ISBN: 978-1-03-283706-2 (pbk)
ISBN: 978-1-315-60238-7 (ebk)

DOI: 10.4324/9781315602387

Contents

**PART I   FUNDAMENTALS OF PROJECT LIFE CYCLE ECONOMICS:
INTRODUCTION TO PART I**

List of Figures

List of Tables

About the Editor

Massimo Pica is a registered engineer in Rome, Italy. After graduating in Chemical Engineering from the Sapienza University of Rome, he spent more than 30 years of his career in the Corps of Professional Engineers of the Italian Army and retired in 2009 as a one-star General. He holds professional qualifications in Systems Engineering and Cost Management. His experiences include running postgraduate engineering courses for about 30 years. He participated in national, international and NATO acquisition programmes and working groups specializing in Life Cycle Cost Management. He is one of the authors of the two NATO publications *RTO TR-SAS-054 – Methods and Models for Life Cycle Costing* and *RTO TR-SAS-069 – Code of Practice for Life Cycle Costing*, as well as being the Italian contributor to the NATO publications *ALCCP-1 – NATO Guidance on Life Cycle Costs* and *RTO TR-SAS-076 – NATO Independent Cost Estimating and the Role of Life Cycle Cost Analysis in Managing the Defence Enterprise*. He also contributed to the updated Italian version of the INCOSE *Systems Engineering Handbook* and to the drafting process of PMBOK® Guide. He is the author of the book *Systems Lifecycle Cost-Effectiveness*, published by Gower in 2014, and of a number of articles in the Italian quarterly magazine *Il Project Manager* and other specialist online journals. He is a regular speaker at national and international conferences and is a member of the International Cost Estimating and Analysis Association (ICEAA) and the European Committee of Construction Economists (CEEC), as well as of the Italian affiliation of the European Federation of Chemical Engineering (EFCE). He has been elected for the period 2015–17 as Member of the Board at AICE, the Italian Association belonging to the International Cost Engineering Council (ICEC).

About the Contributors

Massimiliano Arena is a Project and Programme Manager, with more than 10 years' experience in the industrial and plant engineering sector, particularly the automotive field, and oil and gas and steel-making plants in technical and management roles, always in an international context. He has built up considerable experience in general Project Management, total cost management, contract and claim management, engineering management, risk management and commercial negotiations. He is currently managing a project portfolio involving many Project Management teams in different countries, as well as having to answer to the top management of the company for his Profit and Loss responsibility and acting as an official speaker to clients' management. He is a Certified Senior Project Manager (International Project Management Association) and a Certified Cost Engineer accredited by the International Cost Engineering Council (ICEC); he is also Vice-Chairman of the AICE, the Italian affiliation of the ICEC.

Barbara Boccasini, after her high school certificate from the *Lycée International de St. Germain en Laye* (Paris, France), graduated in Management and Production Engineering. Her experiences include process optimization and SoW/WP drafting at MBDA Customer Support department; KPI rationalization and quick win proposals at BNL-BNP Paribas PMO department; railway signalling system verification and validation at Ansaldo (Madrid); and aerospace quality certifications and internal auditing at Avio (Colleferro, Rome area). She is a financial reporter at the CFO department of Thales Alenia Space in Rome and is involved in an international aerospace project as Italian project director.

David Churcher has been Director and Principal Consultant at Hitherwood Consulting for over seven years. For over 12 years, he has been Principal Consultant at the Sustainable Buildings Group of BSRIA, being specifically responsible for developing practical guidance on life cycle costing (LCC), design activities and deliverables for M&E services and supply-chain relationships. He has delivered training on life cycle costing since 2007 and helps contractors, client organizations, design consultants and product manufacturers understand and implement LCC techniques, including helping new-build projects gain BREEAM credits. He is a UK expert on the Working

Group updating ISO 15686 Part 5 (*Service Life Planning – Life Cycle Costing*). His academic background includes a BSc (Hons) in Civil Engineering – First Class Honours from City University, London and a MBA from the Open University.

Fabrizio Colista is a Project and Programme Manager, and worked for over 14 years in logistics, warehousing and supply chain trade. He is currently in charge of the Project Management Office for business development of tailor-made logistics and integrated solutions in Poste Italiane Group and was formerly in charge of marketing management of the business innovative technological solutions development. He is a graduate in Mechanical Engineering from University of Rome Tor Vergata. His professional qualifications include: PMP® certification, PMI® membership, PM_L7 Project Management Professional Level 7 (ASSIREP) and Accredited Project Management Trainer (*Istituto Italiano di Project Management* – ISIPM). He is also active in Project Management research through a new methodological approach called Project Management and Empowerment (PME) which aims to provide a different view of 'soft skills'.

Federico Minelle has for 20 years been a professor of Business Information Systems in the Computer Science Department of the Sapienza University of Rome, where he also teaches at the University Master Course in ICT Governance and Audit. A graduate in physics, for more than 40 years he has consulted on business organization, information systems and Project Management. Previously as a partner at Accenture and then as a senior partner at the Italian consultancy firm P.R.S. Planning, Ricerche e Studi, he managed and monitored large ICT innovation projects, both in engineering and construction and government industries. He is an honorary member of the ISIPM; he is also editor of the Italian specialist magazine *Il Project Manager*. He co-authored two books on strategies and management of engineering and construction business edited by Industry Associations, while more recently he contributed to the *Guidelines for Quality ICT Procurement* edited by the Government Agency for ICT. He is an author of several articles and is a speaker at seminars on cost/benefit analysis for ICT government projects.

Francesca Montanari graduated in Telecommunications Engineering at the Sapienza University of Rome. She is now Product Development Specialist at Fiat Purchasing in Turin. From 2007 to 2010, she was involved in a cooperative technological innovation project launched by the United Nations to provide technical and financial support for the Iraqi Government. Subsequently she worked for Invitalia as Intranet Project Planner; for CPI Progetti as Junior Analyst in web application development and as Training Area Coordinator; for RAI Trade, MBDA and Altran Italia as Project Management Consultant; and for

Alstom Transport as Engineering Project Planner. Her certifications include: PMP® (Project Management Professional), PRINCE2 Foundation, EUCIP Core Level and ITILv3 Foundation.

Tommaso Panetti has spent more than 12 years in the Information Technology sector following his academic background at the Sapienza University of Rome (Degree in Software Engineering; University Certification in Software Engineering and Automation; University Certification as Software Specialist at the *Scuola Diretta a Fini Speciali in Informatica*). He is Certified Architect in the Cap Gemini University of Béhoust, France. He has held different main positions in IT applications and Project Management, first at Cap Gemini Ernst & Young, then at Spectrum Graphics and finally at mondoesa;lazio (company group: ESA Software/24OreSoftware a Team System Company), where, as Senior Project Manager and in charge of the PMO, he has introduced and consolidated the Project Management culture. His certifications include PMP® (Project Management Professional) and ITILv3 Foundation.

Carmine Russo is in charge of the Project Office at the Agriculture Division of the Auselda AED Group. His international experience (in Europe and the USA) since 1980 covers a wide variety of business applications in the banking, industrial and agriculture sectors, especially the following: Bids, Business Case, Project Management, Programme Management, Monitoring and Control, Software Metrics, Quality Control, FP Analysis and Audits, and Budget Control.

Claudia Spagnuolo is Member of the Board at the ISIPM. Her main experiences are in the areas of Project Management, Publishing, Web Projects and Communication. She is an APMG Accredited Trainer for PRINCE2 and P3O, an IT Security Consultant with experience in identity and Access Governance projects, and an editor and technical writer. Her certifications include: DSDM Atern Agile Approach Certified (Agile Project Management and Delivery); PRINCE2 Practitioner Certified; ISO 27001 Certified – IT Security Techniques – Information Security Management Systems; ITIL® v3 Certified for IT Service Management and IT Service Operation.

Franco Stolfi has consulted for more than 30 years in Business Organization, Information Systems and ICT Project/Service Quality Management. Previously as Director of ICT SMEs and currently as partner of the Italian consulting firm P.R.S. Planning, Ricerche e Studi (delivering professional services in IT monitoring and training), he manages and monitors large ICT innovation projects, both in the government and business sectors. A graduate in Computer Science, he is Assistant Professor in Business Information Systems in Computer

Science at the Sapienza University of Rome, where he also teaches on the University Master Course in ICT Governance and Audit and at a number of seminars to government personnel. He co-authored papers about the quality of websites of Italian public administration bodies, while more recently he contributed to the *Guidelines for Quality ICT Procurement* edited by the Government Agency for ICT. He is a certified PRINCE2 V2 practitioner, lead auditor for IT service management ISO-IEC 20000–1, ITIL V3 and lead auditor ISO/9001 for quality service evaluation. He is a member of the ISIPM and the Information System Auditing and Control Association (ISACA).

Russell D. Archibald (PhD (Hon) in *Strategy, Programme, and Project Management*; MSc and BS Mechanical Engineering; PMI Fellow, Founding Trustee and PMP; Honorary Fellow APM/IPMA; member of the Board of IPMA/ INTERNET 1974–83). In his career of nearly 70 years, he has held engineering and executive positions in aerospace (military pilot, aircraft and missile system designer, and project controls manager during WWII and the Korean conflict), oil and gas, telecommunications, and automotive industries in the USA, France, Mexico and Venezuela. Since 1982 he has consulted to companies, agencies and development banks in 16 countries on four continents; presented expert witness testimony in various USA courts regarding the prudency of the design and construction of nuclear power plants and oil pipelines, and regarding project management information systems; and has taught project management principles and practices to thousands of managers and specialists around the world. He is co-author with Shane Archibald of *Leading and Managing Innovation* (2013, also published in Italian and Portuguese); author of *Managing High-Technology Programs and Projects* (3rd edition, 2003, also published in Russian, Italian, and Chinese); plus 15 chapters in 11 other books and 162 papers and presentations on project management in professional journals and congresses. See http://russarchibald.com

Foreword

RUSSELL D. ARCHIBALD

As indicated by its title, this book combines project life cycles (some prefer to say project life spans) with economics and cost estimation, management and effectiveness, for the general project category of engineering, procurement and construction (EPC) of physical facilities. Those facilities are generally classified as civil, commercial, communications, energy, environmental, high-rise, industrial, residential, ships and transportation. In addition to EPC, facilities projects can also include maintenance and modification, decommissioning and demolition. Generic project life cycle models[1] provide a top-level picture of the basic phases of any project, but to fully understand each of the many kinds of facilities projects, it is necessary to develop much more detailed life cycle models for each project category and sub-category. In these detailed models the generic phases are broken down to include the sub-phases required to accommodate each specific project's category and each project's size, scope, degree of innovation, complexity and risk. These detailed life cycle models provide fundamental tools not only for excellent cost estimation, management and effectiveness, but also:

- enable all individuals concerned with creating, planning, authorizing and executing projects to understand the processes to be followed throughout the life of the project and its product;

- capture and document the best experiences ('lessons learned') within the organization so that the processes within each project phase and sub-phase can be improved continually, integrated with the other related project phases and applied in future similar projects;

- enable all the project roles and responsibilities and the project planning, time and cost estimating, scheduling, monitoring and control methods and tools to be appropriately related to the

---

1   See Figure 3.1 in Chapter 3 for an example of a generic six-phase comprehensive project life cycle model.

overall project life cycle management process – this includes most importantly assigning qualified persons to the roles of Project Executive Sponsor and Project Manager at the proper points in the project life cycle;

- enable the effective implementation of project management software application packages that are properly integrated with all appropriate corporate information systems.

In other words, a well-documented project life cycle model enables us to apply *systems thinking* to creating, planning, authorizing, scheduling and managing the project through all of its phases, and to evaluating both the success and the value of both the project and the results or products that the project has produced. This *systems thinking* is of greatest benefit to the project owner, key stakeholders, the ultimate user of the project results and the social beneficiaries (positive and negative) of those results – whether it is a new process plant, a highway, a new business process or system, or a new product. It may not be of similar interest to a project manager or an organization that only holds responsibility for one phase, or one aspect of one phase, of the entire project. Unless a well-documented, integrated and understandable picture of the overall life cycle process – the model – for each project category/sub-category exists and is properly used, it will be difficult to achieve the full benefits of modern, systematic project management.

This book provides an excellent overview in Part I of the key aspects of the project management discipline, with emphasis on the economic considerations and cost management. Part II provides specific, very useful discussions, processes and methods regarding project cost and value throughout the project life cycle phases of engineering, procurement and construction projects. The four appendices present useful comparative analyses of two widely used project management standards as well as proven methods for improving decision making and project evaluation. Editor and co-author Massimo Pica has effectively integrated the chapters written by his 10 experienced and well-qualified co-authors with the 10 chapters and the other sections written by him, creating a valuable, unique and welcome contribution to the project management literature regarding projects to create physical facilities of all kinds.

Preface
The Right Policy for the Life Cycle of Projects

MASSIMO PICA

> *A good navigator does not suffice to a ship if on-board instruments are not in a good order to assist him.*
>
> Francesco Guicciardini (Florence, 1483–1540)
> – 'Political and Civil Memories'

The meaning of this historical sentence, in the current project management language, can be seen to refer to the problems that may arise from the adoption of project management practices which are thereafter found inadequate to the characteristics of the project organization, whereas they were intended for use by the project manager to improve process performance and cost-effectiveness in projects.

As part of project management policies, significant follow-up benefits in an organization, in terms of performance and cost-effectiveness through the life cycle of projects, can also derive from an efficient adoption of software tools or – more generally – some modelling technique, provided that the selected tool/technique is really appropriate to the characteristics of the organization. If this is not true, negative consequences will inevitably result, so that – as a minimum – the new tool will be discarded and all revenues expected from this investment will turn into costs, which are sometimes quite far from being negligible. The impact could also be even more negative if the organization – assumed as being in itself less mature in managing projects – sees this new software tool as a solution to enable the development of project management practices; in this case, it is likely that the deficiencies of the tool will be considered as deficiencies of the method. This may eventually lead to discontinuing both the software tool *and* the ensuing project management practices; this situation might even deteriorate after the software tool is introduced, as a result of any attempt to select different options for the software tool. This choice is, indeed, highly critical, and moreover complex in a number of cases requiring special attention: complexity essentially derives from the extreme multiplicity of available solutions and from the large number of different variables that have to be considered.

On the other hand, as will be noted again in this volume, the fact that 'all significant innovations are achieved through projects' has been emphasized by Russell D. Archibald and Shane C. Archibald, two worldwide recognized experts in the project management field, in their book *Leading & Managing Innovation*. This, in turn, reflects the inscription on the Nobel Medal for Physics and Chemistry:

> *Inventas vitam juvat excoluisse per artes*

Which means 'those who enhanced life on earth by the art of their inventions', a quotation taken from the poem *Aeneid*, a masterpiece of Latin literature written near the end of the first century BC by Publius Vergilius Maro.

List of Abbreviations

AACE International	Association for the Advancement of Cost Engineering International
AC	Actual Costs
ACostE	Association of Cost Engineers
ACWP	Actual Cost of Work Performed
AHP	Analytic Hierarchy Process
ANSI	American National Standards Institute
AR	Acceptance Review
ASHRAE	American Society of Heating, Refrigerating and Air-Conditioning Engineers
ATB	Amount to be Booked
BAC	Budget at Completion
BAFO	Best and Final Offer
BCP	Baseline Cost Plan
BCWP	Budgeted Cost of Work Performed
BOOT	Build – Own – Operate – Transfer
BOQ	Bill of Quantities
BREEAM	Building Research Establishment Environmental Assessment Methodology
BS	British Standard
BSRIA	Building Services Research and Information Association
C	Cost of project execution
C	Total project cost
C_0	Fixed project cost
CAIRO	Consulted, Accountable, Informed, Responsible, Omitted
CBA	Cost-Benefit Analyses
CBS	Cost Breakdown Structure
C_c	Crash Cost
CCB	Configuration Control Board
CCM	Critical Chain Method
CCSCS	Contractor Cost – Schedule Control System
C_{dn}	Project direct costs in year n
CDR	Critical Design Review
CE	Construction Economics

CEN	European Standardization Committee
CI	Consistency Index
CIBSE	Chartered Institution of Building Services Engineers
C_{in}	Project indirect costs in year n
C_n	Normal Cost
CO	Change Order
CPI	Cost Performance Index
CPM	Critical Path Method
CR	Change Request
CR	Consistency Ratio
CSCW	Computer Supported Cooperative Work
CSF	Critical Success Factor
D	Distance between the actual and the optimal conditions of construction functionality
DACI	Driver, Accountable, Consulted, Informed
DBB	Design Bid Build
DBFOM	Design Build Finance Operate Maintain
DP	Down Payment
DUR	Duration
EAC	Estimate at Completion
EBIT	Earnings Before Interests and Taxes
ECM	Ecodesign Checklist Method
ECSS	European Cooperation for Space Standardization
EFT	Earliest Finish Time
EIA	Environmental Impact Assessment
ELR	End-of-Life Review
EMAT	Economically Most Advantageous Tender
EPC	Engineering, Procurement and Construction
EPCC	Engineering, Procurement, Construction and Commissioning
ES	Early Start
EST	Earliest Start Time
ETC	Estimate to Completion
EV	Earned Value
EWC	Elementary Work Cell
F	Expected output when using an amount R of resources
F'	Actual output when using an amount R' of resources
FF	Finish to Finish
FMEA	Failure Modes and Effects Analysis
FRR	Flight Readiness Review
FS	Finish to Start

GAAP	Generally Accepted Accounting Principles
i	Discount factor
I	Monetary value impact of a risk R
IASB	International Accounting Standards Board
IBR	Integrated Baseline Review
ICB	IPMA Competence Baseline
ICT	Information and Communications Technology
IEC	International Electrotechnical Commission
IFRS	International Financial Reporting Standards
IPD	Integrated Project Delivery
IPMA	International Project Management Association
IRR	Internal Rate of Return
ISIPM	Italian Institute of Project Management
ISO	International Organization for Standardization
ITIL	Information Technology Infrastructure Library
JOC	Job Order Contracting
KPI	Key Performance Indicator
LBMS	Location-Based Management System
LBS	Location Breakdown Structure
LCA	Life Cycle Assessment
LCC	Life Cycle Cost
LCD	Life Cycle Design
LCI	Life Cycle Inventory
LCM	Life Cycle Management
LEED	Leadership in Energy and Environmental Design
LFT	Latest Finish Time
LOB	Line of Balance
LST	Latest Start Time
MADM	Multi-Attribute Decision Methods
MCR	Mission Closeout Review
MDR	Mission Definition Review
MoSCoW	Must, should, could, won't have this time
N	Project duration in years
NCC	Non-conformance Cost
NPV	Net Present Value
OBS	Organization Breakdown Structure
P	Probability that an event takes place
p	Quantity related project unit cost
P3O®	Portfolio, Programme and Project Offices
PBS	Product Breakdown Structure
PDCA	Plan-Do-Check-Act

PDM	Precedence Diagramming Method
PDP	Product/Project Development Process
PDR	Preliminary Design Review
PDS	Product/Project Development Strategies
PERT	Programme Evaluation and Review Technique
PFI	Private Finance Initiative
PILOT	Product Investigation, Learning and Optimization Tool
PLC	Project Life Cycle/Product Life Cycle
PMB	Performance Measurement Baseline
PMBOK	Project Management Body of Knowledge
PMI®	Project Management Institute
PMIS	Project Management Information System
PMO	Project Management Office
PoC	Percentage of Completion
PoC*	Percentage of Completion after contract CO formalization
PPP	Public–Private Partnership
PR	Progress Report
PRINCE	Projects IN Controlled Environment
PRR	Preliminary Requirements Review
PSA	Property Services Agency
PSC	Public Sector Comparator
Q	Quantity in project cost calculation
QR	Qualification Review
R	Owner's revenue 'after the project'
r	Return on Project
R	Risk (the product of I times P)
R_0	Owner's revenue 'without the project'
RACI	Responsible, Accountable, Consulted, Informed
RACI-VS	Responsible, Accountable, Consulted, Informed – Verification and Support
RAM	Responsibility Assignment Matrix
RASCI	Responsible, Accountable, Support, Consulted, Informed
RBS	Resource Breakdown Structure
RCI	Random Consistency Index
RI	Random Index
RICS	Royal Institute of Chartered Surveyors
ROI	Return on Investment
ROM	Rough Order of Magnitude
ROR	Rate of Return
S	Scope change
s	Time-related project unit cost

SCAF	Society of Cost Analysis and Forecasting
SF	Start to Finish
SoC	Stage of Completion
SPI	Schedule Performance Index
SRR	System Requirements Review
SS	Start to Start
SWOT	Strengths, Weaknesses, Opportunities, Threats
T	Variable duration in project cost calculation
T_c	Crash Time
T_n	Normal Time
T_{pb}	Project payback period
TCPI	To-Complete Cost Performance Index
V	Property value after a project
V_m	Market value of a property 'after the project'
V_{m0}	Market value of a property 'without the project'
V_0	Property value before a project
VfM	Value for Money
VIP	Value Improving Practice
WBE	Work Breakdown Element
WBS	Work Breakdown Structure
WLC	Whole Life Cost
WP	Work Package
WT	Work Team

LIST OF ABBREVIATIONS

PART I
Fundamentals of Project Life Cycle Economics: Introduction to Part I

Decision makers will normally approve a project, or a bid, at a certain (risk-adjusted) confidence level in line with organization policy and procedures, and with information provided by their analysts on the so-called 'risk pot' incorporated at that confidence level. Sound financial decision-making processes therefore need to be informed by a good understanding of the impact of risk on both schedule and cost. By and large, analysts are faced with a number of challenges:

- quantitative modelling is often conducted independently on project schedule and cost;

- mixed sources of data are in use at differing maturities, ranging from estimates to firm prices already incorporating at least some risk;

- differing use of terminology for 'risk', 'uncertainty' and 'variability';

- a lack of statistical knowledge in decision makers and in stakeholders providing the input data to the quantitative modelling.

More generally, with reference to the overall project life cycle policies, for example, it has been recently pointed out by the British-established, not-for-profit Society of Cost Analysis and Forecasting (SCAF) that, with frequent headlines on the overspend and overrun of major projects, it is critical that budgets are set and reviewed using robust models and that rich analysis information is provided to decision makers.

Effective Project Management efforts are required to enable 'organizations to accomplish ... the identification and management of project activities both at the early phases of a project and throughout its lifecycle', as stated in BS 6079–1.[1]

In this context, the following statement by Arthur Griffiths, the former Chairman of the SCAF, is also applicable:

> *The task of developing and delivering capital intensive complex engineering projects has probably never been more difficult for engineers and managers particularly in the areas of mitigating potential life cycle cost growth while achieving cost-effective system optimization. With political pressure to minimize expenditure and the drive for value for money with shrinking resources it is essential that people involved today in the delivery of complex projects understand the wide range of often conflicting issues and interests which affect project acquisition.*[2]

In conclusion, as will be seen in more detail in Part II, recurring assertions of project specialists have pointed out the inefficiencies in project organizations leading to delays in bringing projects to successful completion, frequent occurrences of contract claims and subsequent project variants, whereas these shortcomings could have been substantially reduced by optimizing the accurate application of such mechanisms as project verifications and validations, which can be – respectively – intended to make evaluations to assure or confirm that the conditions imposed on project outputs are satisfied and that those outputs comply with the specified requirements.

---

1   BS 6079–1:2010. Project Management – 1: Principles and Guidelines for the Management of Projects. ã BSI 2010.
2   Pica, M., *Systems Lifecycle Cost-Effectiveness*. Farnham: Gower Publishing.

Chapter 1

The Essence of Project Management and its Challenges

MASSIMO PICA

Applicability of Project Management to Specific Projects

It is canonically assumed that every project is an individual event that is not repeatable: if two projects have the same scope or the same objectives, nevertheless the variable influence from environmental, organizational and management factors will make them at best similar, but never identical.

There are, however, two definite connotations in common to all projects: the degree of standardization of activities and processes (which is related to the influencing factors mentioned above) and the degree of management or organizational complexity (which influences the effort required to manage, organize and drive the influencing factors). 'Activity' can be defined (with reference to the PMBOK® Guide) as a component of work executed in a project, whereas 'Process' (from PRINCE2®) is a structured set of activities aimed at a specific objective).

These two 'dimensions' (Figure 1.1) simultaneously define the applicability of Project Management to specific projects. Four situations emerge from this figure: two of them support the Project Management applicability, one is against it and the fourth one appears to be ambiguous.

Quadrant 1 reflects those projects in which the peculiar nature of work (low degree of standardization, high degree of complexity) requires an intensive use of resources.

Quadrant 3 refers to the same categories of projects as in Quadrant 1, but with a lower degree of complexity.

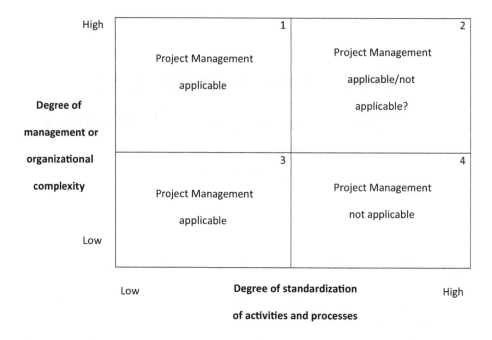

Figure 1.1   Applicability matrix of Project Management in projects

Quadrant 4 collects projects presenting a high degree of standardization of activities and a low degree of complexity. Under these circumstances, the implementation of a Project Management system is not advisable or economically feasible with respect to simple or routinely fashioned activities. The situation in Quadrant 2 will no longer be ambiguous if the level of technology is added as a 'third dimension' (Figure 1.2).

A low technological level of processes and/or activities means that the implementation of a Project Management system is not required, due to the scarcity of non-controllable elements inherent in most cases; therefore, more traditional planning and control systems would be effective enough as part of the corporate governance system instead of the more advanced planning and control system portrayed by current Project Management practices. In the case of a high technological level, on the other hand, the adoption of an existing Project Management system appears to be necessary.

Concisely, whenever a project is envisaged, the feasibility of an advanced Project Management approach depends on the degree of standardization of activities and processes (low to high) and of management or organizational complexity (also low to high). This determines the quadrant in which the project

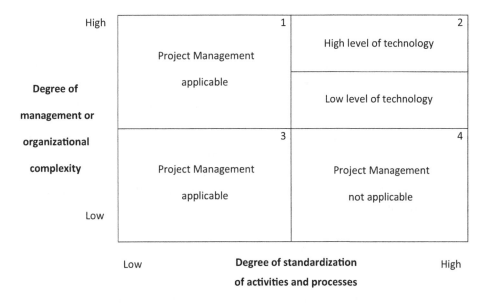

Figure 1.2   Applicability matrix of Project Management in projects: The level of technology is added in Quadrant 2

will be located; in Quadrant 2 projects, an assessment of the technological level will also be required.

Projects, Their Constraints and Challenges

There is a difference in concept between a project and its final output. This can be a new product, a new facility, an ICT system, a new organization, a collection of documents, or any other tangible or intangible end product.

The project is the process by which a new final outcome is obtained. Kerzner (2009) adopts the following definition:

A project can be considered to be any series of activities and tasks that:

- *Have a specific objective to be completed within certain specifications;*
- *Have defined start and end dates;*
- *Have funding limits (if applicable);*
- *Consume human and nonhuman resources money, people, equipment);*
- *Are multifunctional (cut across several functional lines).*

From this definition and other similar and numerous descriptions in the specific literature, the objectives of a project can be identified in terms of final results (for example, products or services) obtained in a certain timeframe and in line with cost and quality standard constraints. Project duration, expected costs and quality of project outputs are subject to a careful planning and checking process; these are the primary elements of projects. These are also interdependent constraints, acting in such a way that if one of them is optimized, the remaining two are adversely influenced; in fact, if a compressed schedule is envisaged, costs will tend to increase and quality will tend to decrease. The best overall result can be achieved by a careful and balanced view of all the aforementioned project variables.

In a certain project, the degree of complexity can be measured on the basis of human, material and financial resources expended, of the resulting degree of coordination and of the degree of involvement of key decision makers of the organization, and a new dimension can be envisaged: the strategic relevance of the project as a determinant for its success. This is portrayed in a new four-quadrant representation with respect to the dimension of project complexity (Figure 1.3).

Projects lying in the first quadrant belong to an area of limited strategic relevance, which means that their effects on the organization breakthrough are

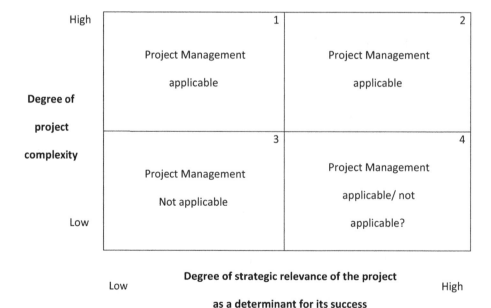

Figure 1.3   Matrix of Project Management applicability to projects

minimal. At the same time, these projects show a high degree of complexity, therefore requiring that Project Management systems be applied; this derives from the massive resource utilization and from the considerable involvement of managers, implying advanced planning and control arrangements for a convenient level of project governance.

As far as challenges in Project Management are concerned, it should be emphasized first that the average level of project performance has been repeatedly reported as being far from satisfactory and that several elements have to be considered to bring about a possible improvement:

- enhancement of top management support;

- increased involvement of final users;

- experience and knowledge of project managers;

- clear identification of project objectives;

- convenient definition of average project size.

With reference to the overall performance of individual company projects, deviations from the combined schedule, cost and requirements constraints are typically experienced. Additional constraints and challenges frequently derive from having to harmonize concurrent projects, coordinate resources conveniently, define and manage priorities effectively and establish suitable assessment criteria for the different initiatives. Investments in projects should therefore reflect specifically a Value for Money (VfM) approach, for which the following definition is provided (HM Treasury 2006):

> VfM is defined as the optimum combination of whole-of-life costs and quality (or fitness for purpose) of the good or service to meet the user's requirements.

This framework reveals the shortcomings of traditional views interpreting Project Management as a collection of techniques and tools. Indeed, current discussions on the essence of Project Management are confronted with original and innovative contexts implying new concepts and definitions for both the terms 'Project Management' and 'Project Manager'; for example, while the latter term primarily identifies individual responsibilities, the former recognizes that projects are cooperative undertakings.

Major Challenges for Projects in the Current Practice

CHALLENGE NO. 1: PROJECTS DO NOT MEET THE REQUIREMENTS OF ALL STAKEHOLDERS

To an excessively large extent, projects are subject to the hazard of failing to deliver cost-effective solutions to owner requirements. Here and in the rest of this book, the following definition (Turner 2007) is adopted:

> We define the owner as the person who provides the money to buy the asset and receives benefit from its operation.

A situation that often occurs is that projects show overruns (with respect to project schedule) and overspends (with respect to project cost). When contracting practices and cultural environments are too rigid and are moving too slowly, there are difficulties in recognizing that the purpose of the project – and hence the customer requirements – may change over time and that the basis upon which the project was launched may tend to become less relevant as a result.

The explanations for this poor performance are deep-seated in certain (maybe too many) organizational cultures. They could be summarized as three categories: poor management; unclear definition of stakeholder roles; and, for certain more advanced projects, the difficulties of technology insertion whenever these are relevant to the project scope and timescales.

CHALLENGE NO. 2: POOR MANAGEMENT

It is sometimes problematic to identify where Project Management goes wrong. Most frequently, a number of weaknesses are encountered in project-based organizations:

- Lack of resources in the early stages – insufficient resources are at times allocated to the early life cycle stages of projects, which means that key decisions are being taken without sufficient information and understanding of the risks involved, thus resulting in much greater expenditure and delays in the later project stages to correct the difficulties.

- Cumbersome approval processes – the approval processes may be time-consuming, leading to substantial postponements and inefficiencies at the project level while failing to deliver effective control.

- Rigid procedures – the existing project governance procedures are not always flexible enough to accommodate the different sorts of project practices that have to be carried out.

- Ineffective contract conditions – sometimes innovative solutions are discouraged by contractual arrangements that tend to be resistant to changing things for the better.

- Prioritizing short-term benefits – when projects are long and complex, the real purpose may get buried and distorted by the objectives and methods applied during the early stages. For example, longer-term metrics, such as life cycle costs – which will be discussed later in this book – are put aside for the sake of short-term cost or delivery benefits.

CHALLENGE NO. 3: UNCLEAR DEFINITION OF STAKEHOLDER ROLES

Where Project Management recurrently goes wrong is in the definition of roles and responsibilities.

On the one hand, project owners have to be clearly identified; in addition, individuals in charge of managing all the various stages of the project life cycle should receive enough authority by delegation so that they can do their jobs effectively. On the other hand, an effective whole-life approach for the project should be made possible by rationalizing the different project processes, from the definition of project requirements down to the subsequent project stages.

CHALLENGE NO. 4: IMPACT OF TECHNOLOGY AND COMPLEXITY

The technical complexity inherent in certain projects is a major challenge to achieving cost and schedule goals. Also, the complexity and differentiation of outputs delivered by projects across their life cycle demands more flexible and shorter procedures.

If projects are technically complex, their cost profile will be difficult to assess accurately at the project implementation stage, when managers are required to produce cost and schedule estimates against which their projects will be measured. Few projects should proceed to the implementation stage unless requirements are well-defined and stable, and the available resources – mature technologies, schedule and funding – are set.

Adequate funding should be made available to meet the project requirements and consider its technical risks.

The Project Life Cycle: Helping Face Project Management Challenges

All projects have a life cycle, irrespective of how many phases can be seen included in it. The name and number of project phases are determined on the basis of the control needs of the organizations involved in the project; it has been suggested (Archibald and Archibald 2013) that:

> *Important improvements can be achieved by applying Systems Thinking to the Project Life Cycle Management System used for each project category.*

Understanding your project life cycle can provide a justification to the actions required to manage a project. As Frame emphasizes in his book (1994):

> *Where you are in the project life cycle will have a strong bearing on what you should be doing and what options are open to you.*

Usually, the project life cycle goes through its phases at a variable degree of intensity. Levels of resources and costs are rather low at the project inception, then the effort progressively increases up to a maximum point in the implementation phase. In the termination phase, a rapid decline occurs. Therefore, resource planning must take place as early in the project life cycle as possible; control activities are expected to be more intense as the project life cycle progresses.

Across the project phases, there is usually a variable influence over the definition of the final project output and also over the final costs and benefits. The highest degree of influence is expected at the beginning of the project; this degree of influence drops as the project proceeds, whereas costs continue to accrue. As a consequence, the ability to add value to the project output decreases from the initial project phases onwards; therefore, early project management efforts should be dedicated to the effective and timely balance of perceived benefits against estimated costs.

There is also, to some extent, another factor that challenges Project Management efforts: a culture of optimism that affects project cost and schedule performance by increasing the difficulty of developing and maintaining realistic estimates. Especially for projects that are technically complex, underestimating these technical elements leads to a larger extent of cost and schedule challenges: technologies may be new and unique, they may combine their interactions and they may require the utilization of expensive resources. This is particularly true at the implementation stage of the project life cycle, when cost and schedule estimates will be used for the assessment of project execution.

References and Further Reading

Archibald, R.D. and Archibald, S.C. 2013. *Leading & Managing Innovation: What Every Executive Team Must Know about Project, Program & Portfolio Management.* West Conshohocken: Infinity Publishing.

Frame, J.D. 1994. *Managing Projects in Organizations.* San Francisco: Jossey-Bass.

Kerzner, H.R. 2009. *Project Management Case Studies,* 2nd edn. New York: John Wiley & Sons, Inc.

HM Treasury 2006. 'Value for Money Assessment Guidance'. Available at: https://www.gov.uk/government/uploads/system/uploads/attachment_data/file/252858/vfm_assessmentguidance061006opt.pdf.

Turner, J.R. (ed.) 2007. *Gower Handbook of Project Management,* 4th edn. Farnham: Gower.

Chapter 2

Project Management, Projects and Their Life Cycles: Historical Views

MASSIMO PICA

Project Management Yesterday, for Today and Tomorrow

The evolution of Project Management practices up to the last 70–80 years of its history shows the promising level of accomplishment that has been mostly achieved so far in the accurate definition of the degree of efficiency in projects, in cost reduction, in optimal resource allocation, in project breakdown techniques, in the formalization of responsibility assignment, in the critical analysis of variances affecting projects and in project risk management. Each of these pieces of the Project Management puzzle has been developed so far by using convenient and accurate techniques. This has been an expeditious way to enable raising Project Management to the rank of a scientific discipline.

Project Management has always been primarily based on planning. Planning is, actually, a daily habit that everyone follows, albeit quite often unconsciously. Daily 'macro-activities' are usually composed of a series of 'micro-activities' that each one of us accomplishes (for example, home-based tasks before going to work in the morning) in line with a personal choice to spend the least amount of time possible in the completion of each macro-activity. In the majority of cases, then, the specific sequence of micro-activities and their timelines are determined by personal preferences in order to minimize the total duration and, maybe, stay in bed somewhat longer. Essentially, human beings are familiar with planning their own actions every day, sometimes instinctively, in their private lives as well as in professional lives or in social relationships: planning is a strongly natural and individual habit, and is also a primeval practice of men and women everywhere in the world.

In the field of construction projects, thousands of years of history witness the survival of great pieces of work that were completed through the support given by often rudimentary systems of governance. The pyramids of Egypt, which were built more than 45 centuries ago, are a representative example of earliest projects, especially the Pyramid of Cheops, the largest one, which – according to historical sources – took more than 20 years to be completed and is still in good shape today. Certainly, the construction enterprise selected by the Pharaohs had to face a number of key challenges: the procurement of material, composed of gigantic stones, that had to be moved for hundreds of kilometres from the mountain quarries, where they had been cut and flattened, down to the site where they were lifted up to the maximum height of 146 metres with the help of simply designed equipment made of wood, which also came from distant sites. On the human side, hundreds of thousands of slaves were engaged in the works, requiring a sound logistic support to ensure the provision of sufficient amounts of food and water; complete personnel changes occurred four times a year, so that at the beginning of every quarter, an enormous number of men had to be moved to the worksite while the survivors of the previous shift were sent back. Therefore, the site manager had to solve a certain number of problems (of which those mentioned above are only a few) every day; this meant that he had to put in place some system – albeit unsophisticated and plain – of operational planning and work advancement control, reflecting an early version of current Project Management systems, as necessary to address these problems. More recently, a similar situation occurred in Athens, where, after the year 500 BC, Phidias successfully managed the efforts related to the construction of the monuments on the Acropolis, the first of which was the Parthenon with its imposing look and its paradigmatic architectural style. Later on, during the third century BC, work on the Great Wall of China was started by connecting individual older pieces, which would be brought to completion no earlier than the fifteenth century AD! Certainly this is the all-time longest project …

In the Roman world, Julius Caesar's personal experience with Project Management[1] (first century BC) showed that certain projects intended for temporary use were not particularly easier than long-life projects. Chapters 17–18 of Book IV of his famous literary work on the Gallic Wars tell the story of his decision to have a wooden bridge built across the river Rhine:

> *Caesar, for those reasons which I have mentioned, had resolved to cross the Rhine; but to cross by ships he neither deemed to be sufficiently safe,*

---

1   The origin of both words 'project' and 'management' is, notably, from Latin language: project derives from *proiectum* (something that is launched or proposed), management from *manu agere* (to handle).

nor considered consistent with his own dignity or that of the Roman people. Therefore, although the greatest difficulty in forming a bridge was presented to him, on account of the breadth, rapidity, and depth of the river, he nevertheless considered that it ought to be attempted by him, or that his army ought not otherwise to be led over. He devised this plan of a bridge … Within ten days after the timber began to be collected, the whole work was completed, and the whole army led over.[2]

It is also worth noting the great works erected during the Roman Empire: main roads, monumental far-reaching aqueducts, entire cities and villages. In each of these works it is not hard to recognize the existence of a preliminary plan, accurately defined and thereafter translated into reality in a methodical and systematic fashion at the command of a comprehensively experienced 'project manager' of that time.

First of all, mention must be made of the Colosseum. In 69 AD, the Emperor Vespasian took power in Rome. His name – as stated in *The Oxford History of the Roman World* – is:

indissolubly linked with the most celebrated of all Roman buildings, the Colosseum, the amphitheatre he provided for the entertainment and gratification of the Roman people.

The Colosseum (for which building began 77 AD, measuring 188 metres and 156 metres on the two axes and at a height of 50 metres) is the most impressive construction of the Roman world as well as one of the most remarkable applications of the architectural genius of ancient times, taking into account the scarcity of resources that were available at that time. Since the Emperor's age could not have allowed him to see the work completed, an amazing organizational plan had to be put in place and the project was executed first by building a cage of pillars in travertine (kind of local white limestone rock) to support the *cavea* vault, then by working in parallel in two huge building sites, one over the other. The entire construction work, resembling the modern process for reinforced concrete buildings, took just over two years!

Also in Rome, the Pantheon – from the Greek word Πάνθεον, meaning the 'temple of all divinities' – that was built from 118 AD (Figure 2.1) witnesses the extraordinary skills of the Romans in designing and building constructions

---

2   English translation by W.A. McDevitte and W.S. Bohn. Available at: http://classics.mit.edu/ Caesar/gallic.4.4.html [accessed 15 December 2014].

Figure 2.1   The Pantheon in Rome

that posed severe challenges during the project execution stage. As attested by *The Oxford History of the Roman World*:

> *The eye is drawn up, immediately and irresistibly, to the superb lines of its coffered concrete dome, at 148 feet in diameter the largest man-made dome in the world until modern times.*

This is certainly sufficient to assert that the Pantheon:

> *is unquestionably one of the great architectural masterpieces of all time.*

Roman aqueducts are also admirable as outstanding works; just before the end of the first century AD, Sextus Julius Frontinus (who was also governor in Britannia in 74 AD) was in charge of ensuring the largest possible water supply to Rome. He laid down his project as *curator aquarum* (water commissioner) in his treatise *De aqueductu urbis Romae* (*On the Aqueduct of the City of Rome*). From a sort of Project Management perspective, his objectives were numerous:

- maintain the quality and quantity of the water supply;

- remove unauthorized side channellings and water losses down the waterways;

- manage channel inspection and maintenance;

- assess the water provisions at the source and at supply points, and update records;

- arrange for agreements with landlords of properties crossed by works;

- document consumption to collect fees and forecast future needs;

- train workers in the use of the most convenient techniques and materials;

- educate users to complying with regulations so that heavy sanctions could be waived;

- request the emperor's permission for the delivery of funds and resources as necessary to ensure the water supply.

Project Management in Later Centuries

Certain examples of constructions designed during the Italian Renaissance (fifteenth and sixteenth centuries AD) show that constructability and siting are some way from being uniquely contemporary issues. In 1423 Filippo Brunelleschi (1377–1446) wins the competition for the dome of the Florence Cathedral, *Santa Maria del Fiore*: he undertook on his own the design as well as the definition of the construction process and of the ancillary works to achieve his completely innovative project, on the basis of a 1/12 model. This helped him to turn his idea into a full-scale construction extending to a diameter of 42 metres.

Brunelleschi's work clearly inspired Michelangelo (born in Tuscany in 1475) for his design of the dome of St Peter's in Rome. Michelangelo was challenged by the replacement of old structures with the massive structures of the walls and pillars that had to sustain the dome's weight. He started by making a clay model of his dome (with the same diameter as the Florence dome, but a height of over 130 metres) in 1557; his death (1564) suddenly interrupted the construction of his masterpiece, which would be completed more than 20 years later.

Some common roots of modern management theories concerning the formulation of scientific methods for management (and, eventually, Project Management) may be ascribed to René Descartes, the seventeenth-century French philosopher who, in his *Discours de la Méthode* (*Discourse on the Method*), expressed the following principles:

1.   Do not accept as being true anything until it is proved to be true.

2.   Break down a problem into sub-problems in order to better understand and solve it.

3.   Follow mentally a logical order developing from simpler and more understandable facts to follow a stepwise procedure towards more complex facts.

4.   Make accounts and controls in such a complete and inclusive way as to exclude all possibility of omission.

Near the end of the very same century, in 1683 and also in France, the already famous military engineer Sébastien Le Prestre, Marquis de Vauban, in a letter written to the Minister of War François Michel Le Tellier, Marquis de Louvois, stated the following:

> *Excellence Minister of War,*
>
> *We have construction works dragging on for years, never finished and perhaps never to be finished. This occurs, Excellence, on account of the confusion caused by the frequent rebates brought into your works, since it is certain that all the breaches of contracts, the broken words and the repeated tenders serve only to attract as Entrepreneurs all the miserable persons who know nothing and the rascals and ignorant fools, while at the same time chasing away from you those who have the means and ability to carry out an enterprise.*
>
> *And I will say further that such rebates delay and considerably increase the cost of the works, which will become increasingly shoddy.*
>
> *And I will also say that the savings realized with such tenaciously sought rebates and discounts will be imaginary, since an entrepreneur who loses is like an individual who is drowning: he clings to all that he can, and clinging to all that he can, in terms of construction,*

means not paying the merchants who furnished the materials, poorly compensating his workers, swindling as many people as he can, having the shoddiest labour force, like that with the lowest price, using the worst materials, finding loopholes in everything and interpreting life now as this and now as that.

Well, this is sufficient, Excellence, for you to see the error of your system; therefore, in the name of God, abandon it; re-establish trust, pay the correct price of the works, do not refuse an honest wage to an entrepreneur who fulfils his duty, this will always be the best deal you can make.

Since that time, and today as well – after more than three centuries – there has been hardly any meaningful change in the construction world.[3]

Much later, in the period between the last years of the nineteenth century and the early decades of the twentieth century, new technologies were frantically developed and the markets saw the appearance of a wealth of new products. Early theories of management processes were formulated to also accommodate some sort of change management (as we currently call it). Systematic and organized management doctrines, however, only originated in the early twentieth century, when Henry L. Gantt developed a simple technique to model manufacturing processes. This initiative derived from the studies undertaken by Frederick W. Taylor, who at the same time had approached the review of problems connected to work organization in factories. Taylor introduced the basic rules of work assignment and allocation of operational activities in order to increase individual productivity; Gantt proposed to represent each single activity of the manufacturing cycle in a two-dimensional chart using a horizontal bar whose length was proportional to its planned duration.[4]

An entire project life cycle, including the actual realization of the project, could, since that time, be represented by a graphical arrangement of bars along the time axis, following the order of the project sequence. The bars are arranged in accordance with the specific steps of the project procedure up to

---

3   On both sides of the construction projects context (public and private), financial outlay and the subsequent pursuit of the greatest extent of cost reduction are allegedly deemed to be major concerns. This may, quite unreasonably, cause – on the contractors' side – less attention to construction site safety, work performance and the specialization of personnel in charge of organizational and operational tasks.

4   Fortunately, the graphical two-dimensional representation technique had been also introduced in the seventeenth century by René Descartes!

its implementation. This enables an overall and comprehensive visualization of the entire project; more importantly, Gantt charts require reasoning in terms of pre-planned activity durations. The real innovation introduced by Gantt was the possibility of identifying a timely allocation of individual operations and obtaining, as a result, a more accurate assessment of the time required to complete the whole set of operations.

One of the quotations by H.L. Gantt that is worth mentioning with reference to its recognizable adaptation to Project Management is the following:

> *Without efficiency in management, efficiency of the workmen is useless, even if it is possible to get it. With an efficient management there is but little difficulty in training the workmen to be efficient. I have proved this so many times and so clearly that there can be absolutely no doubt about it. Our most serious trouble is incompetence in high places. As long as that remains uncorrected, no amount of efficiency in the workmen will avail very much.*

The 1940s

Contributions to the evolution of Project Management were due, in this timeframe, to the application of advanced mathematical theories, especially in the areas of graph theory and probability theory and, along with these, the development and use of electronic computers.

The first exhaustive and effective application of Project Management can be related to the atomic bomb studies carried out in the USA under the leadership of Lieutenant General Leslie Groves from 1942 to 1947. Robert Oppenheimer was assigned in 1942 the task of coordinating the research efforts of several scientists and technicians at Los Alamos in the Manhattan Project. Oppenheimer proved to be highly skilled not only as a technician, but also as a team leader; as a result of successful Project Management efforts, in a two-year period the first uranium bomb could be successfully tested for further operational use.

The 1950s

This period witnessed the complex post-war reconstruction era in which engineering and construction companies were engaged in a massive effort, giving rise especially to innovative organizational models emphasizing the potential role of project engineers as project managers.

In a famous and repeatedly quoted article written in 1959 in the *Harvard Business Review*, Paul O. Gaddis prophetically stated that:

> *If we are to grow as advanced technology grows, we must realize the new importance of the project manager.*

At the same time, more and more sophisticated techniques were introduced to update and improve the applicability of the simple graphical representation created by Gantt, using graph theory in network charts to connect elementary planned activities so that logical relations between these could be identified and emphasized for the benefit of comprehensive models of production processes. In 1957, Morgan R. Walker and James E. Kelley, Jr. formulated the rules controlling the network analysis according to their Critical Path Method (CPM).

CPM was then refined for use in the US Navy Polaris submarine project where the new Programme Evaluation and Review Technique (PERT) was introduced. For this, due acknowledgement should be paid to Russ Archibald, whom I met personally in Rome in early 2013 for a day-long private talk. Archibald began his memorable 60-year career in Project Management working in the Polaris project, applying PERT in the planning of the Polaris missile propulsion system. In our conversation, Archibald strongly expressed his view that, irrespective of some traditional interpretations, the influence of PERT in the successful outcome of the project was not so significant as the guidance given to the project by the chief project manager, Admiral Raborn, who managed to coordinate at best the enormous industrial efforts expended in the project while sacrificing a limited part of the project scope to successfully make up for all project delays.

The US Department of Defense (DoD) certainly made a major contribution to the development and implementation of the new network techniques to ensure the timely compliance of all the military and space research programmes launched during and after this decade. First of all, the DoD began to introduce for its internal use suitable progress control systems in the various projects under its responsibility; subsequently, the DoD's contractors were required to use similar systems. In addition to schedule control-oriented techniques, emphasis was extended to the control of economic achievements and to the improvement of project organization. Some basic concepts of the project life cycle were introduced and became familiar: the statement of project objectives, the definition of functional specifications, operational planning (along with the cost and schedule estimation), engineering design and so on.

The 1960s

Having so far established solid foundations for modern Project Management, this decade saw the development of maturity in the successful outcome of the Apollo space programme, culminating in 1969 in the moon landing mission led by Neil Armstrong.

Secretary McNamara led the DoD to successfully implementing several Project Management tools, especially the Contractor Cost – Schedule Control System (CCSCS), by which project cost and schedule variances could be analyzed and controlled using the newly earned value techniques.

Aerospace and construction companies, which at the end of the period accounted for about 20 per cent of the gross domestic product (GDP) of most advanced countries, were massive users of Project Management techniques in the achievement and utilization of their economic power.

While traditional functional arrays evolve towards new organizational models (matrix, task force), conflict resolution strategies in project teams were considered. Institutionally, the main event of the period was the foundation of the Project Management Institute in 1969.

The 1970s

During this period Project Management techniques saw their ultimate consecration. The management of the Trans-Alaska Pipeline System (TAPS) project can be considered as a typical example of application of these techniques: three years of hard work from 1974 to 1977 involved 70,000 people building an 800-mile pipeline at a total cost of more than $8 billion. The result of this hard work was, however, not completely successful. As Russell Archibald has personally pointed out:

> *In 1983–84 I was retained by a law firm in Washington, DC as one of several Project Management consultants to evaluate the management of this project for the State of Alaska. This consultant team included Dr. David Cleland and senior managers from Bechtel Corporation,*

which ... was initially involved in the TAPS Project but withdrew very early in its life cycle because of serious concerns that Bechtel had about the owner structure and Project Management approach that was being implemented. Our consultant team concluded that about $2 billion (of the $8 billion) were imprudently wasted during the planning and execution of that project, and recommended that this amount be excluded from the 'base cost' for [the] purposes of calculating the per barrel royalties that the owners had to pay the State of Alaska. Of course this exclusion created substantially increased royalty payments to the State. So the management of this major project by the consortium of 7 or 8 oil company owners actually was not very good.[5]

The 1980s

This was a period of further widespread dissemination of Project Management methodologies and techniques, achieving a full level of maturity and supported by the growing availability of personal computers along with specific early versions of Project Management software.

Hardware and software resources were the foundations of the development of ICT systems and for the application in the manufacturing of healthcare products and automotive products. Car manufacturers applied Project Management techniques and resources to the launch of new models to harmonize budget and schedule targets for a successful outcome. For example, Toyota was able to reduce its time to market to 36 months, that is, about half the usual duration up to that point, whilst bringing their engineering effort down from 3 million to 1.8 million hours.

This was also a period of severe budget constraints for various nations, forcing their governments into undertaking privatizations in specific less institutional areas, which also gave rise to the application of project financing techniques to BOOT (Build – Own – Operate – Transfer) projects through the creation of companies in charge of managing the full spectrum of business cycles, beginning with the provision of the economic resources needed for work funding, as required for the cost-effective execution of capital projects and the operation of their products for the entire capital recovery period, ensuring the expected return on investment.

---

5   Private correspondence.

The extension of management efforts on projects to cover the operational phase of their life cycle broadened the scope of Project Management from a purely tactical value to a more strategic connotation based primarily on the cost and schedule control of work, but also on the assurance of profitability of the initial investment. This created a context for project risk management techniques.

The 1990s

The last decade of the twentieth century saw the remarkable development of Information Technology, creating the possibility of really integrating project control systems into the existing ICT facilities. Corporate networks and client-server architectures enabled a comprehensive and integrated view of project data, along with the availability of management modules to control project schedule, project costs, resources, project reporting and documentation, graphical interfaces and risk analysis. Remote project information exchange and management were made much easier by new technologies and especially by the growing use of Internet tools and, for the benefit of group work, Computer Supported Cooperative Work (CSCW). To a large extent these developments supported project team members in:

- communicating internally through email facilities or conferencing systems;

- sharing databases and filing systems;

- using common application software.

CSCW was notably practised in the Boeing 777 project, which assembled more than 200 expert teams to work on the same 3D aircraft model as the basis for their institutional tasks.

Conclusions

In summary, century after century, a large number of projects have been brought to final completion depending primarily on the careful control of the status of the work under the responsibility of skilled individuals who were constantly under pressure from various organizational, logistic and economic difficulties.

While it is true that the success of these projects was largely derived from the competence, ability and knowledge of operators, it is likewise certain that at all times, some sort of methodology, albeit simple and ordinary, has been constantly applied to schedule operational tasks and to assess their actual performance.

In recent times, the construction site has been identified as the place where, often, deferred design issues have to be finally resolved. Renzo Piano[6] stated:

> *I love construction sites. They are extraordinary places where everything is moving at all times, is a continuous discovery and innovation. It is not true that everything resides in design processes.*

And, maybe unintentionally looking at a life cycle perspective:

> *Construction sites have no end, as well as buildings and cities are endless or unfinished works.*

---

6   Renzo Piano, born in Genoa in 1937, is one of the most famous Italian architectural designers of this time. Some of his most notable works are in London (the Shard building), in Paris (*Centre Pompidou*, with R. Rogers) and in Berlin (*Potsdamer Platz*), as well as in Genoa (port area) and outside Europe.

Chapter 3

Projects and Their Life Cycles: Some Current Views

FRANCESCA MONTANARI

Basic Notions and Definitions

In recent years, Life Cycle Management (LCM) has become a major subject for debate in every business environment and, especially, among experts in Programme Management (PgM) and Project Management (PM), who try to align their views on this subject while recognizing its value as an approach to increase efficiency and effectiveness in their organizations.

In this context, the characterizations of Project Life Cycle and Product Life Cycle are carefully considered, and the boundaries between them are examined closely. Currently, this topic is under continuous discussion as had already occurred in the past when these two terms were defined in the form of numerous and sometimes contradictory enunciations and models, depending on the needs and peculiarities of the corporate environment and of the reference background.

The substantial difference between the two life cycles reflects the same terminology difference existing between a project and a product. If the conventional definition given by the PMBOK® Guide for the term 'project' as 'a temporary endeavor undertaken to create a unique product, service, or result' is considered, then projects are identified by various attributes, and especially by their limited duration and defined schedule. This is not true for the term 'product', which identifies the result of a project (although this might also be represented by a service or documentation instead of a material product) – in principle, a product might be conceived as having an unlimited lifetime (as if it were a monument or a historic building like the Colosseum in Rome or the Parthenon in Athens).

Concisely, a single Product Life Cycle could accommodate several Project Life Cycles, each one aiming at the realization of the whole product or part of it.

Project Life Cycles

Project Life Cycles typically encompass the sequence of activities running from the time that the project is initiated to the delivery of project product to the final user or owner (located inside or outside the project organization). The traditional project structure, according to the PMBOK® Guide, is generically composed of the following phases: starting the project, organizing and preparing, carrying out the work and closing the project.

STARTING THE PROJECT

The essential details of the project are defined in terms of scope, resources, schedule and costs. A project manager is appointed and relevant tasks are defined. The project charter is then issued.

ORGANIZING AND PREPARING

The project is managed and detailed plans are defined for the management of specific areas (scope, time, costs, resources, quality and so on). The project management plan is issued.

CARRYING OUT THE WORK

The project is executed in line with the decision made in the development phase. Project deliverables are accepted.

CLOSING THE PROJECT

The project is formally closed and the resources are released.

Managing a Project

A certain project can be managed as a single entity from its beginning to its completion or, depending on its nature and complexity, it can be separated in a number of phases and sub-phases, which do not necessarily follow the aforementioned structure.

Each phase is identified by the need to manage it as an individual and specific segment of the whole project, characterized by defined input requirements, schedule/cost/resource constraints and output deliverables: it is therefore required that each phase be managed through the application of convenient Project Management methodologies.

In typical conditions, project phases are sequential. In a sequential relationship, the beginning of each phase requires inputs from the outputs of the previous project phase; under certain circumstances, depending on the arrangement of inputs and outputs of different phases, it is also possible that they overlap totally or partially ('overlapping relationship') in order to reduce the project duration (this is called the 'fast-tracking' technique).

In PRINCE2® methodology, great importance is attached to project phases since at the transition from a particular phase to the subsequent one, the project undergoes an overall re-assessment process, that is, a 'go – no go' decision that involves a comprehensive review, including a confirmation of project feasibility.

This is the mechanism on which one of the primary principles of PRINCE2® is based – the 'Continued Business Justification', which requires a number of conditions to be satisfied prior to undertaking a project:

- the existence of a justified reason to initiate the project;

- that the justification remains valid through the project duration; and

- that the justification is documented and approved.

The first condition is satisfied by the preparation of the 'Business Case', which is an essential pre-requisite for all decisions regarding the viability of the project. The two remaining conditions are the real innovations introduced by PRINCE2®; at the same time, they represent some of its primary strengths. In fact, at the conclusion of each phase, it is required that the Business Case be updated and reviewed, using it to re-assess the project, which can then be carried forward to the following phase or terminated if the conditions for its extension are no longer met.

Project Life Cycles can be categorized in accordance with the arrangements made for managing the project phases, the scope change requests and the requirements documentation. Hence, the following classification can be envisaged:

- Predictive Project Life Cycles – project products and deliveries are defined initially; all changes to the project's scope are managed very carefully.

- Iterative/Incremental Project Life Cycles – these are particularly advantageous for complex projects and whenever project goals and the project scope are expected to be subject to modifications. At each project phase or at each iteration, one or more project actions are intentionally repeated in order to add functionalities sequentially to the product.

- Adaptive/Agile Project Life Cycles – the most significant feature of these is the considerable process flexibility, ensuring on the one hand the application of more traditional Project Management methods and principles, but nevertheless reducing the typical formalism of complex frameworks such as those of PRINCE2® or PMI® so that the response to the continuous evolution and growth of market demands can be as expeditious and effective as possible.

For each of these categories, to date, a number of Project Life Cycle models have been conceived to accommodate different development contexts and different organizational, industrial and technological environments. A common example of the Predictive Life Cycle, in the ICT field, is the Prototype Model, in which the final product is gradually executed through the release of intermediate software prototypes, thus allowing the release of intermediate software prototypes, while the user is assisted in the final characterization.

Agile Project Life Cycle models have been largely considered, more recently, for applications in the ICT area, in which convenient methodologies and specific techniques are created to handle the challenges due to evolving market demands and to predictable user expectations for the delivery of increasingly innovative products in less time and at lower cost.

Extreme Programming and SCRUM are examples of agile models. Extreme Programming is based on the work of programmers in pairs who carry out continuous verifications on the code while it is being written; continuous test sessions are also carried out as part of the development phase. SCRUM methodology is based on the concepts of Sprint, Backlog and daily SCRUM meetings to assess the status of the work done.

The Product Life Cycle

The Product Life Cycle traditionally begins with the formulation of an idea for the product, which is later realized as a result of a design phase and is then introduced into service until its final retirement.

The individual phases of a typical Life Cycle are examined below.

CONCEIVE

The analysis of a single user's needs, along with the creation of a product or service for which a market demand exists, can provide impetus to a product concept stage, in which the product is imagined, conceived and broadly defined.

DESIGN

In this stage, the whole work leading to the product realization will be planned and organized in detail.

REALIZE

Here the product is actually realized and delivered to its users.

SERVICE

This occurs when the product undergoes its utilization.

RETIREMENT

The product is withdrawn from utilization. Conversely, a *relaunch* stage may take place when a new Product Life Cycle begins.

Similarly to the Project Life Cycle, depending on the intended applications, for a Product Life Cycle, it is also possible to find different models and definitions. Referring again to the ICT sector for specific examples, the framework given by the Information Technology Infrastructure Library (ITIL) can be taken into consideration as a *de facto* standard in the management of IT services. In the 2007 edition of the ITIL, the service life cycle is identified by the following structure:

1.   Service Strategy.

2.   Service Design.

3.   Service Transition.

4.   Service Operation.

5.   Continual Service Improvement.

For software products, the life cycle is described in the ISO/IEC 12207 standard as follows:

1.   Acquisition.

2.   Supply.

3.   Development.

4.   Operation.

5.   Maintenance.

Finally, ISO/IEC 15288 describes the life cycle of a generic system as composed of the following stages: Concept; Development; Production; Utilization and Support; and Retirement.

Distinctive Characteristics and Interconnections

From a conceptual point of view, it can be recognized that the boundary between the Project Life Cycle and the Product Life Cycle is determined by the distinction between the two terms 'project' and 'product'. However, some definitions that are reported tend to shorten the distance between these concepts, so that the boundary between the two life cycles becomes rather unclear.

In the aerospace sector, for example, projects are strongly interacting with products. The European standard ECSS-M-ST-10C Rev. 1, published by the European Cooperation for Space Standardization in 2009, provides the following structure for Project Life Cycles:

1.   Phase 0: Mission Analysis/Needs Identification.

2.   Phase A: Feasibility.

3.   Phase B: Preliminary Definition.

4.   Phase C: Detailed Definition.

5.   Phase D: Qualification and Production.

6.   Phase E: Utilization.

7.   Phase F: Disposal.

It should be noted that Phase 0 and especially both Phases E and F are included in the Project Life Cycle, although they are typically related to the product.

'Extended' Project Life Cycles are currently becoming rather common. They tend to emphasize the intentional incorporation of some additional activities into the Project Life Cycle. Some of these additional activities, which had been previously considered as external to the Project Life Cycle, are particularly related to the identification of owner/market needs. On the other hand, there are provisions in PRINCE2® for the preparation of Business Plans inside the Project Life Cycle during Pre-project and Initiation stage.

Russell D. Archibald and Shane C. Archibald have recently published a book (Archibald and Archibald 2013) illustrating a Six-Phase Comprehensive Project Life Cycle Model, which includes a Project Incubation/Feasibility Phase preceding the Initiation Phase of traditional standard models and a Post-Project Evaluation Phase after the standard Project Closure Phase (Figure 3.1).

This approach realistically reflects the circumstances in which the existence of a project originates before the traditional starting phase (Figure 3.1) and that its products/results, as already mentioned, continue their existence and have to be assessed after project closure, so that the project's success – and especially its value – can be measured. It is therefore deemed that both the Project Incubation/ Feasibility phase and the Post-Project Evaluation phase should be rightfully considered in the project context.

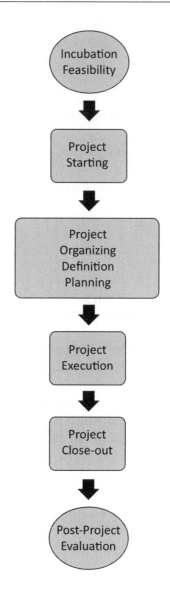

Figure 3.1   Six-Phase Comprehensive Project Life Cycle Model

Source: Archibald and Archibald (2013).

References and Further Reading

Archibald, R.D. and Archibald S.C. 2013. *Leading & Managing Innovation: What Every Executive Team Must Know about Project, Program & Portfolio Management.* West Conshohocken: Infinity Publishing.

European Cooperation for Space Standardization 2009. *ECSS-M-ST-10C Rev. 1. Space Project Management. Project Planning and Implementation.* Noordwijk: ECSS.

ISO/IEC 12207:2008. *Systems and Software Engineering – Software Life Cycle Processes.* Geneva: International Organization for Standardization.

ISO/IEC 15288:2008. *Systems and Software Engineering – System Life Cycle Processes.* Geneva: International Organization for Standardization.

ITIL 2007. *The Official Introduction to the ITIL Service Lifecycle.* London: The Stationery Office.

OGC 2009. *Managing Successful Projects with PRINCE2®*, 5th edn. London: The Stationery Office.

PMI® 2013. *The Guide to the Project Management Body of Knowledge*, 5th edn. Newtown Square: Project Management Institute.

Chapter 4

Introduction to Project Life Cycle Cost, Schedule and Requirements Management

FEDERICO MINELLE and FRANCO STOLFI

Project Processes in the Project Life Cycle Environment

According to most acknowledged Project Management (PM) approaches, which hopefully are also the most frequently used approaches, the main process groups that encompass the whole Project Life Cycle (PLC) are the following, with nominal variations. The activities/products most related to cost/schedule and benefit issues (if the necessary requirements were fulfilled) are emphasized:

1. Initiating, where overall significance of the whole project has to be defined, at a very high level: objectives and scope, business justification, requirements and stakeholders' expectations, main deliverables and time/cost budget, selection of a Project Manager and success criteria.

2. Planning, where the baseline for the whole project has to be prepared, at different granularity levels: work breakdown structure (WBS) and organization breakdown structure (OBS), responsibility matrix for work package (WP) assignment, time schedule/plan (usually according to CPM network logic, or PERT or CCM) and the relevant Gantt chart (pinpointing main intermediate milestones/ target), cost estimate/plan, risk analysis and corrective action plan, progress checkpoint plan, quality plan, communication plan and so on.

3. Executing where, at the time of actual project development and delivery, the following have to be done: work and work team (WT) coordination, progress report (PR) processing and editing, distribution of relevant information to stakeholders, changes and contingency management, risk monitoring and corrective actions implementation, etc.

4. Monitoring and controlling, where, at the same time, the following tasks are expected to be done: deliverables and progress data collection, critical issues and variances analysis vs. current baseline, root causes identification and evaluation of updated time/cost estimate-to-complete (including corrective actions and required changes implementation), revision of baseline (if necessary and approved properly), business justification update/approval, etc.

5. Closing, where, at the end of the project, the following tasks are expected to be done: administrative/contract(s) closure, capitalization of lessons learned knowledge, human and other engaged resources release, business justification revision, etc.

Figure 4.1 below shows how the process groups are usually overlapping (with a different effort level), while they could be repeated in the event that the project would be implemented in subsequent phases (or 'stages', as stated in the PRINCE2® language).

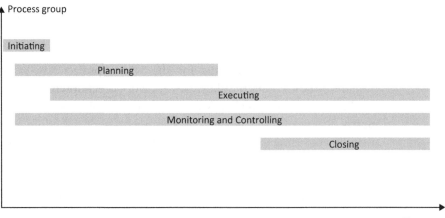

Figure 4.1   Project process groups effort

According to other sources, an 'incubation' process has to be considered as the starting point, while a 'post-project benefits evaluation' plan is also valuably prescribed in the 'Closing a Project' process of the PRINCE2® methodology.

The post-project benefits evaluation plan should be included whenever we want to be sure that overall significance of the whole project (see process 1) has been actually achieved, while at the end of the project (see process 5) we can get only a 'proxy' evaluation, namely, time/cost spent (input) and scope/quality of deliverables (output), but not yet an after-the-fact measure of the true benefit (outcome) provided to stakeholders.

The same PRINCE2® methodology states that business justification has to be confirmed as a go/no-go criteria for each project stage approval, including any 'evolutionary' approach to its definition.

As a conclusion, we can state that the success of a project (besides any process approach) has a solid foundation only when stakeholders achieve the promised benefits – that is the ultimate goal for Project Managers or Project Steering Committees!

Another significant activity to be included in the whole PLC – and Product Life Cycle too – is Requirements Engineering. In many industry sectors (for example, construction, defence, ICT and electronics), it is already a standard practice, with a variable degree of depth and thoroughness according to the maturity of the organization (or maybe imposed by contract clauses) because, according to Brooks:

> *the hardest single part of building a system is deciding precisely what to build: no other part of the conceptual work is as difficult as establishing the detailed technical requirements; ... no other part of the work so cripples the resulting system if done wrong; no other part is as difficult to rectify later.*

As is unfortunately proved in many circumstances, the cost/schedule (and quality) impact of a requirement change is closely related to project progress; in other words, the same change request has a more significant impact when the project is closer to its completion, which is subsequently delayed.

This is the payoff for starting immediately, even in the very first process group (that is, initiating or – by and large – during the Feasibility Study), the activity of requirements elicitation and documentation which, after a

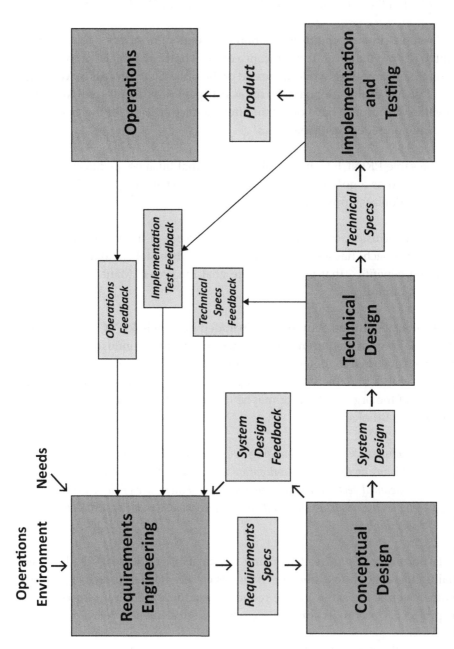

Figure 4.2   Requirements Management approach

management/stakeholder feedback approval, unambiguously determines 'what' has to be delivered by the project and its performance criteria.

This also creates a check-reference tool, which will be further detailed/updated under management (and stakeholders) control throughout the PLC, until final test of project 'product' and feedback on operations, as shown in Figure 4.2.

Project Risk Components in the PLC Stages

Every project has its own level of uncertainty as a result of various intrinsic factors (primarily the following: complexity, size, organization, innovation, lifetime span and extent of changes), which are likely to have an impact on project performance and relevant outcome unless they are properly managed.

A basic question: what does 'risk' really mean and how is it related to uncertainty? A sound definition follows – one of a number to be found in the literature, encompassing either scope and comprehensiveness issues – taken from PRINCE2®:

> *A risk is an uncertain event or set of events that, should it occur, will have an effect on the achievement of objectives. It consists of a combination of the probability of a perceived threat or opportunity occurring, and the magnitude of its impact on objectives.*

This assertion stresses the two faces of risk: it may bring either negative or positive impacts, respectively called 'threats' and 'opportunities'. The aim of risk management is to keep under control the intrinsic project uncertainty, working both to decrease the impact of threats and to develop opportunities.

Risks may have different nature/sources (for example, technology, business, economy/finance, sociology and politics) and may have an impact on project activities or its outcomes, as well as on related extents not attributable directly to the project. In addition, depending on whether they have an internal or an external source, they are respectively easier or harder to foresee and manage.

Risk management cannot be by any means an 'offhand' task, but it must be an ongoing process along the whole PLC: managing risks means carrying out the following activities:

- Detect risks – find out any project-related risk. Detection begins with project context analysis, isolating significant uncertainties on project assumptions/estimates and evaluating their potential impact on project performance/outcome. In order to detect a meaningful risk list, various approaches would be adopted, for instance:

  - Risk catalogue – if such a catalogue is available for the specific industry/project characteristics (for example, in engineering/construction: manufacturing or chemical plant, civil works/real estate, etc.; in defence: aircraft/submarine prototype, etc.; in ICT: information system/communication network, etc.), it makes it possible to have a comprehensive list of risks, usually categorized by nature/source, where each risk has a standard grade of importance and a suggested range of effective countermeasures (based on industry-wide 'lessons learned').
  - Risk analysis checklist – depending on the type pf project, a specific checklist may be applicable: answers to each question serve to detect main uncertainties and a preliminary list of project-related risks.
  - List of risks experienced in previous similar projects – with the support of the 'lessons learned' knowledge, risk selection/ranking is reliable and, by the same token, effectiveness of related countermeasures is more trustworthy. This selection approach can be easily integrated with the previous ones (see the previous two bullet points).
  - Brainstorming technique – Project Managers (and hopefully Project Sponsors) in association with Project Team leaders may arrange an open discussion meeting to discover additional undetected risks, which are usually linked to project-specific or product-specific features. The payoff of this organizational effort is to gain a more comprehensive risks list, combined with their ranking and (possibly) suggested countermeasures; as a secondary positive effect, the whole Project Team will gain a larger awareness of risks and would be more committed to facing them.

- Evaluate/quantify risk – rank and quantify the probability of risk occurrence and its impact level. Both values can be graded on a quantitative scale (for example, from 0 to 5) or a qualitative scale (for example, High/Medium/Low): it is usually not very valuable to obtain a numerical detailed value (for example, x.xx per cent or y.yy £ or z days/hours), except in very specific conditions. In order to gain the probability and impact evaluation, various techniques/ tools can be applied, depending on project confidence and the type of risk (for example, Decision Tree, FMEA analysis, what-if analysis and SWOT analysis). Risks under evaluation are ranked in decreasing order of their severity; thus, attention will be focused on the critical risks. A useful measure of the overall project risk level is the algebraic sum (+ and -) of the impact of threats and opportunities: it shows whether the overall risk level is consistent with tolerances allowed for the project. Risk evaluation and quantification approaches are detailed in this chapter.

- Plan risk responses – find convenient strategies to restrain risk consequences. Values given to both probability and impact, as pointed out above, determine the severity level of each risk and its position in the Risk Matrix (see Figure 4.3); therefore, it gives a sound hint for countermeasure strategy selection. The strategy of risk restraint must be carefully defined and periodically reviewed in order to select countermeasures according to these criteria; they

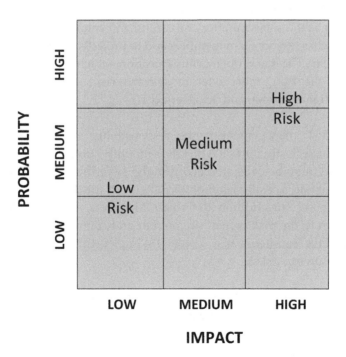

Figure 4.3   Risk Matrix

are proportionate to risk and applicable to more risks, minimizing residual risk and preventing side-effect risks.

- Implement plan and monitor risks – implement countermeasures strategy according to the previously defined plan (see above). Implementation means actually performing selected countermeasures (according to the planned project timeframe) or arranging an appropriate 'emergency plan' to be implemented when the related risk event actually occurs. In the latter case, an individual responsible for risk monitoring and controlling (the risk owner) must be appointed, together with individuals responsible for implementing related countermeasures. All the main risks should be continuously monitored in order to check actual risk occurrence vs. forecasts and to update the risk register (see below), deleting overcome/not-shown risks and adding newly detected risks. The latter risks are subject to an iterative evaluation process, as detailed above. Furthermore, the adequacy of the project time and cost provisions must be checked and, if necessary, revised.

In order to have the best payoff from risk restraint strategies, risk analysis results must be the subject matter of a careful and continuous communication process to either Project Team members and to project stakeholders (as far as it concerns them). Clear and open communication, which should be undertaken throughout the PLC, must refer to selected risks (threats/opportunities), planned restraint strategy and actual effects.

Project risk management is the responsibility of a Project Manager. Whenever project structures (WBS/OBS) identify sub-projects, risk analysis responsibility may be delegated accordingly; nevertheless, Project Managers must maintain an overall vision of all risks, both for detection and monitor/ control purposes. In addition to Project Managers, support roles may be defined, such as the 'risk owner' (to monitor and control specific risks or sets of risks) and the 'countermeasure owner' (to implement planned or emergency countermeasures to risks).

A basic tool to effectively manage risks is the Risk Register, which lists all detected risks and related tracking along the whole PLC. More specifically, the forms of information to be registered are (as a minimum):

- risk identification;

- risk description (cause/effect);

- event or date linked to risk occurrence;

- risk type/nature;

- risk evaluation/quantification (probability, impact and severity);

- risk owner;

- risk status (forecast, occurred/countermeasured, overcome/not shown);

- planned countermeasures or emergency plan;

- countermeasure owner.

A careful, correct and ongoing update of the Risk Register, in addition to its completion by the Project Manager and the Project Team at the end of the project (including evaluated strengths and weaknesses of the risk management process), is a basic component of the 'lessons learned' knowledge capitalization for future projects, and/or can be used to increase the company experience included in the risk catalogue (whenever this is provided).

Identifying and Applying the Risk Management Process to Cost and Schedule

The main reason for managing cost and schedule risk is to keep the project aligned with its baseline or, when necessary, to proceed with an alternative and agreed-upon baseline, which reasonably preserves its value for the stakeholders, or otherwise to efficiently close it, without wasting additional resources.

Being aware of the probabilistic environment of any project (and of the common optimistic approch to any estimate), a risk analysis must be undertaken, mainly by the Project Manager and approved by the Steering Committee (and for special items even by selected stakeholder segments) and put into action throughout the entire life cycle of the project.

Risk management activities to be carried out include, first of all, the acknowledgment that risks would be of a certain magnitude (both in terms of probability and relevant consequences). Therefore, in order to pragmatically manage them (Pareto's Law really works!), they must be ranked according to their 'expected impact' = Risk Probability * Risk Impact.

Top priority risks are then selected, and an action plan developed, following some basic strategies. Before going into detail, it is worth recalling that a 'visualization' of the risk map through the Risk Matrix (see Figure 4.3) would be instrumental for strategy selection for different risk classes.

Risk classes and preferred strategies are as follows:

- High risk – remarkable impact on cost/time or quality of deliverables (namely, on promised benefits): an action should be planned and performed well in advance (before the risk arises) under tight management control (high priority).

- Medium risk – pertinent impact on cost/time or quality of deliverables (namely, on promised benefits): early action would be desirable, but in any event, action must be planned and then performed in a timely fashion (when risk occurs), alerting management control (medium priority).

- Low risk – minimal impact on cost/time or quality of deliverables (namely, on the promised benefits): usual management supervision.

The preferred categories of strategies to combat risks are as follows:

- Risk Avoidance: 'risk is not acceptable', so a different project approach/option should be selected. This action works on the root cause and hopefully removes risk, driving it towards zero probability (for example, by changing the technical solution or softening the functional/technical requirements). The project is safer, but there is a certain downside to this: cost/time increases and stakeholder expectations/benefits decrease.

- Risk Mitigation/Reduction: an action lowering the probability or the impact of the risk should be selected in advance. Specific countermeasures would operate in order to keep the risk under control, applying an ongoing evaluation and developing an emergency plan. Projects employing this method are less safe than those following the former strategy, but, on the other hand, performance declines are lower (in a probabilistic sense).

- Risk Transfer: early action has to be taken in order to allocate the impact of risk (whenever it occurs) elsewhere. It could be (for instance): a typical business insurance against risk (which is common in the construction industry), a contract clause that makes the other party responsible for any consequence of the selected risk for a project contracted by the owner to the upplier (this works both ways, expecially in ICT contracts: pay attention to fine-print clauses!). Therefore, the management of that risk becomes someone else's issue.

- Risk Acceptance: being aware of the wide range of potential risks, no action will be taken until a risk actually occurs, then in the event of its occurrence, a convenient emergency action will be adopted. A 'wait and see' attitude or, more precisely, a 'monitor and react' management approach would be applied.

How should classes of risk and strategies to tackle them be better matched? There is no single answer to this question, but an overall relation profile could be outlined (see Table 4.1).

The approach described in the table takes into account risks which, in their usual sense, are probabilistic threats to project performances. A similar approach can be applied to the positive side of risks, when there are opportunities to improve project performances. In the latter case, strategies have different names:

- exploit opportunities to achieve a positive impact;

- share opportunities to a thid party more suited to generate an improvement in the project performance;

- increase the probability of occurrence of an opportunity or/and its positive impact;

- accept the positive impact on project performances of an opportunity that should occur.

Table 4.1   Risk class and risk strategy: Overall relationship profile

Risk strategy	Risk class		
	High	**Medium**	**Low**
Avoidance	Best choice (often mandatory)	Sometimes applied (provided project perfomances are slightly affected)	Not considered (no payoff)
Mitigation/ Reduction	Second choice (when no other strategy is viable)	Usual choice (early action time/cost largely offset by reduced impact)	Not considered (no payoff)
Transfer	Always to be explored (provided there is a counterpart willing to accept)	Always to be explored (provided there is a counterpart willing to accept)	To be explored (provided a viable payoff for both counterparts)
Acceptance	No way (too risky)	Alternative choice (when no other strategy is viable)	Usual choice (monitoring time/ cost offset by minimal impact)

Since these lucky occurrences happen to be usually very few in number, this summary hint looks to be sufficient!

The Value of Cost and Schedule Risk Management

Why are cost/schedule risks so frequently present? Even before the present financial and economic crisis, innovation has been considered a strategic factor in order to achieve business objectives aligned to enterprise mission (applicable to any organization, whtheer private, public or not-for-profit). At present, in the middle (or, hopefully, near the end) of the financial/economic crisis, innovation projects have to be carried in a very short timeframe and with limited (or no) additional resources. This constraint drives any organization towards a more careful governance on projects, on projects, either in progress or at the initiation, with an ongoing check on business justification.

A few words on the project organization which is, by its nature, temporary and cross-functional: it includes not only the Project Team, headed by the Project Manager, but usually also an ad hoc Management Steering Committee, having an oversight/strategic decision role, while stakeholders represent the clients whose requirements are to be accomplished. The various PM Methodologies or PM Competence Guidelines feature some differences and suggest additional/

useful roles, but the four above-mentioned roles are adequate for the purposes of this chapter.

The approach to cost and schedule risk management, which will be discussed below, has its basis in the guidance it offers to the Project Manager (and to the project steeering committee) in order to evaluate and select a convenient action plan when external or internal forces/accidents seem to drive the project off the planned path.

In addition, cost/schedule risk management allows Project Managers (and project steering committees) to respond to any foreseen event that may occur (remembering Murphy's law!) and that could negatively affect project performance and, as a consequence, could lead to re-baselining the project cost/ schedule.

In order to adopt this approach, an effective time-saving project control might be reinforced if this approach is also coupled with the 'management-by-exception style' (that is, only events/outlooks, besides suggested solutions, that actually or eventually drive the project outside a pre-defined tolerance range are passed to the steering committee for its evaluation).

As a further assumption to this approach, a clear definition of roles and responsibilities is required, both in the Project Team (including the Project Manager) and the steering committee or active stakeholders. This sharing of risk/opportunities issues with stakeholders, applying a proper communication (two-way) plan, enables a sound expectation management, reducing the risk of project failure.

The Value of Impact Analysis (Business Case Justification)

In the competitive market in which we are usually engaged, limited resources are available and/or the expectation level of stakeholders is very high. Therefore, it is crucial to thoroughly evaluate project feasibility in order to take the right decisions about investment relating to the project. What it does really mean? Typically it means: project scope, implementation time and cost, product (output) quality, risks and expected benefits (outcome). The optimal/ accepted configuration of these elements, which becomes the project business justification, also represents the reference framework for ongoing project evaluation throughout the whole PLC (and Product Life Cycle too). As a matter of fact, when the main project milestones are achieved or when a significant change in the project occurs (in any of above-mentioned elements), a re-assessment of the impact on the project is required in order to check if the initial business justification is still applicable. This approach enables a sound update and possible approval of the affected items, which are no longer aligned with the initial goals of the project, to be carried out.

Impact Analysis in a project environment, as previously highlighted (see also Chapter 9 and Appendix 4), forms a comprehensive and integrated approach to prove the existence of the initial pre-requisites that enable the project start-up/implementation and financial viability (not only until the completion of the project, but also throughout the whole Product Life Cycle).

It encompasses:

- the usual financial/economic investment evaluation;

- evaluation of other types of benefit that are not easily measurable in financial terms, but nevertheless are quantitatively defined and measured accordingly.

The financial/economic evaluation refers to well-known methods/tools widely applied in any financial investment evaluation (for details, see Appendix 4); to be more specific, time-phased cash flow has to be considered, which usually includes:

- Cash outflow:

  - the entire cost/expenditure required to achieve project implementation;
  - the differential costs/expenditure required to operate the project output (that is, products or any other output in comparison to the status quo ante without the project (either a technical product or an organizational initiative).

- Cash inflow:

  - the differential income/revenues (cost savings or increased revenues) generated by the deployment and operation of the project output;
  - in the event that the project owner is a governmental institution, these amounts should include possible cost savings (or

increased revenues) for external users of the project output (namely, citizens, enterprises and other institutions: the above-mentioned stakeholders).

The evaluation of other types of benefit encompasses non-monetary effects of the investment, which cannot be easily considered in the financial/economic evaluation. This category includes:

- potential increases in operational efficiency (for example, for an innovation project in the ICT area, the number of empowered 'knowledge operators' and the number of 're-engineered processes'), due to re-engineering of organizational structures or business processes;

- increases in the effectiveness of services delivered to users/ stakeholders, both internal (for example, management, employees and salesmen) and external (for example, customers, suppliers and citizens/enterprises/institutions) to the organization;

- in the event that the project owner is a governmental institution, measures of increased citizens democratic participation and access to 'open government' should also be considered.

The Impact Analysis timeframe should be adjusted according to the PLC phases (or stages in PRINCE2® language), following a suitable approach in each phase/stage.

An early 'pre-project evaluation' is strongly recommended before any decision about the project start-up (see the 'initiating' phase of the project process mentioned above), while 'in-progress evaluation' should be repeated along the various phases of project planning and implementation (see the 'monitoring and controlling' phase of the project process mentioned above) in order to check if the costs and benefits are still aligned with the stated goals. A 'post-project evaluation' is mandatory after the end of the project (that is, at the end of the product deployment period) in order to compare the achievement of expected benefits to the actual costs (project and operational ones). The true advantage comes from the use of a specific impact model throughout the PLC, based on consistent criteria and measurable values.

Project evaluations based on Impact Analysis yield several advantages at different levels. At the Project Management level, they make it possible to:

- have a clear and objective evaluation of the whole set of benefits, either on the financial side and the other quantitative (and often more important), non-monetary side;

- understand which services/products implemented by the project yield actual benefits and to what extent;

- any causes that prevented the achievement of the expected benefit levels in the 'business case' evaluation;

- be (fairly in advance) aware of countermeasures to be adopted in order for the project processes and its implemented services/products to achieve its expected benefit levels;

- have, throughout the PLC, factual metrics established to measure the achievement of cost/benefit pre-project values or (in the event of project changes) re-align them according to business strategic objectives. In the post-project phase, the very same metrics provide the actual measure of the operational benefits achieved.

At the programme/portfolio management level, this makes it possible, applying an objective benchmark approach, to improve:

- the expected performances of different projects, activating/empowering those which maximize return on investment or non-monetary benefits;

- the actual performances of different projects, highlighting 'best practices', risk profile and relevant countermeasures to be employed as 'lessons learned' for incoming/future projects;

- the effectiveness of services/products delivered in order to demonstrate the provision of benefits expected from investment (project/operations).

References and Further Reading

Archibald, R.D. 2013. *The Six-Phase Comprehensive Project Life Cycle Model – Including the Project Incubation/Feasibility Phase and the Post-Project Evaluation*

Phase. Manno: University of Applied Sciences and Arts of Southern Switzerland (SUPSI).

Archibald, R.D. and Archibald S.C. 2013. *Leading & Managing Innovation: What Every Executive Team Must Know about Project, Program & Portfolio Management*. West Conshohocken: Infinity Publishing.

Brooks, F. 1987. No Silver Bullet: Essence and Accidents of Software Engineering. *Computer*, 20(4), 10.

OGC 2009. *Managing Successful Projects with PRINCE2®*, 5th edn. London: The Stationery Office.

PMI® 2013. *The Guide to the Project Management Body of Knowledge*, 5th edn. Newtown Square: Project Management Institute.

Chapter 5

Initiating the Project

CLAUDIA SPAGNUOLO

Introduction

Several cost elements may be included in a project; not unusually, some of these elements are neglected in the cost-estimating process. Before committing to any investment, it is essential to get a correct picture of all project costs: it would be pointless, for example, to realize during project execution that a very expensive Project Manager is involved for 30 per cent of the time – or maybe up to 80 per cent – in reporting to apprehensive stakeholders looking for assurance in relation to the project's performance. Time and money could have been saved by creating a communication management strategy including monthly reports.

As a consequence, at the project initiation stage, a careful approach is essential to the preliminary requirement analysis and to cost estimates, while providing for an effective management methodology – 'fit for purpose' – that is, tailored to the peculiarities of the project in question.

The Importance of a Good Project Initiation

The significance of the initiation stage is greater than for the later project stages. If the Project Management team is unable to implement the correct level of rigorousness early in the initiation stage, there will be a risk of misinterpretations preventing the achievement of stipulated benefits or requiring continuous adjustments, leading to harmful increases in terms of costs and time.

This, however, does not imply any exemption from having to provide for corrective actions at a later stage; nevertheless, it is necessary to prepare strong foundations well in advance.

Preliminary activities will include the following:

- identification of a business justification to initiate the project – this will be documented in a Business Case, including key risks and expected benefits;

- review of lessons learned from previous experiences in similar projects;

- selection of a Project Life Cycle model;

- identification of key stakeholders and definition of a communication strategy; and

- definition of the organizational structure that will be in charge of Project Management, carefully providing for roles and responsibilities to be assigned to project team members.

The Reference Model for Project Management: PRINCE2®

It is convenient to select a Project Management model as soon as possible: the choice of a good, possibly well-established model ensures that defined processes are available and that there is no need to 'reinvent the wheel' each time.

Good models are particularly capable of responding to recurring questions in different project environments – for example:

- In an unexpected circumstance, can decisions be made autonomously or do they have to be scaled up? To whom should this be reported?

- Who has authority to give support or indications? Who decides?

- What types of information has to be provided in reports – and by which deadlines?

- Where can useful information be found?

The discussion in this chapter is based on PRINCE2®, including its management products (documents) and a Project Life Cycle that, as a result of the project responsibility assignment, is composed of the following stages:

- Starting up a project (start-up stage).

- Initiating a project (initiation stage).

- Controlling a stage (first delivery stage).

- The next delivery stages.

- Closing a project and the last delivery stage (last stage).

Post-project activities, in turn, will include the ascertainment of the benefits not achieved before project closure.

Specifically of interest in this chapter will be the two earliest stages of the project, namely the start-up stage and the initiation stage, which respectively lay the foundation for the subsequent stage and for the entire project.

The peculiarities of project environment shall, of course, be taken into account to customize the application of this approach, so that a certain project might include a significantly smaller number of stages. On no account, however, should the initiation stage be excluded: this, in fact, controls the entire project platform and ensures that no meaningless project is started.

In the start-up stage the pre-requisites for the project to be initiated are identified. Effort is expended, to the least extent possible, to gather all necessary information prior to deciding whether the project investment is worthwhile. The pre-requisites for project initiation are the following:

- Existence of a valid business justification for initiating the project, while avoiding the waste of time and funds that may occur whenever project assumptions are unreasonable (justifications should be incorporated into a preliminary Business Case).

- Existence of authorizations that are required (or adequate confidence in their forthcoming release) and absence of constraints irrevocably preventing the completion of the project or the achievement of benefits.

- Availability of sufficient information on the scope of the project in order for the Project Brief to be prepared.

The subsequent initiation stage provides the project with firm roots before committing to a major economic effort, in addition to supporting the customer organization in quantifying project resources to achieve a successful completion. The following activities are included:

- Careful analysis of project justification, expected benefits and risks likely to influence the project (these factors will be the guidelines for the detailed Business Case).

- Amalgamation of the project scope by identifying the deliverables (with respect to any effort that is excluded from the project) and defining the delivery plan in terms of procedures, schedules and costs for the agreed project outputs to be handed over.

- Definition of the decision-making process (who will be involved and what responsibilities will be assigned to them).

- Clarification of quality management procedures and costs relevant to the achievement of the required level (as stipulated in the quality management strategy).

- Definition of the procedures for managing risks, issues and modifications and, if necessary, for allocating specific budget lines, for example on the basis of a Risk Management strategy and of a Configuration Management strategy; Risk Management will be uninterrupted throughout the project, but as soon as possible, the extent of risk exposure will have to be appraised so as not to exceed customer needs.

- Identification of procedures for project performance control.

- Identification of information and communication management procedures (a Communication Management strategy will be issued to incorporate internal and external stakeholder relationships).

Following these steps, detailed indications will be provided for the preparation of project cost estimates. It is impossible to estimate costs accurately before ensuring a preliminary definition of Risk Management procedures, quality management procedures, management team structure and their costs. In addition, it is important that – among management costs – certain cost elements are not overlooked; for example, documentation management costs are frequently neglected, whereas not unusually they happen to be significant with respect to the entire range of project costs.

Planning for future project controls takes place in the initiation stage, in accordance with the overall Project Plan and in parallel with the preparation of the Project Initiation Documentation (PID).

Project plans include the planned costs and management stages encompassed in the project, key milestones and all checkpoints that are deemed essential; a summary of these will be also incorporated into the Business Case. Project plans are utilized by the Project Board to monitor the project performance at given points in time, especially when comparing the results achieved with the planned progress.

Identification of Key Factors Influencing Cost Analysis

If a realistic cost analysis and an accurate investment appraisal are to be performed, some preliminary investigations are needed in the early stages of the project; their purpose is to gather information elements that are significant to understand the project merit and its expected cost.

More exactly, in order for project success probability to be enhanced and for project costs to be accurately identified, the following step-by-step procedure should not be left aside:

- prepare the Business Case;

- define the scope and agreed quality;

- identify activity costs for the execution and management of the project;

- identify stakeholders and define the communication strategy;

- prepare the project plan;

- prepare the benefit measurement plan;

- consider utilizing a Project Management Office (PMO).

The details of this procedure are explored below.

PREPARE THE BUSINESS CASE

Every project should be accompanied by a justification driving its decision-making processes, ensuring alignment to strategic objectives and constantly looking at the feasibility of achieving the expected benefits.

Whenever deviations from strategic objectives or failures in the achievement of benefits occur, projects must be terminated in order for funds and resources to be switched over to more profitable initiatives.

In the development of the Business Case, several issues can be discovered requiring early provisions to ensure a minimal impact on the project; alternatively, unbeatable constraints can be identified in order to avoid investing in a project that will be 'doomed to failure'.

While reiterating that there must be a reasonable business justification for a project to be initiated and executed, nevertheless it is likely that this justification will be subject to change over time. What is essential is that the new justification is in line with the strategic objectives.

Justifications must always be documented in a Business Case. This document, in its initial formulation, might just be roughly outlined, whereas during the initiation stage, a more accurate version is required. The Business Case is a dynamic document and is subject to continuous update, requiring that the justification included in it be regularly checked for reasonableness.

In adherence to the PRINCE2® guidelines, a Business Case should, first, emphasize key points such as expected benefits and economic returns from the project investment. It is also recommended that it address: the reasons to undertake the project initiative; the business options (do nothing, minimal action or do the right thing); the benefits (in measurable terms); the counter-benefits (that is, final outputs that may be perceived as negative by some stakeholders, irrespective of risks that may materialize or not); the timelines for project execution and benefit achievement; a summary of costs, including operational and maintenance costs; an investment appraisal, by means of agreed metrics such as return on investment (ROI), net present value (NPV) or internal rate of return (ROR) – key project risks, related to uncertain events that, should they occur, could have an impact on the project.

It should be emphasized that the justification of the business option that will have been selected is also required for projects of a mandatory nature. In fact, several options might have to be considered, with a range of potential solutions – in terms of cost, benefit and risk – presenting very different peculiarities.

DEFINE THE SCOPE AND AGREED QUALITY

Overall project schedule and cost estimates are only possible after defining the project scope, that is, the entire range of project products to be delivered, besides the quality criteria relevant to product appraisal, incorporated into the quality management procedures.

Quality costs – including those to be incurred for non-conformance verification and management – are an integral part of production costs and cannot be disregarded. The notion of quality that is relevant in this context is the compliance of the project product with the agreed requirements in terms of the demonstrated adherence to stipulated expectations and specifications.

There are two basic approaches that a project initiative can adopt with respect to scope and quality (reflecting the series of requirements that the project output must comply with):

- 'traditional' – in which there is a fixed scope and, whenever a problem should arise, cost and/or schedule constraints would have to be revised; conversely, should no schedule/cost revision be envisaged, it would be necessary to remove some of the quality constraints;

- 'agile' – in which no modification is possible except for the project scope, in order for deliveries to occur at specified dates and in line with the stipulated quality.

The latter approach, in contrast to what can be expected, may be also applied to construction projects; a relevant reference can be derived from the true story of a stadium that was designed for the Athens Olympic Games of 2004. Having specified a certain date for the delivery of a stadium to be built, the delivery on time would not be guaranteed without certain project provisions, especially the preparation of a Product Breakdown Structure (PBS) and the prioritization of individual project elements. For example, the stadium cover could have a low priority, while safety requirements could have a high priority. Were the delivery of the entire stadium prevented by some circumstances, the works for the cover could be deferred, with no impact on the specified date at which the stadium would be delivered in a perfectly operational condition.

From an economic point of view, missing the delivery date of the stadium in operational conditions would be extremely harmful to the customer, far beyond the loss deriving from not having built the stadium cover. Clearly, this solution should be agreed in advance with the customer as well as contractually formalized.

'MoSCoW' is a technique used to prioritize the lists of project requirements or of the project scope components. This acronym was derived from the names attributed to the four priority levels that may correspond to elements in a list:

- Must – vital project requirements. Were a project activity or project solution not in adherence to this requirement, it would not be considered 'acceptable'.

- Should – essential or high-priority project requirements. Their achievement should always be assured, otherwise benefits expected in the Business Case could be compromised.

- Could – desirable project requirements. Their achievement is not strictly necessary.

- Won't have this time – project requirements that are not achieved by a certain stage or in a certain release, but that could be reconsidered at a later stage.

Priority allocation is required in cooperation with the customer and/or final user, who is aware of business needs and of requirements to be achieved in order for the project output to be 'fit for purpose'.

Should the customer agree to de-scoping the project, in this case, part of the deliverables would not be released.

IDENTIFY ACTIVITY COSTS FOR THE EXECUTION AND MANAGEMENT OF THE PROJECT

In a number of projects, the effort of cost estimation processes is reduced to the activities required to deliver the project product, for example, either a building or a software application, whereas general Project Management activities are not considered, although the resources spent on such activities would have to be budgeted for.

In some projects, management costs are underestimated; for example, 10 per cent of the total cost is allocated, whatever the project complexity and the number of stakeholders concerned with it, leading to the possibility of a massive increase in the final costs.

Especially for those projects in which team members are in charge of both management and production, the management effort is often incorrectly estimated whenever it is not recognized as 'real' work, inclusive of extended, resource-consuming tasks, such as preparing documentation, making phone calls, sending or receiving emails, all of which have a marked influence on cost, quality and delivery dates. Therefore, if management costs are disregarded, project costs will be miscalculated.

IDENTIFY STAKEHOLDERS AND DEFINE THE COMMUNICATION STRATEGY

Stakeholder identification is extremely important. Whether an individual, a group of individuals or an organization are identified as stakeholders, as long as they influence – or are allegedly influenced by – a project, this occurrence can be considered either as a threat or as an opportunity for the project.

In order for engagement of interested parties – besides communication among them – to be ensured, the following step-by-step procedure is suggested by the best practice MSP® (OGC 2011):

1.   Identify stakeholders.

2.   Create and analyse stakeholder profiles.

3.   Define a communication strategy to involve stakeholders.

4.   Plan the involvement.

5.   Implement participation and communication.

6.   Measure the effectiveness of the strategy application.

Having identified the stakeholders – which can be grouped in accordance with affinity criteria – the analysis process consists of an understanding of their influence levels on the project, as well as of their positive or negative attitudes, so that it can be determined whether they should be given more or less attention.

Taking into consideration stakeholder interests – whether they are deemed more or less reasonable – is required even though some of these stakeholders may have a wrong perception, which nonetheless might potentially influence a successful project outturn.

Whenever a quantification of benefits and disbenefits – as they are perceived by individual stakeholders – is feasible, this information becomes useful for the purpose of a benefit management strategy and also of a communication strategy (for example, in terms of information to be supplied, rate of supply, communication channel, source and destination).

It is essential that the effectiveness of communication be monitored, that convenient information be conveyed to the intended destination and that all the main interested parties be kept informed. New stakeholders might be identified and new needs might arise over the project lifetime: this new context requires rapidly updating and adapting communication strategies.

While stakeholder management is a continuous effort, it can also become an extremely onerous effort, whenever – for example – meetings have to be scheduled with hundreds of shareholders or expensive express mail service has to be used. This effort is, in any case, required in order to prevent potential threats to the project.

PREPARE THE PROJECT PLAN

Project plans are essential mechanisms to ensure that provisions are made for project cost monitoring and control; first of all, they dictate how and when agreed objectives are to be achieved, but they also define key checkpoints.

In adherence with PRINCE2® guidelines, a summary project plan description is suggested, emphasizing the key points. Subsequently, the following elements should be included in the plan: pre-requisites influencing project success; external dependencies (if present) that interfere or might interfere with the plan; planning assumptions made that affect the project plan; lessons learned from previous projects and adapted to the current plan; project monitoring and control data; project budget; tolerances on schedule, cost and scope, besides other variables relevant to the project; description of the project product (all and only the products included in the scope of the project); and visual descriptions such as bar charts or histograms.

Whenever project costs are to be estimated, consideration should be given to the resources required to prepare and maintain the project plan. This is initially an overall plan; more details will be refined and formalized sequentially during the stage plan.

PREPARE THE BENEFIT MEASUREMENT PLAN

The benefit measurement plan is a management document defining how and when to evaluate the achievement of the expected project benefits; projects are initiated because the customer organization intends to realize benefits besides the delivery of project outputs *per se*.

There have been examples of good Project Management practice, in which – although the project requirements were successfully achieved and also planned costs and delivery dates were met – expected benefits were disappointingly missed. Failure to achieve benefits means loss of profit and reputation; concurrently, had the customer been informed on time, this might have led to the decision to terminate the project and switching funds over to alternative investments.

The list of expected project benefits is included in the Business Case and is regularly updated. The measurement plan defines procedures and schedules for the assessment of benefits achieved from the project.

Benefits shall be measurable so as not to incur risks of disputes arising from 'subjective' interpretations.

The importance of the benefit measurement plan cannot be overemphasized: as is repeatedly noted, customer satisfaction relies not only on completion of the project in adherence to requirements, but also on the achievement of the expected benefits. This is the reason for having in place a mechanism to actually ascertain whether the benefits have been attained and the conditions for this.

Project cost estimates shall consider resource requirements related to preparing and maintaining the plan besides costs to be incurred for the actual ascertainment of benefits during the Project Life Cycle.

CONSIDER UTILIZING A PMO

Certain organizations are in favour of *ad hoc* practices for managing individual projects. Conversely, PMOs can be created to support the adoption of best practices in projects, while conveniently monitoring their performance, in order for all internal resources to be optimally utilized, besides reporting as required to support strategic decisions.

PMOs, for example, are present in those organizations in which several projects are to be managed or in highly burdensome projects where some strategic value is seen as inherent in project performance for successful business.

The costs incurred for using PMOs may be charged either to the organization or to the project, depending upon the selected cost allocation model.

In some organizations, a network of PMOs, who are effectively inter-related, may be envisaged as the backbone conveying all elements of information and all reports to be provided to senior management for the purpose of controlling the good health and the performance of projects; successful outcomes are guaranteed to a project if vital information is provided, besides accurate cost management. In UK, P3O® (Portfolio, Programme and Project Offices) (OGC 2008) is the standard reference for PMO types of organization.

Tasks assigned to these offices are subject to extreme variations, as is required in certain cases. Typical functions include the following:

- provide consultancy to project teams on specific matters – legal, financial, stakeholder interface;

- analyse and monitor risks;

- provide administrative and operational support;

- support the widespread utilization of standards (for example, in the area of document preparation, adhering to industrial practices, or for the application of management methodologies);

- provide for in-house training in Project Management and specialized areas;

- provide/identify skilled staff.

The duration of the initiation stage can be conveniently shortened to a significant extent and the performance will be better if a PMO is involved in supporting the earliest period of the project, for example:

- by transferring expertise to the project team;

- by providing a list of documents to be completed, as required to obtain authorizations from public authorities;

- by providing assistance in cost management.

Note

PRINCE2®, P3O™ and MSP™ are Registered Trade Marks of AXELOS Limited.

References and Further Reading

OGC 2008. *P3O™ – Portfolio, Programme and Project Offices*. London: The Stationery Office.

OGC 2008. *Managing Successful Projects with PRINCE2®*. London: The Stationery Office.

OGC 2011. *MSP™ – Managing Successful Programmes*. London: The Stationery Office.

Chapter 6

Estimating and Budgeting for Project Activities: Project Work Breakdown Structures and Cost Breakdown Structures

TOMMASO PANETTI

Work Breakdown Structures: Definition and Examples

Using the PMI definition, the work breakdown structure (WBS) is a deliverable-oriented hierarchical decomposition of the work to be executed by the project team to accomplish the project objectives and create the stipulated deliverables. The WBS organizes and defines the total scope of the project. Each descending level represents an increasingly detailed definition of the project work. Finally, the WBS is broken down into work packages and activities. The deliverable orientation of the hierarchy includes both internal and external deliverables. The internal deliverables are used by the project team for producing the external deliverables. This is not a unique understanding; in some cases, Project Managers use to build a WBS activities oriented, which means that activities and work packages are on the top WBS levels.

In most cases, using a deliverables-oriented approach helps the team and the Project Manager to reach the '100 per cent Rule' (Haugan 2002). This is one of the most important principles guiding the development, decomposition and evaluation of the WBS. This rule states that the WBS includes 100 per cent of the work defined by the project scope and, by doing so, captures all the work to be completed. The rule applies at all levels within the hierarchy: the sum of the work at the child level must equal 100 per cent of the work represented by the parent. Moreover, the WBS should not include any work that falls outside the actual scope of the project. This means that the WBS cannot include more than 100 per cent of the work.

Table 6.1　　**Outlined WBS**

Example Project A	Phase I	Deliverable I.I	Work package I.I.I	Activity I.I.I.I
				Activity I.I.I.2
			Work package I.I.2	Activity I.I.2.I
		Deliverable I.2	Work package I.2.I	Activity I.2.I.I
			Work package I.2.2	Activity I.2.2.I
				Activity I.2.2.2

Let's imagine how this is important for a fixed-charge contract! The WBS starts to establish the work to be done within the project, no less and no more! Who has to create the WBS? The WBS can be a very powerful tool if it is created by the entire project team under the supervision on the Project Manager. Using this approach, the Project Managers assure themselves that there are not missed work and start to create team cohesion. The example in Table 6.1 is of an outlined WBS.

An example of a graphical WBS is given in Figure 6.1 on the left.

Projects can also be organized into phases. As stated by the PMI® (PMI® 2013), the definition of a phase is a collection of logically related project activities that culminates in the completion of one or more deliverable. Dividing a project into phases makes it possible to lead it in the best possible direction. Through this organization into phases, the total workload of a project is divided into smaller components. This is very important

BILLING SYSTEM DELIVERY	
Initiation I.I	Evaluation and Recommendations I.I.I
	Develop Project Charter I.I.2
	Project Sponsor Reviews Project Charter I.I.3
	Project Charter Approved I.I.4
Planning I.2	Create Scope Statement I.2.I
	Build Project Team I.2.2
	Develop Project Plan I.2.3
	Project Plan Approved I.2.4
Execution I.3	Project Kick-Off Meeting I.3.I
	Verify User Requirements I.3.2
	Design System I.3.3
	Build System I.3.4
	Testing Phase I.3.5
	Install Live System I.3.6
	User Training I.3.7
Control I.4	Project Management I.4.I
	Risk Management I.4.2
Closeout I.5	Audit Procurement I.5.I
	Document Lessons Learned I.5.2
	Gain Formal Acceptance I.5.3
	Archive Project Files and Documents I.5.4

Figure 6.1　　**Graphical WBS**

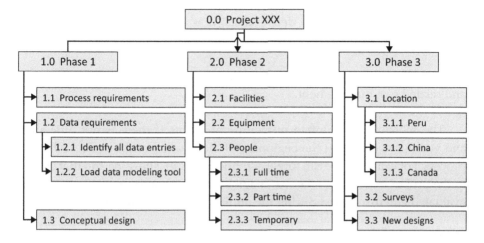

Figure 6.2   Project phases and deliverables

Source: Figure 6.2 is based on Figure 6 'An example of a work breakdown structure (WBS) based on project phase'. Available at: http://cnx.org/content/m32170/latest/ [accessed 10 October 2014]. Licensed by Merrie Barron, PMP, CSM and Andrew R. Barron under creative commons. See http://creativecommons.org/licenses/by/4.0

for large projects. Phases can be also organized into different contracts. For example, the project phase budget can be tuned and approved at the end of the previous phase: phases help the organization to reach a better project estimation. Figure 6.2 above represents a project with three phases at the top level and deliverables at the second level.

Do you want to improve your organization in terms of projects expertise? You can start immediately creating a collection of WBS templates for use by the Project Managers. Organizations very often perform projects that have a many similarities among them. WBS templates help the companies to standardize the different project elements. Different projects may have similar work package names and activities; therefore, the turnover of team members can be sustained more efficiently. The Project Management Office (PMO) should be the owner and maintainer of WBS templates.

Benefits Related to the Creation of the WBS

The creation of the WBS is the basis for an effective Project Management. We can say that there is not a project without a WBS! In fact, it is not possible to manage a project without understanding the scope of the project. Then, the WBS defines what is included and what is not included in terms of the scope of the project and its deliverables: it is clear that the WBS prevents many misunderstandings.

A clear and complete WBS is the basis for an accurate project estimation and related cost management.

The schedule can contain numerous problems if there is not a detailed and well-formed WBS at the beginning of the creation of the project schedule process. For example, we can forget activities that must be done and that belong to the project critical path. Let us imagine how this can be a problem if this is evaluated and discovered during the implementation of the project.

The WBS is a powerful tool for allowing the project stakeholders to understand the project scope and 'to buy into' the project. In fact, due to the creation of the WBS, at the beginning of the project life, the stakeholders regard the project as their own project.

The WBS helps Project Managers manage the project as a whole, without gaps, including the management of the outsourced service providers, for example, suppliers or owners, in addition to internal project team members.

The WBS creates accountability. In fact, it makes it easier to hold people accountable for completing their tasks. A well-defined task can be assigned to a specific individual, who is then responsible for its completion.

Picking the Right WBS Approach for Creating a High-Quality WBS

Using the PMI's approach, it is important to define how to manage the scope within the Scope Management Plan. This means that, for each project, the Project Managers, the team and the involved stakeholders must answer the following question: 'Which one is the right WBS approach for this project?' Finding the answer to this question, and to the related questions, means analysing:

- the project charter that initiates the project within the organization;

- the requirements;

- the organizational process assets.

For large projects it is important to divide the projects into phases and to re-estimate, by means of a full WBS, the nearest phase where the result plan can be of the appropriate accuracy level.

Past experiences and the PMI standard identify the need to create a deliverable-oriented WBS: the deliverable must be at the top level.

The 100 per cent rule must not be overlooked: all the project scope must be described and managed by the WBS.

The WBS must arrange all major and minor deliverables in a hierarchical structure; in this way it is possible to show the dependencies among deliverables.

This hierarchical representation of the WBS enables a full and deep understanding. Moreover, the graphical representation is very useful during project meetings.

It is important to use a code within the WBS. By means of coding each item of the WBS, the team has the possibility of identifying it in a unique way, without misunderstandings. The example in Figure 6.3 below explains that the 'Roles and tasks correlation' deliverable is composed by the 'Key users identification', 'Matrix roles and tasks' and 'Contact list' work packages.

Regarding the terminology, it can be useful to use nouns and adjectives, not verbs. For example, a good WBS item is 'Requirement documentation', while a bad one is 'Write the requirement documentation'.

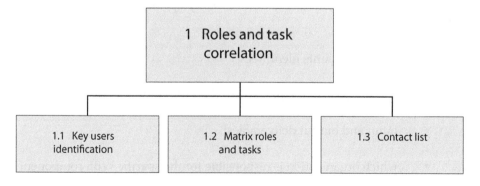

Figure 6.3   Hierarchical structure of a WBS

The WBS can evolve along with the progressive elaboration of project scope, up to the point of scope baseline, and thereafter in accordance with project change control. In this way, it is possible to allow a continual project improvement.

Last but not least, a high-quality WBS is not the product of an isolated Project Manager. Teams, stakeholders and sponsors must be coordinated and forced by Project Managers to give their contributions to the creation of the WBS. The WBS can also be refined in a final brainstorming meeting where graphical representations can be reviewed and refined, to be delivered subsequently.

A result of the creation of the WBS must be to define work packages and activities. A work package is an aggregation of activities. An example of work package is 'Solution Design', while examples of activities are 'Conceptual design', 'Logical design' and 'Physical design'. Different work packages can be allocated, for example, to different functional divisions within the organization or to different teams within the project. Moreover, work packages can be managed by external suppliers. Activities can be allocated, for example, directly to project team members. The activities are then enriched by attributes and used in the schedule.

WBS Dictionary

The WBS dictionary describes each WBS component. The format and structure of the description per component may vary based on organizational practices and project guidelines, but – broadly speaking – should cover the following items:

- code of accounts identifier;

- a description of the purpose of the WBS component;

- input and output deliverables;

- which organization is responsible for the specific WBS component;

- schedule activities (start and end dates) with their schedule milestones;

- resource and quality requirements;

- cost estimates;

- acceptance criteria;

- technical information required for the proper performance of work;

- other relevant references; and

- related contract information.

The WBS dictionary must be consulted before starting any work package/ component in order to ensure that proper standards, procedures and quality control measures are being followed. Due to ever-changing circumstances, the WBS dictionary is the subject of constant revision. Therefore, it is important to frequently review its contents in order to ensure the proper management of the project.

The WBS dictionary, managed by a PMO, can be easily re-used in other projects. The PMO is also responsible for maintaining the WBS dictionary template. Table 6.2 gives an example of a simple and light WBS dictionary.

Table 6.2   WBS dictionary

WBS ID	WBS element name	Description
1	Roles and task correlation	The aim of this work package is to correlate roles and task within team members and other stakeholders
1.1	Key user identification	By means of key user identification activity, all the key users are identified. It is important to underline the related office and key user goals within the company
1.2	Matrix roles and tasks	To produce a matrix where roles/key users and tasks are correlated
1.3	Contact list	The contact list is a document that is always updated with all the key users' name and surname, job description, goals, phone number, email, mobile phone number

*WBS Number: 1.1	*WBS Name: Plan Requirements	*WBS Author: Jane Smith
WBS Predecessor(s): N/A Which WBS components must finish before this starts	**WBS Description:** Document the description of this component in a few sentences here	
WBS LOE: 10 FTEs for 3 months		
Must Start: A must start date		
Must Finish: A must finish date	**Assumptions and constraints:** Identify any assumptions or constraints that could help project/scheduling	

Figure 6.4   WBS dictionary with component descriptions

Figure 6.4 above shows an example of a complete WBS component description within a dictionary.

The WBS Synthesis: Control Accounts

One of the goals of WBS is to allocate each work package to a control account. A control account is a management control point (PMI® 2013) where scope, budget, cost and schedule are integrated and compared with the earned value for performance measurement.

Each control account can include one or more work packages. Each work package must be associated only with one control account. Control accounts must have defined responsibilities within project teams: for example, for team leaders, functional leaders or Project Managers themselves.

Control accounts help the Project Manager to keep the project under control and to measure the project variances during the execution of the project in order for trends to be evaluated and any corrective actions to be initiated. The approach at the root of the control account is Plan-Do-Check-Act (PDCA), where the control account is used within the Check phase with the aim of employing the proper corrective actions.

Project Estimating and Budgeting

The WBS approach and creation that we have discussed previously has been useful mainly for the definition of the scope of the project.

Now, we move on to deal with the estimating and budgeting task. The aim is to define the resources needed for each project activity.

Something that is very beneficial for this purpose has been a golden rule used in the previous chapter: recognize the role of individual project activities so that each one can be easy to estimate and manage. Breaking down the more complex work into small activities will help the Project Manager and the project team to estimate the project in a more accurate way.

Breaking down is also employed as another very useful tool for estimating the 'Resource Breakdown Structure' (RBS). By means of the RBS, it is possible to start from the main resource categories (human resources, equipment, computers, etc.) and to provide details for the required resources (surveyor, press, laptop, etc.).

Identification of Estimation Approaches

It is possible to identify several techniques and estimation approaches. In a project it can also be useful to employ different techniques for different work packages. In fact, opportunities deriving from historical data, expertise, etc. can provide guidance for choosing the right estimation approaches.

ONE-POINT ESTIMATING

This type of estimate takes one estimate per activity. The disadvantages of this process are many:

- the estimator might buffer his or her estimate;

- it can result in an estimation that no one believes in, thus decreasing the buy-in of the team to the Project Management process;

- if somebody estimates an activity for the duration of 30 days and it is completed in 20 days, this could be considered as an unacceptable result because the estimation is incorrect.

This type of estimation should be used only for very simple projects/activities where a very reliable plan is not required.

ANALOGY ESTIMATING

Analogy estimating uses a similar past project to estimate the duration or cost of your current project; it is also known as top-down estimating.

This approach can be used when there is limited information regarding the project. The main benefit of using the analogy estimating technique is that it is less costly than other estimating techniques. The downside of using this technique is that it is also generally less accurate.

With this approach, experience and judgement must be applied, as it is considered a combination of historical information and expert judgment.

With the aim of producing a quality estimation, the project team must have access to adequate information about the previous project:

- Scope statements – the team will be unaware of whether two projects are in fact similar unless descriptions of the project and product scopes can be compared.

- WBS – the WBS from the previous project is also necessary to ensure that similar processes and steps will be followed in the current project. Differences in the two projects could affect the accuracy of cost estimates.

- Performance reports – actual costs are the most important information from the preceding project.

PARAMETRIC ESTIMATING

Parametric estimating uses statistical relationships between historical costs and other programme variables such as system physical or performance characteristics, contractor output measures or manpower loading.

A closely correlated concept to parametric estimating is the learning curve: individuals who perform repetitive tasks reveal an improvement in performance as the task is repeated a number of times. The main conclusions of the learning curve theory are the following:

1.   The time required to perform a task decreases as the task is repeated.

2.   The amount of improvement decreases as more units are produced.

3.   The rate of improvement has sufficient consistency to allow its use as a prediction tool.

HEURISTIC

The heuristic method is also known as a rule of thumb. An example is the assertion that 'the design activity is 15 per cent of the total project'.

It is based on experience and on statistical models. It is a very quick estimation process, but it can produce estimation errors due to a lack of knowledge about project risks, project peculiarities, etc.

THREE-POINT ESTIMATING

Three-point estimating is an analytical technique to determine and improve the accuracy of estimates of cost or duration.

The project team or the estimator produces three estimates:

- the most likely estimate (M);

- the optimistic estimate (O);

- the pessimistic estimate (P).

The expected value is determined as follows:

$$\text{Expected value} = \frac{P + 4 * M + O}{6}$$

The Main Types of Estimating Error

In conclusion, why do Project Managers and team happen to make a wrong estimate? The following is a list of the most frequent errors:

- Scope omissions – these derive from items accidentally left out of the estimate: soft costs (permits, fees, etc.), hard construction costs or work packages and activities. Omissions may be due to items missing from the plans and specification.

- Wrong assumptions – these are items that were assumed to be covered under a contractor's or subcontractor's bid, but actually are not.

- Insufficient use of historical data – often organizations have a lot of useful information that sometimes is not completely used by the project team during the estimation phase. A PMO, if present, can improve the re-use of historical data for estimation purposes within organizations.

- Inadequate allowances – an estimate may be submitted by a contractor or subcontractor with a material allowance that is too low.

- Price changes – material or labour costs may rise following the estimation and project start date. If necessary, it is important to check the material and labour costs before approving and starting the project.

- New materials and techniques – each new material or building technique has a learning curve.

- Low level of expertise – specific projects require specific expertise.

Analysis of Reserves

Project managers must reserve budget for managing risks that have not yet been discovered. It is important to execute a very high-quality risk analysis and to identify as many risks as possible, as well as to allocate budget and resources for individual risks; on the other hand, it is always possible that new risks will arise and the reserve must assist the Project Manager in managing them.

The following kinds of reserves are envisaged: contingency reserves and management reserves.

The contingency reserve is the cost or time reserve that is used to manage the identified risks ('known unknowns'). It is controlled by the Project Manager, who has authority to use it when any identified risk occurs.

The management reserve is the cost or time reserve that is used to manage unidentified risks ('unknown unknowns'). It is not an estimated reserve; it is defined in line with the organization's policy (for example, three per cent of the total project).

Developing the Final Budget: The Cost Breakdown Structure (CBS)

The following is an example of the creation of the project budgeting process – the criteria used is bottom-up from activities at the bottom to full-cost budget on the top.

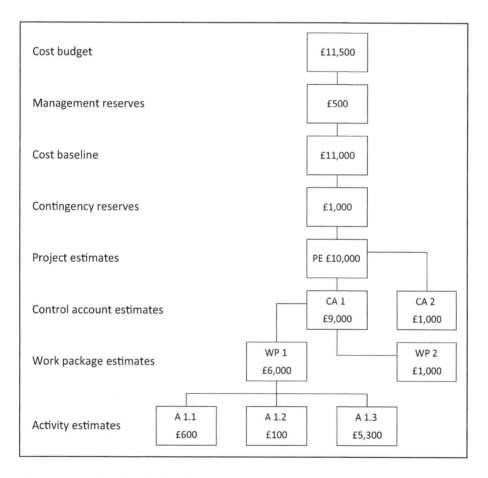

Figure 6.5   Project budgeting process

Within the CBS, costs are allocated to the lowest level of the WBS and are aggregated into work packages. The structure of the CBS is often the same as for the WBS at the lowest level, but this is not mandatory. Certainly, the elements of the CBS must be correlated to the elements of the WBS. The tasks at this level can often be subdivided into discrete activities to be completed by different departments: therefore, one task may have several cost elements. Once costs have been assigned to tasks, it is possible to monitor the project in terms of actual, forecast and earned costs on a task.

The budget process starts from the activities and concludes with the cost budget for the entire project, applying contingency and management reserves.

What must be included on the budget? The answer is all the economic items that are related to the project, for example:

- cost of quality;

- risk management cost;

- labour costs;

- material costs;

- miscellaneous costs.

Costs under consideration may belong to any of the following categories:

- variable costs, for example, depending on material quantities;

- fixed costs, for example, rental costs;

- direct costs directly attributed to the project, for example, travel costs;

- indirect costs related to several projects, for example, taxes.

During the life of a project, it is possible that several levels of the project budget are required at different times: early budgets can be refined later in a more accurate fashion. Therefore, it is very important that, when a budget is produced, its level of accuracy is always stated.

The usual levels of budget accuracy are as follows:

- A 'rough order of magnitude' (ROM) estimate is the least accurate estimate. ROMs are -50 to +50 per cent accurate; the range may be even greater. They are used very early in the project when there is limited information on the scope of the project.

- A budget estimate is a preliminary assessment either of the funds projected to be available to a company or agency, or of the funds required to complete a project. These estimates provide valuable information for planning purposes, but are not the final step.

- In Project Management, a definitive estimate is a good one. There is the possibility of some variance from the estimate, but definitive estimates are -5 to +10 per cent accurate.

Once the first version of project budget is produced, it will be taken into account for variances and trend analysis. Other project budget versions can be released later and compared with the first one, that is, the baseline.

References and Further Reading

Haugan, G.T. 2002. *How to Build a Work Breakdown Structure, the Cornerstone of Project Management.* Arlington: ESI International.

Norman, E.S., Brotherton, S.A. and Fried, R.T. 2008. *Work Breakdown Structures: The Foundation for Project Management Excellence.* New York: John Wiley & Sons, Inc.

PMI® 2013. *The Guide to the Project Management Body of Knowledge,* 5th edn. Newtown Square: Project Management Institute.

Chapter 7

Developing and Managing the Project Schedule

TOMMASO PANETTI

Introduction

The aim of this chapter is to provide concepts and tools for developing an effective project schedule. Time can be an enemy of project managers or can become their best friend: it depends on how well the schedule is designed, how precisely it is realizable and how closely it is shared between project team members and stakeholders!

Schedule Overview

Using the PMI language, the project schedule presents linked activities with planned dates, durations, milestones and resources.

There are different levels in which the project schedule can be presented. It can be influenced, for example, by whom the schedule is addressed to. If the schedule is addressed to Executive Management and sponsors, it should be at a higher level of abstraction in order for them to be able to glean key information on the project. On the other hand, if we have to discuss the schedule with the customers, we can focus our representation on key input and output. If we have to discuss with team members the status of project activities, we will probably use the maximum level of details (see the examples given in Figures 7.1, 7.2 and 7.3 on the next page).

Moreover, the level of schedule representation depends on the maturity of the project. In fact, we can develop a project schedule in the initial phase of

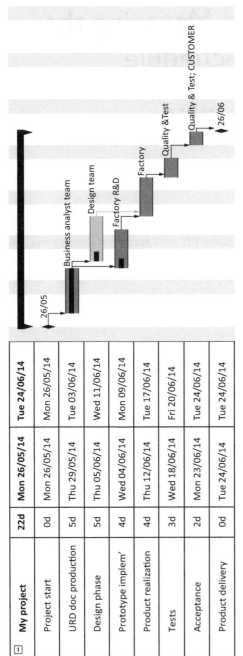

My project	22d	Mon 26/05/14	Tue 24/06/14
Project start	0d	Mon 26/05/14	Mon 26/05/14
URD doc production	5d	Thu 29/05/14	Tue 03/06/14
Design phase	5d	Thu 05/06/14	Wed 11/06/14
Prototype implem'	4d	Wed 04/06/14	Mon 09/06/14
Product realization	4d	Thu 12/06/14	Tue 17/06/14
Tests	3d	Wed 18/06/14	Fri 20/06/14
Acceptance	2d	Mon 23/06/14	Tue 24/06/14
Product delivery	0d	Tue 24/06/14	Tue 24/06/14

Figure 7.1   Example of a Gantt chart for Executive Management and sponsors

My project	17d	Thu 22/05/14	Fri 13/06/14
Project start	0d	Thu 22/05/14	Thu 22/05/14
User req't definition	5d	Thu 22/05/14	Wed 28/05/14
URD doc't delivery	0d	Wed 28/05/14	Wed 28/05/14
Design	10d	Thu 29/05/14	Wed 11/06/14
Project closing	2d	Thu 12/06/14	Fri 13/06/14

Figure 7.2   Project schedule for discussion with customers

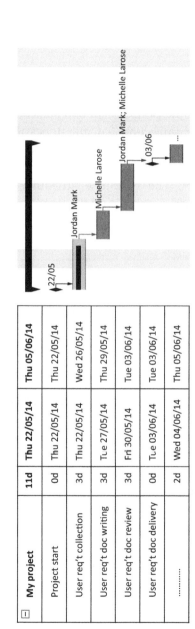

My project	11d	Thu 22/05/14	Thu 05/06/14
Project start	0d	Thu 22/05/14	Thu 22/05/14
User req't collection	3d	Thu 22/05/14	Wed 26/05/14
User req't doc writing	3d	Tue 27/05/14	Thu 29/05/14
User req't doc review	3d	Fri 30/05/14	Tue 03/06/14
User req't doc delivery	0d	Tue 03/06/14	Tue 03/06/14
……….	2d	Wed 04/06/14	Thu 05/06/14

Figure 7.3   Project schedule for discussion with team members

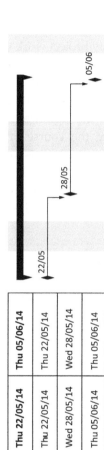

My project	10d	Thu 22/05/14	Thu 05/06/14
Project start	0d	Thu 22/05/14	Thu 22/05/14
User req't doc delivery	0d	Wed 28/05/14	Wed 28/05/14
Design delivery	0d	Thu 05/06/14	Thu 05/06/14

Figure 7.4   Project milestone schedule

project planning. This can be a summary level schedule which highlights the principal activities and tasks and their estimated duration. It can serve as an early communication tool for an initial buy-in for the project with upper-level management and other stakeholders.

At a later stage, a detailed schedule can be derived for the project. This is an operational schedule intended to help front-line managers in directing hourly, daily or weekly project work tasks.

Last but not least, a very important schedule is the milestone schedule. This is a summary level schedule that allows the project team and stakeholders to identify all of the significant and major project-related milestones that may appear during the course of a project. Because of its easy-to-read format, the milestone schedule is recommended for status reporting to top-level management and external stakeholders. The milestone schedule is often referred to throughout the project life cycle. Figure 7.4 on the previous page is an example of milestone schedule.

Schedule Terminology

The following is a list of terms and definitions that are useful for understanding and managing schedules.

SCHEDULES

This consists of a list of project activities with intended start and finish dates.

MILESTONE

This is a key event during the life of a project, usually at the completion of project deliverables or another noteworthy achievement.

GANTT CHART

This is a popular Project Management bar chart that tracks tasks over time. When it was first developed in 1917, the Gantt chart did not show the relationships between tasks. This has become common in current use, as both time and interdependencies between tasks are tracked.

CRITICAL PATH

This is the sequence of activities that must be completed on time for the entire project to be completed on schedule. It is the longest duration path through the project plan. If an activity on the critical path is delayed by one day, the entire project will be delayed by one day unless another activity on the critical path can be finished a day earlier than planned.

TOTAL FLOAT

This is the total amount of time whereby a scheduled activity can be delayed from its early start without delaying the project finish date or violating a schedule constraint. It is calculated by using the critical path method technique and determining the difference between the early finish dates and late finish dates.

FREE FLOAT

This is the amount of time whereby a scheduled activity can be delayed without delaying the early start date of any immediately following schedule activities.

Identifying the Schedule

The starting point for identifying the schedule is the generation of the activities list, which follows the WBS definition. More specifically, the WBS shows a decomposition of the project scope into work packages; each work package can be broken down into activities. The main characteristics of an activity are that it must be easily estimated and addressed.

The following tasks are useful for identifying the schedule with a step-by-step approach:

- create the project network diagram that explains the logical connections between activities;

- determine the network schedule information (duration, total float and free float, etc.);

- develop the entire and final schedule using a precedence diagram.

The details of the step-by-step approach are explained over the following few pages.

CREATION OF A NETWORK DIAGRAM

A network diagram is a sequence of steps (activities), commonly represented by blocks, that are connected to each other in the logical sequence of their occurrence. There are four standard types of dependencies between activities:

- Start to Start (SS) – 'A SS B' means that B cannot start before A starts (or that Activity B can start after Activity A has started).

- Start to Finish (SF) – 'A SF B' means that B cannot finish before A starts.

- Finish to Start (FS) – 'A FS B' means that B cannot start before A is finished (or else Activity A must be completed before Activity B can begin).

- Finish to Finish (FF) – 'A FF B' means that B cannot finish before A is finished (or that Activity A must be completed before Activity B can finish).

An example of graphical representation is provided in Figure 7.5 opposite. FS is considered a 'natural dependency'. In fact, typically, each predecessor activity would finish prior to the start of its successor activities. Figure 7.6 gives an example of a network diagram for our case study.

Dependencies can be modified by leads and lags. Both leads and lags can be applied to all four types of dependencies. The PMBOK® Guide (PMI® 2013) defines 'lag' as:

> *the amount of time whereby a successor activity will be delayed with respect to a predecessor activity.*

It also defines 'lead' as:

> *the amount of time whereby a successor activity can be advanced with respect to a predecessor activity.*

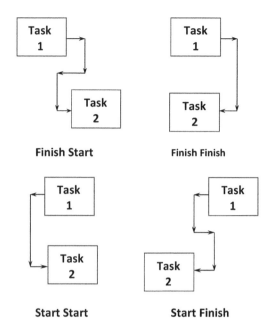

Figure 7.5   Dependencies between project activities

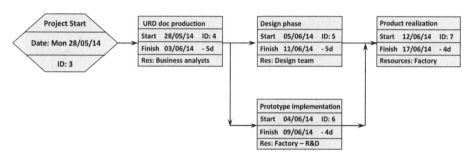

Figure 7.6   Network diagram example

NETWORK CALCULATION: CRITICAL PATH, TOTAL FLOAT AND FREE FLOAT

The network calculation is based on the following main concepts:

- critical path definition;

- how to calculate the 'early start dates';

- how to calculate total and free float.

These basic concepts will be defined before they are used in preparing a precedence diagram.

CRITICAL PATH DEFINITION

The critical path is the longest path for a project. This is the minimum amount of time needed for the completion of the project. The critical path identification and analysis is a critical aspect of schedule management:

- the activities along this path must be accelerated in order to speed up the project;

- on the other hand, delays in these activities would cause delays in the project.

An example of a critical path is shown in Figure 7.7 below.

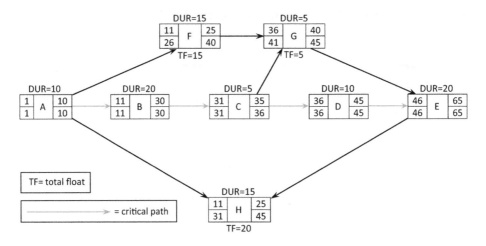

Figure 7.7   Example of a critical path

HOW TO CALCULATE THE 'EARLY START DATES'

The early start (ES) date for an activity is the earliest date at which the activity can begin. Starting dates can be assigned to each activity by executing a forward pass. The forward pass consists of proceeding through the network diagram from left to right, beginning with the project start date. The estimate considers durations and resource availability calendars.

These steps should be followed to calculate the early start dates of subsequent activities, assuming FS relationships among activities:

- add the predecessor activity duration to its start date;

- add the lag time or subtract the lead time;

- refer to the resource calendar(s) applicable to the people and equipment necessary for the activity, and add the number of days that the activity requires;

- assign the calculated date as the ES date of the successor activity.

TOTAL AND FREE FLOAT

The total float is the difference between the finish date of the last activity on the critical path and the project completion date. Any delay in an activity on the critical path would reduce the amount of total float available on the project. A project can also have negative float, which means that the calculated completion date of the last activity is later than the targeted completion date established at the beginning of the project.

If activities that are not on the critical path have a difference between their ES date and their late start date, those activities can be delayed without affecting the project completion date. The float on those activities is called free float.

PREPARING A PRECEDENCE DIAGRAM

As a consequence of the previous steps, all the tools and concepts useful for preparing a precedence diagram are now available.

When assembling the precedence diagram, each task is normally represented as a box, and tasks are linked with arrows to show their predecessors.

Figure 7.8, on the next page, represents two correlated tasks and shows how you can include in the graphical representation all the useful information for the network analysis, even the float information.

It is possible to draw the precedence diagram from left to right with the final task on the right. The following list summarizes the information that is relevant to an activity:

- DUR – the duration of each activity (how long the activity will take to complete);

- EST – the earliest start time (the earliest an activity can start without interfering with the completion of any preceding activity);

- LST – the latest start time (the latest an activity can start without interfering with the start of any subsequent activity);

- EFT – the earliest finish time (the earliest an activity can finish);

- LFT – the latest finish time (the latest an activity can finish without interfering with the start of any subsequent activity);

- FLOAT – the 'float' time of an activity (the time available to perform the activity less the time needed, or the time available minus the duration of the activity).

The critical activities are those with zero float; for a critical activity, EST = LST.

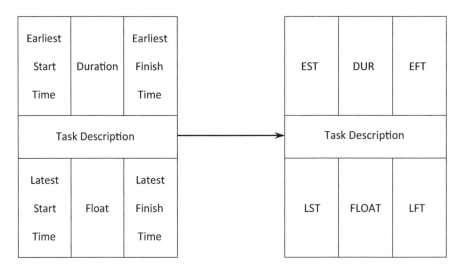

Figure 7.8   Correlation of tasks in a precedence diagram

The following approach can be adopted to insert all the relevant information within the precedence diagram:

- establish activity dependencies;

- establish activity duration;

- execute the Forward Pass:

  - calculate the EST and the EFT for each task proceeding through the network from the beginning to the end of the project.

- execute the Backward Pass:

  - calculate the LST and the LFT for each task processing the network from the end of the project to the beginning of the project.

- calculate activity float (LFT – [EST + DUR]);

- identify the critical path, the path with the 'zero' float in each activity.

The final precedence diagram will be similar to our example given in Figure 7.9 below (the critical path is in bold).

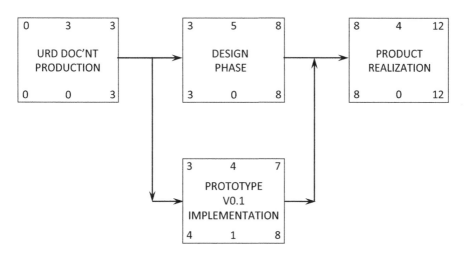

Figure 7.9   Example of a precedence diagram

Summary of the Procedure

1. Estimate the time required to complete each project activity.

2. Calculate the time available to complete each activity (considering resource estimation, for example, the 'three-point method').

3. Create the precedence diagram identifying the critical path (zero float activities).

4. Calculate the total project duration.

5. Agree the resources needed and their availability with the Executive/Project Board. Adjust resources and/or schedule if necessary.

6. Agree the schedule with the project team and other stakeholders.

7. Prepare and publish the project schedule.

   (Steps 1 to 6 can be iterated several times!)

Many commercial software products for Project Management are able to support the project manager in the creation of the schedule. Figures 7.10 and 7.11 give an example created by means of a dedicated software at different levels of detail.

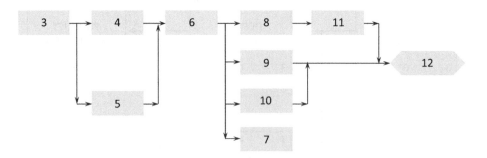

Figure 7.10   The precedence diagram at a glance

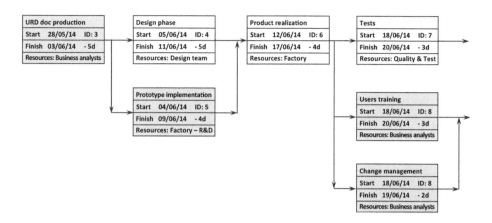

Figure 7.11   Detail of the precedence diagram: Boxes with a white background are placed on the critical path

References and Further Reading

PMI® 2013. *The Guide to the Project Management Body of Knowledge*, 5th edn. Newtown Square: Project Management Institute.

Chapter 8

Resource Issues in Schedule Management

TOMMASO PANETTI

Introduction

One of the main tasks of a Project Manager is to effectively manage the resources assigned to the project. The resources are of several typologies: builders, testers, inspectors, labour hours of the designers, etc. Managing the subcontractor labour is also included. Very often the Project Manager must manage the equipment used for the project and the material needed by the people for building the project deliverables. All of them are resources assigned by the organization as part of the Project Manager's responsibilities.

There are typically several issues that the Project Manager will encounter regarding resource management throughout the life of the project, for example:

- issues concerning the attitude of project human resources towards communication, procedures, roles in the project team and external stakeholders;

- issues about resource quality and quantity – this is applicable both to human resources and material/equipment available for the project;

- issues about the time needed to complete the project or its individual work packages;

- issues relating to the question 'how much human resources buy the project?';

- issues about shared resources among different projects.

The aim of this chapter is to provide useful tools and approaches for effective resource management while taking into consideration the above issues.

Organization Categories and the Responsibility Assignment Matrix

Probably, too many times work environments are found where roles, processes and procedures are not clear. The Responsibility Assignment Matrix (RAM) is a tool that enables the Project Manager to avoid misunderstandings within the project organization and with the project team and the company organization.

Now, it is important to think about the different categories of organizations that Project Managers can encounter in their work; a RAM can be used as a management tool for dealing with these different categories in the best possible way. The following description characterizes organizations from the lowest to the highest level in terms of project culture.

In a functional organization the Project Manager has absolutely no control over the project budget or its resources. He or she acts more as an assistant than as a Project Manager. Functional managers are responsible for budgeting and for the allocation of resources.

In a 'weak matrix' organization, projects are managed by functional staff while functional managers are in charge of managing the budget and resources of their projects. In this arrangement, the Project Manager is really understood as a project expediter with a lower level of authority.

In the 'balanced matrix' organization, there is a recognized need for Project Managers, but the idea is that they should work side-by-side with functional managers to manage projects. Project Managers and functional managers share the budget and resource responsibilities, and work together in a sort of 'balanced' authority.

The 'strong matrix' organizations usually have a Project Management Office (PMO) in place where the organizational Project Management standards are clearly defined and enforced. Company managers request the assistance of a Project Manager from the PMO. When the Project Manager is assigned to the project, he or she is responsible for the resources and budget of the project. Project team members report to the functional managers and the Project Manager.

In the 'projectized' organization, that is, the top level of the maturity model from the point of view of a Project Manager, the business handles projects and has no true functional management roles other than perhaps payroll and human resources. The project team members report directly to the Project Managers. Employees in these organizations continuously work on projects. When the organization runs out of projects, there is no work for the staff. The Project Manager reports to clients and PMOs.

This clearly means that for a Project Manager, it is more difficult to work in a functional/weak environment that in a strong/projectized one. The RAM tools are always useful in these organizations, but in a functional/weak environment, they are merely regarded as a sort of a survival tool: therefore, the basic recommendation to Project Managers is to understand your company organization and keep the right tools in your toolkit!

A RAM, also known as a RACI matrix or Linear Responsibility Chart (LRC), describes the participation of various roles in completing different tasks or deliverables for a project or stages in a business process. RACI is an acronym derived from the four key responsibilities most typically used:

- Responsible – those who do the work to achieve the task. There is typically only one Responsible who is shown in a RACI matrix, although others can be delegated to assist in the work required.

- Accountable – those who are ultimately in charge of the correct and thorough completion of the deliverable or task, and the one to whom a Responsible reports. In other words, an Accountable must sign off/approve the work under his or her responsibility; there must be only one Accountable specified for each row of the matrix.

- Consulted – those whose opinions must be taken into account.

- Informed – those who are always kept up to date on the progress of the project and with whom there is only one-way communication. Often, informed people are involved only on the completion of the task or deliverable. In a project it is possible that many people are informed of a single task.

Figure 8.1 on the next page gives an example of a RAM, the RACI chart.

Function	Project Sponsor	Business Analyst	Project Manager	Software Developer
Initiate Project	C		AR	
Establish Project Plan	I	C	AR	C
Gather User Requirements	I	R	A	I
Develop Technical Requirements	I	R	A	I
Develop Software Tools	I	C	A	R
Test Software	I	R	A	C
Deploy Software	C	R	A	C

Figure 8.1   The RACI chart

The following are some benefits of using a RAM matrix:

- it reduces the problems arising from a lack of knowledge about working responsibilities of project team members;

- it keeps all the necessary people in the loop and reduces miscommunications;

- it lets the organization know if some people are assigned with too many or too few responsibilities;

- it keeps everybody up to date on who is accountable for a particular task;

- it helps develop a simple communication system to keep those in the 'Informed' category informed, for example, through emails, while involving only those in the 'Consulted' category in meetings and interactive communication. This saves a lot of working time and avoids a lot of misunderstandings; in turn, it can be a very useful input of business processes, especially in certain technological areas.

The following are useful suggestions for creating an effective RAM matrix:

- make sure that every task has at least one individual assigned for the 'Responsible' and 'Accountable' roles. It is possible that both roles are assigned to the same individual;

- make sure that every task has only one individual assigned as 'Accountable'; remember that responsibilities can be shared, but accountabilities must be allocated to a single individual;

- if there are too many people in the 'Consulted' category, it is necessary to consider moving some of these to the 'Informed' category in order to reduce loops and delays at work.

There are a number of variations of the RAM/RACI model and these can be applied according to the nature of the project:

- CAIRO, which uses 'O' for omitted;

- DACI, where 'D' represents the driver of the project activity;

- RACI-VS, which includes two roles for verification and support;

- RASCI, which includes the provision for a support function.

Duration Compression Techniques: Crashing and Fast-Tracking

A typical situation in which the schedule has to be compressed is correlated to the fact that the required resources cannot be available when needed.

Schedule compression shortens the project duration without changing the scope of the project in order to meet imposed dates, other schedule constraints or other schedule objectives. The following techniques, as reflected in the PMBOK® Guide (PMI® 2013), are widely used for schedule compression:

- crashing;

- fast-tracking.

CRASHING: MEET THE DATE AND IMPROVE COSTS

In schedule crashing, the Project Manager reviews the critical path and identifies which activities can be completed before the scheduled date by adding extra resources. The goal of this analysis is to find activities that can give the greatest reduction by adding the least amount of resources or least extra cost.

This technique often affects the project cost. Therefore, the trade-off between cost and schedule is taken into account and is used to achieve maximum schedule compression for a minimal cost increase.

Once the Project Manager qualifies those activities, he or she can add extra resources to finish them before their planned completion date.

Crashing usually affects the quality of work. In fact, using additional resources does not always guarantee better results; a critical aspect is the time needed to train the new resources.

Moreover, the communication quality within the team can be worse after introducing a crashing approach.

Figure 8.2 below shows an application of the crashing technique to improve cost in accordance with the following crash ratio formula:

Crash Ratio = (Crash cost – Normal cost)/(Normal time – Crash time)

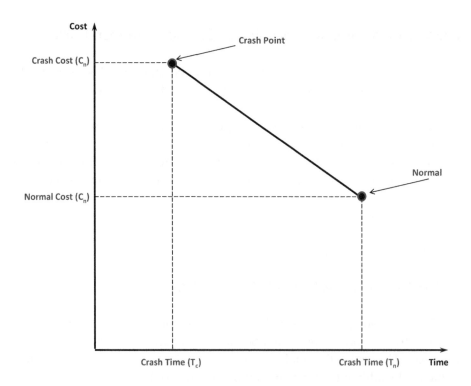

Figure 8.2 **Example of the crashing technique**

It is possible to compare different crashing approaches for a given schedule, using the crash ratio value directly.

Figure 8.3 below represents the impact of crashing technique by comparing the arrangement of two consecutive activities before crashing and after crashing.

Before crashing

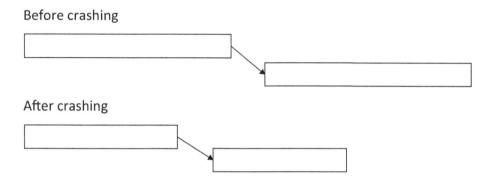

After crashing

Figure 8.3   Impact of the crashing technique on consecutive project activities

SCHEDULE FAST-TRACKING: MEET THE DATE WORKING ON THE SCHEDULE

In schedule fast-tracking, the Project Manager reviews the critical path with the aim of identifying which activities can be performed in parallel or partially in parallel to each other.

Obviously, the Project Manager will take into account the activities on the critical path because on other paths, activities are having the float; as such, there is no need to shorten the duration of such activities.

Moreover, it is interesting to also analyse other paths whose path duration is nearly equal to the critical path duration because they are candidates to be the next critical paths after the schedule compression carried out by the Project Manager.

The selected activities will be performed in a parallel way to reach the schedule compression goal. Typically, using the schedule fast-tracking approach does not result in an improvement in the cost of the project.

Before fast tracking

After fast tracking

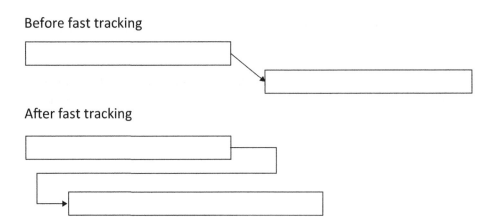

Figure 8.4 **Impact of the fast-tracking technique on consecutive project activities**

Figure 8.4 above represents the impact of the fast-tracking technique by comparing the arrangement of two consecutive activities before fast-tracking and after fast-tracking.

In addition, using the fast-tracking technique results in a loss of schedule constraints among activities, such as FS relationships. This approach, if badly managed, can lead to reworks and to unwanted results.

Resource Levelling

Resource requirements are often represented in the form of a resource histogram. A resource histogram shows the amount of time assigned to a resource for a time interval.

The resources assigned for more work hours than available hours must be considered 'over-allocated'. Figure 8.5 shows a simple example of a resource histogram where single resource allocations are compared in a given project timeframe.

The levels of resource availability are shown on the vertical axis for comparison purposes in a period of four quarters. This sort of representation primarily helps to identify if there are resources that are over-allocated or under-allocated.

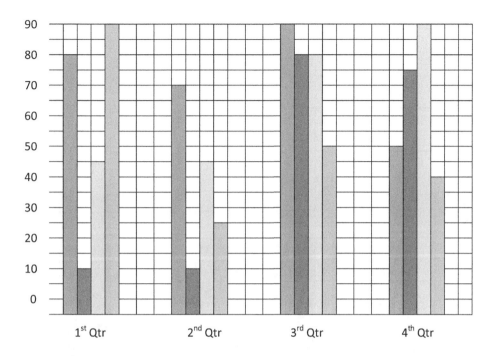

Figure 8.5   Resource histogram

Another interesting perspective is to understand how the number of different resources varies across the entire project or single stage duration. Figure 8.6, on the following page, represents the number of project team members varying across a project timeframe of four months: from January to April.

Moreover, it is very interesting to understand the variation of labour in correlation with the project time. This representation is similar to a Gaussian curve where fewer resources are used at the beginning and in the closing phase of the project, with a peak value around the mid-point of the project. This behaviour is supported by the following assumptions:

- At the beginning, the Project Manager and the other main stakeholders are involved in creating the Project Management plan, defining the scope and setting up the entire project.

- At the closing stage, effort must be focused on checking the status and acceptance of deliverables and on closing the contracts.

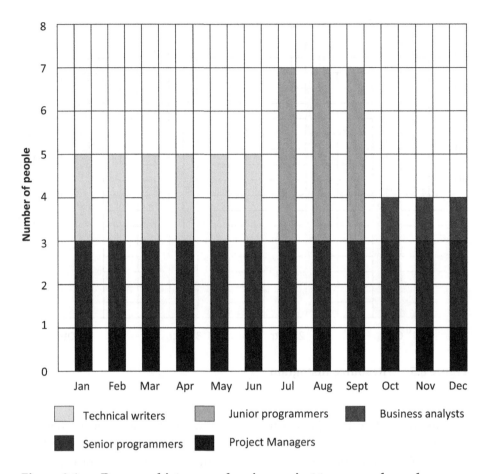

Figure 8.6   Resource histogram showing project team member roles

- Around the mid-point, effort must be maximized to enhance the project performance.

Therefore, resource levelling is a Project Management technique that is used to examine a project for an unbalanced use of resources over time and to smoothen out the allocation of resources. The aim of this analysis of human resources is, essentially, to resolve over-allocations or conflicts in the project schedule.

The Project Manager, by means of resource levelling, must always have the assurance that:

- resource demand does not exceed resource availability;

- the shared resources or critical resource requirements are well managed;

- resource usage is kept at a constant level during specific time periods of the project work.

Last but not least, the resources must be gathered and provided to the project by devising an advance notice period for the benefit of the organization and the better management of project resources.

References and Further Reading

PMI® 2013. *The Guide to the Project Management Body of Knowledge*, 5th edn. Newtown Square: Project Management Institute.

Chapter 9

Measuring, Monitoring and Controlling the Project Performance

FEDERICO MINELLE and FRANCO STOLFI

Project Risk and Project Success Criteria

This chapter has the aim of focusing on the correlation between project risks and success criteria in order to facilitate a timely selection of an appropriate set of countermeasures to be available for the Project Manager or for the person assigned to ongoing risk analysis.

While project risk definition has already been spelled out in Chapter 4, before proceeding it is useful to understand what project success criteria really mean: the whole set of items, mainly structured as indicators, which constitutes the reference to compare estimated or actual values, in order to evaluate project performances and results (both in terms of output and outcome). Several items could be entitled to be part of this set, but the usual items include compliance with the planned project time/cost/scope, product quality (along the whole product life cycle) and the risk/benefit profile, in accordance with the principles of PRINCE2®.

In order for a project to reach its success criteria, a systematic approach to Project Management is required, in which risk management plays a significant role.

The ability to detect and control the various risks that could affect success criteria values is a powerful tool for ensuring the overall success of the project initiative.

It is well known that uncertain events that generate project risks are very numerous and very different in their cause/nature; therefore, risks should be grouped into main categories (see Figure 9.1 below), where the risk drivers list is by no means an exhaustive one!

Risk class	Risk drivers (examples)
Size	Project/product volume, according to: • number of organizational structures which are impacted by project/product implementation; • number of correlated projects which are in process at the same time; • number of solutions/components which are integrated in the project 'product' (output); • size/volume of product to be implemented by the project (for example: civil works/plant size, software/hardware volume).
Organization	Impact of induced changes on stakeholders organizations and their relevant operating processes: • complexity of affected processes and their operations; • use rate and benefit driven by implemented operations; • complexity/diversity of training participation; • effect degree on department/offices operations; • change extent on operating processes.
Contract	Impact on management of contractual constraints and clauses between customer/owner and supplier/contractor: • definition of objective criteria for measuring/accepting products delivered by the project; • definition of quality standards for delivered (intermediate and final) products; • formalization degree of the penalties process.
Innovation	Innovation extent (technology, process, organization, and so on) of project products/solutions to be implemented: • new (or state-of-the-art) devices and/or technology platform; • new operations mode; • organization innovative solutions; • upgrade in operating processes maturity; • involvement degree of personnel/stakeholders in the innovation process.

Figure 9.1   Risk class and risk drivers (examples)

Each project is unique and has its own characteristics, because even similar projects, which could have the same management approach, would certainly be different, at least because they are caused by the different implementation environment/context (size, organization, resources, timing, etc.). Therefore, the definition of the set of success criteria for a specific project must be carefully undertaken: for each item, the relevant metrics (often more than one) should be settled, as well as the feasible target values. On the other hand, in order to prevent any bias in relation to success criteria definition, risks which could influence project/product performances must be detected and then linked with potentially affected success criteria. An example of the above-mentioned relevant correlation between risks and success criteria is shown in Figure 9.2 below.

Risks related to \ Success Criteria	Cost	Time	Quality	Scope	Benefits
Size		•			•
Organization		•	•		
Contract	•		•	•	
Innovation	•				•

Figure 9.2   Success criteria and influence of risk classes (example)

Correlation marks can be graded according to a qualitative scale (that is, high/medium/low) or a quantitative scale (that is, 3/2/1/0 or a different scale). In addition, both success criteria and risk classes may be marked by a relevance level (that is, by an assigned weight on a three-value scale). A tentative graduation (only qualitative) is shown in Figure 9.3 below, which stresses that different projects may have a customized grading (H = High, M = Medium, L = Low).

Risks related to \ Success Criteria	Cost	Time	Quality	Scope	Benefits
Size	M	H	M	L	H
Organization	M	H	H	L	M
Contract	H	L	H	H	L
Innovation	H	M	M	L	H

Figure 9.3   Success criteria and influence of risk classes (qualitative example)

The summary statement of risk/success criteria correlation would make it possible to detect the most suitable countermeasures to be implemented in order to contain the negative effects on success criteria values and, as a consequence, on project/product performances. To be more specific, according to the risk classes and success criteria involved, the countermeasures that are more focused on the proper action can be selected. Figure 9.4 below shows an example of countermeasures grouped into four main categories (as defined by McFarlan).

Action category	Risk countermeasures (example)
External integration (outside project team)	1. Plan and execute frequently scheduled project review with the user, in order to check requirements alignment/coverage/fulfilment with design/implementation solutions. 2. Predefine and schedule integration points with other project which are instrumental to the proper and full deployment of project product. 3. Promote the implementation of the User Committee (representatives from management and operational ranks).
Internal integration (within project team)	1. Plan and execute project review with stakeholder or functional/technical experts, in order to check feasibility and suitability of design/implementation solutions. 2. Assess skills, capabilities and stability of the project team. 3. Install an adequate process for managing changes requests and their evaluation/approval/implementation, strictly related to contractual clauses. 4. Involve other related project representatives in progress meeting and plan review (milestones control, integration issues check, and so on).
Formal project management (team and stakeholder)	1. Use project management scheduling techniques (for example PERT, CPM, CCM) supported by software tools. 2. Apply systematic control on progress vs. plan (for example baseline, milestones, earned value) 3. Structure project activities/deliverables according to a WBS model. 4. Define team organization/tasks according to a Responsibility Matrix model. 5. Define formalized method to compute project 'Estimate To Complete' and manage related corrective actions. 6. Assign task responsibility and allotted time/effort to team members, referring to industry productivity standards. 7. Install a formalized Configuration Management procedure. 8. Communicate routinely to main stakeholders progress and trends on project performances and expected results/benefits.
Quality assurance or control	1. Apply QA policies/targets for project processes and product/services delivered by the project (also at an intermediate stage). 2. Define quality targets and formal methods to trace their implementation. 3. Use relevant metrics and settle target values to check for acceptance all the products/services delivered by the project. 4. Perform cause analysis of quality deviation and formally manage related corrective actions.

Figure 9.4   Action categories and risk countermeasures (example)

The approach outlined above makes it possible to define a risk restraint strategy that is strictly focused on critical issues and on the sensitivity of success criteria to risks, and thus seeks to increase project success probability.

Impact Analysis for Ongoing Project Evaluation and Portfolio

As already mentioned in Chapter 4, project business justification is an ongoing process throughout the whole project life cycle (and product life cycle too). Impact analysis should be updated upon the achievement of major milestones or at least close to the completion of each project phase (following PRINCE2® methodology). In addition, if a significant change in the project baseline should occur, a re-assessment of project impact would be required in order to check if the approved business justification were still applicable.

In the initial evaluation process, ongoing impact analysis encompasses both financial/economic investment evaluation and the evaluation of other quantitative benefit types that are not easily measurable in financial terms. Of course, the evaluation will be focused on the items clearly perceived as heavily affected by baseline changes. In the event that the project is still aligned with initial (or updated) project goals, a new project baseline can be approved and becomes the current baseline for future Project Management checks.

For instance, assuming that the project goal is to deliver the first batch of a new consumer product (it might be a smartphone, a TV set or anything similar) that includes a technological breakthrough, let us consider different scenarios where each of the three usual main project success driving factors (time, cost and quality) are affected:

1. Project time schedule delay: the focus of financial analysis would be on cashflow slippage (both outflow and inflow: sliding of project/ product costs and revenues), while other quantitative impacted indicators would consider adverse customer/competitor behaviour (due to delays in product deployment) and a poorer market share or brand image. How can the latter be measured? If it is a significant issue, the same method must be applied as in the project business justification at the initiating process, of course!

2. Project cost overrun: the focus of financial analysis would be on the increase in outflow (project/product costs), while other quantitative impacted benefits would consider a lower customer acceptance due

to an increase in the product selling price likely to be settled as a countermeasure in order not to reduce the unit margin.

3.   Product quality decrease (as a usual consequence to avoid the other above-mentioned scenarios): the focus of financial analysis would be on inflow variation (a foreseen decrease in revenues) due to lower market acceptance of the new product, while other quantitative impacted indicators would consider market share or brand image.

Besides this simplistic example, the integration of ongoing impact analysis must be stressed, because it provides the Project Manager (and also the Project Management Steering Committee) with a powerful tool to support/ drive main decisions on alternatives for project success (or even for an immediate termination).

If the project is embedded in a portfolio/programme environment, the quantitative data on its foreseen impact (not only on its progress) are essential in order to evaluate in due time individual project foreseen performances and to select where organization resources (financial, human, infrastructural, knowledge, etc.) should be effectively allocated. Instead of strenuously trying to 'straighten' a hopelessly downgrading project, a timely and orderly managed termination is not a pure loss, but a more effective way to exploit opportunities. Of course, it would be better to find out a 'magic solution', but we are usually short of it!

In summary, for any project in progress, impact analysis should include the following actions, which are all related to the business case justification:

•   verify if project progress is still aligned with the initial assumptions of the cost/benefit analysis;

•   detect appropriate countermeasures (if necessary) in order to preserve the planned impact profile;

•   evaluate and eventually approve any change to the planned impact profile relevant to the updated project baseline (if necessary);

•   review and update the cost/benefit plan.

References and Further Reading

McFarlan, F.W. 1981. Portfolio approach to information systems. *Harvard Business Review*, 59(5), 142–50.

OGC 2009. *Managing Successful Projects with PRINCE2®*, 5th edn. London: The Stationery Office.

PMI® 2013. *The Guide to the Project Management Body of Knowledge*, 5th edn. Newtown Square: Project Management Institute.

PMI® 2013. *The Standard for Program Management*, 3rd edn. Newtown Square: Project Management Institute.

Chapter 10

The Percentage of Completion as a Metric of Project Control: Concepts and Calculation Methods

MASSIMILIANO ARENA

Introduction

As described and explained in previous chapters, the complete and reliable control of a project calls for metrics and Key Performance Indicators (KPIs), which give a concise, consistent and coherent measure relevant to a specific project status parameter.

Among the available metrics, the Percentage of Completion (PoC) is one of the most widely accepted and used in the construction and plant engineering project sectors, where, according to a contract specification, the construction of facilities, production of goods and provision of services are delivered to a customer.

This metric is at first considered as an accounting method which yields the progress of completion of the project according to the International Financial Reporting Standards (IFRS) – a set of accounting standards developed by the International Accounting Standards Board (IASB) – that is becoming the global standard for the preparation of public company financial statements. In this case the PoC is also called SoC (Stage of Completion). Similarly, the PoC is also recognized as a standard method by the US Generally Accepted Accounting Principles (GAAP).

It is important to note that, in contrast with other metrics and methods which account for the project progress, such as Earned Value (EV), the Cost

Performance Index (CPI), the Schedule Performance Index (SPI) and others, the PoC is a common language metric between the financial sector and the more operational Project Management environment.

If we consider the ever-increasing influence that project financing has in the evaluation and fostering of project success, we can easily understand that finding parameters which account for the progress of projects and are accepted by a financial investor may play an essential role.

The following aspects will be described in this chapter:

- definition and application of the PoC;

- the focus of PoC components;

- calculation methods;

- utilization of the PoC.

Definitions of the PoC Method

The PoC method is used as a metric (that is, figures which tell us what we have accomplished or give us an indication of performances and trends) for construction contracts. The following considerations are required in order to suitably apply the PoC method:

- a clear definition of the services to be rendered and goods to be supplied;

- seller (contractor) and buyer (customer) are able to meet their contractual obligations, as clearly stated in a contractual form;

- a justifiable, rational and fact-based cost estimation relevant to the contract contents is possible.

The PoC calculations are carried out using the 'cost-to cost' formula, which consists of the ratio between the costs incurred by a project at the evaluation time ('timenow') and the estimation of overall project total cost performed in the same 'timenow':

$$PoC = \frac{\text{Actual total costs}}{\text{Currently estimated total costs}} * 100$$

According to this approach, it will also be possible to calculate partial revenues and profit or losses during the entire project life cycle progress. This will be done using the percentage of the project that has been completed at a certain stage.

We will focus on a detailed description of the terms in the previous formula in the following sections.

Costs Relevant to Project Progress

These costs are all the costs incurred during the project execution at the point of the time evaluation (timenow), which are directly attributable to the project and which contribute to its progress.

It is important to note that costs incurred which are not relevant to progress in the project completion process will be calculated as inventory costs, but do not contribute to the PoC.

Typical costs of this class are:

- costs incurred for change orders that are not yet formalized;

- costs for materials or equipment which will be used at a later stage and not yet at the timenow.

In this situation, the following costs cannot be considered relevant to progress and do not contribute to the PoC:

- Commissions for acquisition:

  - these are relevant to an activity carried out during the bid phase and do not influence the completion of the project.

- Parasite costs due to currency fluctuations:

  - these have no relation with operative progress.

The scheme in Figure 10.1 sums up the concepts that have been outlined. Considering a typical project execution balance sheet, we can calculate the

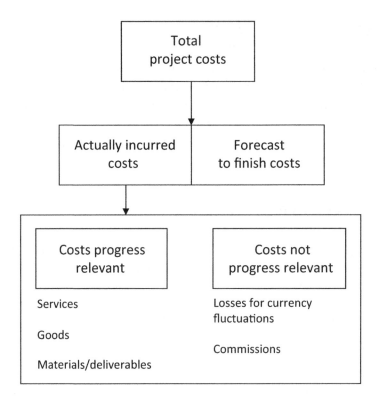

Figure 10.1   Total project costs

	Original Budget	Actual Budget	Actual Costs	Actual Forecast
		BCWS	AC	FCST (EAC)
Total Sales	22,640,000-	22,640,000-	1,973,831-	22,640,000-
Direct Costs of material	16,768,156	16,768,156	1,130,234	16,768,156
Other direct costs	928,707	928,707	192,636	928,707
Contingencies	1,132,001	1,132,001		1,132,001
Project provisions				
CONTRIBUTION MARGIN	3,811,136-	3,811,136-	650,962-	3,811,136-
Direct prod. costs	1,246,825	1,246,825	505,748	1,272,853
Sum of order costs (OC)	20,075,689	20,075,689	1,828,617	20,101,717
EBIT	1,132,001-	1,132,001-	5,223-	1,105,973-
Corporate tax	339,600	339,600	1,567	331,792
Project EVA	792,400-	792,400-	3,656-	774,181-
PoC (OC AC/OC FCST)	0.09			

Figure 10.2   Calculation of the PoC

PoC taking into account the actual costs and the cost estimation to finish (Figure 10.2).

The main concern in the analysis of the PoC is to take due account of the cost classes which contribute to the progress of the project. It is worth examining some cost classes which are often on the 'borderline' when they have to be considered:

- advance payments;

- provisions;

- risk contingencies;

- change management costs and change costs;

- claims and opportunities.

Before delving into the details of the above-mentioned items, it is worth recalling a principle which should be applied in the evaluation of elements that contribute to building up the economic analysis and the consequent calculation of the PoC. It is the 'materiality principle' which states that the analysts are allowed to ignore an accounting standard if the net impact of doing so has such a small impact on the financial statements that a reader of the financial statements would not be misled.

ADVANCE PAYMENTS

In the event that advance payments have been made to suppliers for services or goods which are relevant to deliverables to the client, according to the contract definitions, these shall be considered as progress relevant.

Advance payments can be included proportionally in the progress calculation, as shown in Figure 10.3, where:

(2)   Down Payment (DP) issued to supplier.

(3)   Service/deliverables performed by supplier, at timenow.

(4)   Value relevant to services provided by supplier, correspondent to the percentage of DP.

Of course, the calculation described in Figure 10.3 can be easily extended to the case in which services performed by supplier are 100 per cent of the value, corresponding to the total recognition of cost relevant to the progress of the project.

		Currency	
Suppliers orders	(1)	500,000	
Advance payment	(2)	150,000	30 per cent
Services/ goods by supplier	(3)	450,000	
Proportional value correspondent to advance payment per cent	(4)	135,000	30 per cent
Cost progress relevant	(5)	135,000	

Figure 10.3   Inclusion of advance payments

PROVISIONS

Provisions are generally defined as obligations arising from an existing condition, situation or set of circumstances involving a high degree of uncertainty. This uncertainty is relevant to the existence, timing or amount of the obligations. Typical of such provisions are warranty obligations, penalties or losses on onerous contracts.

In project budgeting management and project economics, these classes are often defined as 'unknown unknowns'.

Provisions can be considered as contributions to the PoC as part of the estimated total costs. For instance, losses which may realistically occur will be carefully considered and the corresponding provisions can be attributed as estimated associated costs. Similarly, other components of provisions can be inputs to the estimated total costs depending on their level of uncertainty.

The calculation of provision as a part of the cost forecast should be the result of a documented and sound analysis carried out by the Project Manager and the project control team, who perform the evaluation under well-defined guidelines.

Because of the uncertain nature of this 'cost class', the relevant evaluation will be conducted as a periodic review, along with the assumptions made to take them into account.

From the operational point of view, in many industries and project execution cases, provisions are often not taken into account for the PoC; this approach is very dependent on the specific field of application and in any case will be outlined in the economic status reports.

It is worthwhile briefly focusing on the following sources of provisions:

- Losses on contracts – if the ongoing evaluations of project costs or revenues indicate a real potential loss, it is necessary to consider the creation of dedicated provisions. This amount has to be adjusted and reflected in the PoC with respect to losses incurred or those most likely to be incurred.

- Liquidated damages and penalties – these provisions can be shifted to period costs when they become actual costs.

- Warranties – provisions for warranties can be created when risk is transferred to the client, generally after a Preliminary Acceptance or Final Acceptance (depending on the business model). If from the original budgeting phase onwards they are well defined, they do not contribute to the PoC.

All the above-mentioned classes can be translated from provisions to risk contingencies (see below) to actual costs, provided a consistent analysis is carried out based on ongoing actual circumstances in the project.

RISK CONTINGENCIES

Risk contingencies are a budgeted evaluation of 'known unknown' situations which can happen during the project development. They can also be seen as a budget reserve which can be used to implement plans to mitigate or eliminate risks.

Risk management is, in fact, a continuous estimation of costs potentially involved in relation to risks in the project which influence the forecasted total project costs. This will be considered in parallel to the increase of the PoC.

In this case the risk contingencies can be seen as a specific component of costs, contributing to the overall project cost forecast, evaluated at timenow and being a part of the Estimate at Completion (EAC).

It is useful to recall the general formulation of risk in its most simple and known form:

R = I * P

Where, in our case, I is the monetary value impact of a risk R, and P is the associated probability that the event takes place.

While this definition refers to the probability of incurring a certain cost, the cost budget estimate, considered as a baseline estimate, is deterministic in its nature.

The costs actually incurred, due to the implementation of mitigation plans, will accordingly be included in the actual costs, while the pure risk contingency will be included in the estimated costs (Figure 10.4).

The component of risk contingency is by definition a probabilistic component containing an element of uncertainty. The basis for its calculation can vary significantly, depending on the model applied.

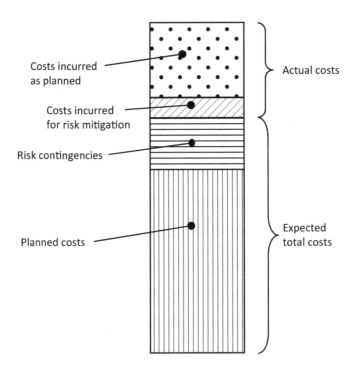

Figure 10.4   Estimated costs

The simple form of the risk equation can be made much more complicated or aligned to the actual conditions, which are indeed made complex by different interactions. The theories behind risk analysis are beyond the scope of this section, and we briefly here recall two possible approaches belonging to advanced methods.

CONDITIONED ('*A POSTERIORI*') PROBABILITY

This method allows a more accurate usage of the probability figure, taking into account the probability of one event occurring once another event is known to have occurred.

Denoting by p (A | B), the *a posteriori* probability of event A happening given the event B has already happened, and by A^c, the complementary event of A, we have:

$$p (A^c) = 1 - p (A)$$

so that the conditional probability p (A | B) is:

$$p (A \mid B) = \frac{p (B \mid A) \; p (A)}{p (B \mid A) \; p (A) + p (B \mid A^c) \; p (A^c)}$$

It is therefore possible to utilize this more complete probability information to build up a simple risk evaluation such as that shown above.

THE MONTE CARLO METHOD

This method consists of a stochastic simulation technique which utilizes a random sampling algorithm to create a series of possible scenarios. It then analyses, in *a posteriori* fashion, the resulting distribution. By using the random sampling, a possible value is selected from each probability distribution in the input; with the data obtained, it is possible to perform a calculation of the value obtained for the variables. This process is repeated thousands of times (sampling amplitude) to achieve an empirical distribution of the results, which represents the consequence on the outputs of the uncertainty of the inputs.

In our case, the object of analysis can be the monetary values attributable to a specific event, and after the simulation the bid manager can build up a risk charter comprising the risk elements associated with the most likely numerical value, based on statistics and suitably simulated probability distributions.

In spite of the theoretical risk model used, during the initial budgeting phase, the determination of contingency is often carried out taking into account a percentage of the overall budget cost. This contingency figure is derived from similar previous projects, that is, based on overall historical data.

Nevertheless, assumptions, probability definitions and statistical extrapolations shall be made in accordance with the best knowledge and belief of the project or bid management team.

The contribution of provisions will not be included in the risk contingency in order to avoid double counting of the cost impact.

The consideration of risk contingency results, of course, in decreasing the PoC value, compared to the bare 'deterministic' content of the estimated costs (Figure 10.5).

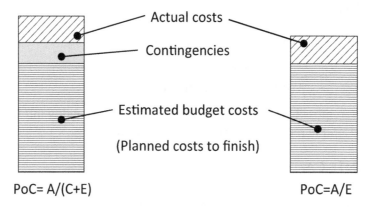

Figure 10.5   Different PoC values

In certain business sectors or according to certain company policies, sometimes the management choice is not to take into account contingencies in the PoC calculation (as shown above). This approach is also possible provided that it is well understood in financial and economic reporting.

A careful risk analysis and a continuous risk management plan update are essential not only for proper Project Management and control, but also to avoid unstable and sudden changes in PoC values, including all relevant cost risk elements, as mentioned above.

If there are significant changes in the results of risk evaluation from period to period as the project progress is assessed, the PoC is in general consequently affected.

CHANGE ORDERS AND POC

Even middle or low complexity projects are very often affected by change orders (COs). In these cases, the calculations of project progress shall be duly adjusted, according to a change in:

→ scope of supply (S);

→ allocated budget (i.e. cost relevant increase estimate);

→ actual costs incurred (relevant to S).

once the change order is contractually formalized. In this case, these costs (actual and estimated) will be relevant to the progress:

$$PoC^* = \frac{AC + AC_S}{EAC + EAC_S}$$

PoC*= after contract CO formalization

where:

S = scope change

EAC_S = budget allocated to S

AC_S = actual costs incurred relevant to S

Accounting for costs (both actual and forecast) as a result of COs without a formal contract amendment is not correct practice and therefore is not recommended.

CLAIMS AND OPPORTUNITIES

Claims

Claim management usually results in monetary compensation for a loss (tangible or intangible) suffered by a party executing a project.

Claims are generally due to delays, execution or specifications mistakes and lack of fulfilment of contractual obligations, for which one party may charge the other(s).

Project costs incurred for claims shall be included as part of the project-relevant actual costs and the expected total costs related to these claims have to be added to the total estimated project costs. This applies both for incoming and outgoing claims (that is, from/to customers, suppliers, partners, etc.).

Opportunities

Some of the most common sources of opportunities are:

- additions to the scope of work (that is, COs);

- cost reduction;

- project schedule crashing.

The opportunity for cost reduction (on materials, equipment, etc.) clearly has an impact on the calculation of planned costs (forecast total costs) and the PoC is influenced accordingly. The possibility of reducing the project duration, without incurring additional costs in speeding it up, can also be seen as improving efficiency and bringing about subsequent cost reductions as well (for example, resulting from a reduction in work hours, infrastructure costs and tool rental costs). Also in this case, a realistic evaluation can be ensured by a sound analysis, possibly supported and shared by the main levels of personnel involved in the project team.

Note

Claims, change orders and opportunities will be calculated in the determination of revenues only when they have been formally recognized (that is, have become legally binding).

Cost Estimation at Completion: Approaches and Calculations

In the previous sections, an analysis of the cost classes contributing to the estimated costs has been carried out. The calculation of the Estimate At

Completion (EAC) is considered below, showing some peculiarities and examples.

It has been shown that the EAC can be expressed as:

$$EAC = ETC. + ACWP$$

where:

ETC = Estimate To Completion

ACWP = Actual Cost of Work Performed (sometimes shortened to AC)

and also:

ETC = BAC – ACWP, with BAC = Budget At Completion (project budget)

In addition, it can be useful to include in the ETC the additional contributions of contingencies, claims and opportunities, possibly considering the provisions as explained above:

$$ETC = BAC – ACWP + CONT + CLAIM + OPP + PROV$$

Therefore, in general, we can write:

$$PoC = \frac{ACWP}{EAC}$$

It is worth recalling some expressions of the EAC, calculated as a function of fundamental performance parameters, which are the basis for Earned Value analysis:

$$EAC = ACWP + \frac{BAC + BCWP}{CPI} = \frac{BAC}{CPI}$$

$$CPI = \frac{BCWP}{ACWP}$$

where CPI is the Cost Performance Index and BCWP the Budgeted Cost of Work Performed.

It is worthwhile noting that this calculation can be modified if the BCWP and the BAC take into account recognized contributions relevant to contingencies, claims and opportunities as specified.

Revenues Recognition Using the PoC

After the PoC is calculated, it is utilized for the determination of revenues to be recognized in a specified timeframe.

The total project revenues (R) are multiplied by the PoC to calculate the revenues relevant to a period t_1. In a similar way, the project income (I) at t_1 can be calculated as the product of PoC with the term (R – EAC).

In case of contract amendments or revenues from successful claims, these will be calculated only after finalization and, as explained above, the corresponding costs will be accounted for in the AC and the EAC, whichever is appropriate.

Adjustments to the PoC During Project Execution

Despite the accuracy of estimation and the sound approach adopted, supported by management judgement, imprecise evaluations may take place, which will affect the estimated total costs.

As a consequence, it may be necessary to make adjustments in certain evaluation periods where it has been detected that previous estimations are incorrect.

If $EAC_{t1} > EAC_{t0}$, then $PoC_{t1} < PoC_{t0}$ and of course the actual costs are updated on an actual basis and are not affected. This means that the PoC was higher than the correct one at timenow t_0.

What is the effect of this on the revenues? The revenues were incorrect and overestimated in t_0, and therefore it is necessary to allocate a part of them in t_1 period by reducing the PoC in t_1. This adjustment, sometimes called 'cumulative catch up', can result in a loss in a certain period (that is, in t_1).

In order not to create more errors, it is necessary to detect mistakes promptly, avoiding the need of substantial adjustment at a later stage (Figure 10.6).

In other words, the PoC trend against time is also an indicator of the cost control quality and reliability. Table 10.1 opposite provides a numerical example of this.

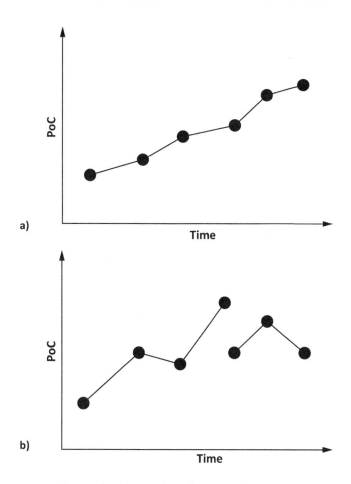

Figure 10.6   PoC trends: (a) regular; (b) irregular

Table 10.1   Example of calculations

Period	1	2	3	4
Total revenue	100	100	100	100
EAC	80	90	90	90
Gross margin	20	10	10	10
AC	40	40	80	90
PoC	50%	44%	89%	100%
Progress revenue	50	44	88.9	100
Progress margin	10	4	9	10
'Catch up'		-6	5	1

Note: Rounded figures.

As a further exercise, the reader can easily figure out how the increase of revenues, for example, in period 2 or 3, influences the PoC trend.

Use of the PoC for Determining Costs in Excess or Billing in Excess

Excess costs, with respect to excess billings, represent basically the difference between the PoC method of accounting sales and the accounts payable by the customer (progress billings).

The use of these figures is quite important since it can show whether the project is basically financed by the customer or by the contractor (seller). The applicable scheme is described in Figures 10.7 and 10.8.

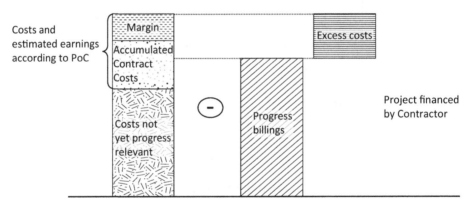

Figure 10.7   Project financed by the contractor

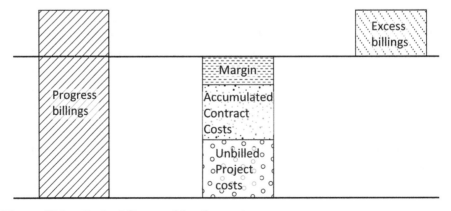

Figure 10.8   Project financed by the customer

In short:

PoC revenues + costs not progress relevant – progress billings = amount to be booked (ATB)

If ATB > 0 ➔ Costs in excess, project financed by contractor (supplier)
If ATB < 0 ➔ Billings in excess, project financed by customer

These definitions can of course be considered as KPIs for the project.

Numerical Example Using PoC

In the final section of this chapter, we give a numerical example which includes most of the elements discussed, making use of a general project business balance sheet.

Contract value/ Total revenue	€850,000		Total Bdgt Cost	€650,000
PoC (per cent)	method			
	Year 1	Year 2	Year 3	Year 4
Yearly cost	€150,000	€250,000	€150,000	€100,000
Cumulated cost	€150,000	€400,000	€550,000	€650,000
Estimated total cost (current year est.)	€650,000	€680,000	€650,000	€650,000
PoC (per cent) – cost to cost	23 per cent	59 per cent	85 per cent	100 per cent
Revenues (per year)	€196,154	€303,846	€219,231	€130,769
Revenues (cumulated)	€196,154	€500,000	€719,231	€850,000
Margin (yearly)	€46,154	€53,846	€69,231	€30,769
Margin cumulated	€46,154	€100,000	€169,231	€200,000
Turnover	€100,000	€300,000	€200,000	€250,000
Turnover cumulated	€100,000	€400,000	€600,000	€850,000
Cost/Billings – in-excess	€96,154	€100,000	€119,231	€0
Payment received	€75,000	€250,000	€275,000	€250,000
Payment cumulated	€75,000	€325,000	€600,000	€850,000
Receivables	€25,000	€75,000	€0	€0
Actual payments	€50,000	€200,000	€250,000	€150,000
Actual payments cumulated	€50,000	€250,000	€500,000	€650,000
Liabilities	€100,000	€150,000	€50,000	€0
Cash balance (per year)	€25,000	€50,000	€25,000	€100,000
Cash balance cumulated	€25,000	€75,000	€100,000	€200,000
Working capital	€21,154	€25,000	€69,231	€0

Figure 10.9   Numerical example using the PoC

References and Further Reading

Davison R.P. and Mullen, J. 2009. *Evaluating Contract Claims*, 2nd edn. Hoboken: Wiley-Blackwell.

Harvard Business School 2007. *Understanding Finance*. Boston: HBS Press.

Hollmann, J.K. (ed.) 2006. *Total Cost Management Framework: An Integrated Approach to Portfolio, Program, and Project Management*. Morgantown: AACE International.

International Accounting Standards Board 2007. *International Financial Reporting Standards*. London: IASB.

Kerzner, H. 2011. *Project Management Metrics*. New York: John Wiley & Sons.

Michaels, J. 1989. *Design to Cost*. New York: John Wiley & Sons.

Panneerselvam, R. and Senthilkumar, P. 2009. *Project Management*. New Delhi: PHI Learning.

Chapter 11
Project Change Management

FABRIZIO COLISTA

Introduction to Project Change Management

Great emphasis is frequently placed on Change Management in a number of different corporate environments: this term, in fact, is generally intended to refer to a full range of activities involved in an organization-wide 'change'. First of all, it is essential to provide a definition for 'change' in order for a clear understanding to be established. In a general context, 'change' is a transition from a current status (an 'as-is' condition) to a future status (a new 'to-be' condition), which postulates the implementation of a careful action plan along with the quantification of risks and benefits. Change Management therefore addresses changes by adopting well-structured methods in an efficient implementation of modifications involving people, organizations, technological facilities, etc.

A macro-breakdown enables a detailed analysis of the two possible sets of actions. Change Management, in fact, implies two similar but different contexts that may frequently be recognized as components of a single programme (that is, a group of correlated projects): it may be interpreted either in a 'narrow sense' or in a 'broad sense'. The difference is by no means artificial and for the sole purpose of a better analysis, but the two approaches are really opposite in terms of how their management processes are conducted; both have to be considered for a successful completion of the project.

Change Management is focused on Project Managers. They must be conscious that their project will introduce innovations in their organizations, or – more specifically – that, as asserted by R.D. Archibald and S.C. Archibald (Archibald 2013: 3): 'All significant innovations are achieved through projects'. Conversely, no project can be brought to a successful completion – in line with schedule, cost and quality constraints – without a Project Manager. Accordingly, Project Managers will also act as Change Managers.

The 'Broad Sense' of Change Management

Change is a crucial process. It must be prepared carefully in order for the organization to be able to enhance its culture and its consciousness in its 'new' operating behaviour. Against this process, there are major hurdles created by human factors, as long as any attempt at re-designing a status quo may be a threat to well-established organizations, work procedures, competences, behaviours and personal inter-relationships. As emphasized by Turner (Turner 2007: 294):

> *Changes will usually be required to meet higher hurdles than the project itself. The reasons for this are:*
>
> • *many changes are nice-to-have, and so should be subjected to greater rigour – changes to avoid show-stoppers will have infinite IRR[1] and therefore have no problem being accepted.*
>
> • *the benefits are usually over-egged, and the costs understated.*

According to Wikipedia,[2] Change Management can be defined as follows:

> *Change management is an approach to transitioning individuals, teams, and organizations to a desired future state. In a Project Management context, change management may refer to a Project Management process wherein changes to the scope of a project are formally introduced and approved.*

Having defined organizational change as modifications planned to improve organizational performance, changes are – accordingly – the result of an intentional combination of analysis capability and management skills.

The 'broad sense' of Change Management can be better described with reference to the remarkable case of organizational change. This may be the consequence of either a planned change or an unplanned change.

Planned changes result from specific efforts that are achieved through a sequence of stages. Change agents are required in change processes to support

---

1   IRR = Internal Rate of Return.
2   See http://en.wikipedia.org/wiki/Change_management

the change system. Change agents, change objects and knowledge of change processes are essential conditions of a planned change.

Accurate planning processes are the essence of the success or failure of Change Management.

Organizational changes may also take different designations depending on their influence within the corporate system; there may be 'total changes' or 'evolutionary changes':

- 'Total changes' are massive changes involving the organizational system in its entirety. In the current management environment, these changes are induced by crucial events such as company mergers. Total changes are highly complex and challenging for corporate management as long as they lead to real cultural changes.

- 'Evolutionary changes' are much less ground-breaking and can be categorized as ordinary organizational re-arrangements that might incorporate, for example, new technologies or processes, launch new products leading to alterations of company nature, etc.

Organizations are to be considered as systems consisting of interdependent elements. Accordingly, changes in the organizational structure can lead to alterations to the operating environment or processes, while new strategies can lead to modifications of organizational structures.

Focusing now on a quick overview of organizational changes, three different cases can be identified:

1. Changes of structures and organizational strategies – these are mainly relevant for corporate management.

2. Changes of processes and work environment – these may involve measures affecting the employees' quality of life.

3. Cultural changes – these affect changes of values, standards, attitudes and corporate behaviours.

Analysis of project stages for organizational changes identifies five stages that are representative of broader categories of changes:

1.   Define the environment of changes – some questions have to be answered, such as:

    – to what extent is the current situation progressing towards a change?
    – does the change have a structural, technological objective?
    – does the change involve organizational stakeholders and tasks?

2.   Identify hurdles against changes and understand their levels, sources and connotations.

3.   Plan for changes – design and support changes through an effective system for overseeing objectives and accordingly monitoring hurdles that have been identified; change risk analysis is a crucial step, as is usual for every project.

4.   Promote changes – especially through such provisions as:

    – persuading others of the need for change;
    – involving change agents (stakeholders);
    – encouraging employees to express their uncertainties, worries and hesitations, as well as their hopeful beliefs and expectations concerning changes in progress (to be supported by stakeholder engagement);
    – ensuring that changes are actually in place, supported and retained.

It should be evident that the completion of a project for change requires the results to be carefully scrutinized and lessons learned to be taken on board for future use whenever the organization is subject to further evolutions.

If an organization misses opportunities for its evolution, it will no longer be able to survive market-driven changes.

Accordingly, it should be emphasized that Change Management is a comprehensive and structured approach to the transition from a current status to a future status involving expected business benefits, as well as helping organizations to integrate and bring people, processes, structures, culture and strategy into line.

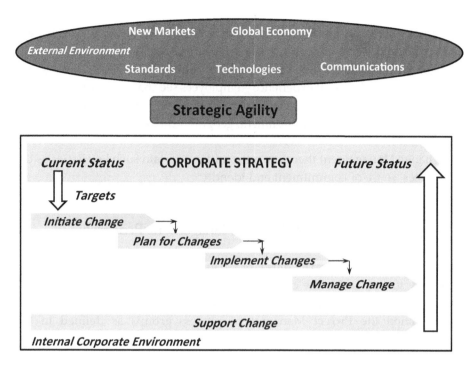

Figure 11.1   The concept of Strategic Agility in a corporate environment

Evolutions of successful organizations are never random processes. These evolutions proceed through intentional and dynamic strategies anticipating and effectively addressing external trends that emerge with a fluctuating behaviour. Therefore, Strategic Agility in organizations can be defined as their capability to capture a continuously changing business environment proactively and to their best advantage.

Figure 11.1 schematically captures this essential concept as reflected in the current literature. It has already been mentioned that people are affected by changes which have been introduced; in order for their impact to become much less upsetting and more effective, provisions can be made by considering, addressing and managing human factors as appropriately as applicable. Employees will then have to be involved in initiatives leading to decisions and organizational changes (the concept of Stakeholder Engagement applies). Whenever changes occur, communication and stakeholder involvement assume major prominence, more so than in other periods. Project cost and performance will also be significantly influenced. Confidence is the key element ensuring support and participation.

Furthermore, consideration should also be given to the perception of changes at the different corporate levels: while senior managers, broadly speaking, see changes as opportunities both for the business and for themselves, conversely – and according to the usual experience – employees see changes as disappointing and hostile practices, and potentially harmful in relation to their position, status, benefits, cooperative work environment, geographical location, etc.

Change Management therefore must address certain such key issues as the employees' sense of commitment and identity.

Change Management and Project Management Processes

Having discussed the 'broad sense' of Change Management above, it is now necessary to emphasize the close connections between Change Management and Project Management. These connections will be explored taking into consideration the Project Management process groups as defined in the PMI® standard:

- Initiating:

  - identify resources;
  - identify interested parties and their interest in changes;
  - coordinate activities for project and programme Change Management;
  - define changes;
  - define management environment;
  - initiate change communications.

- Planning:

  - collect change requirements and define scope of changes;
  - define sequences and obtain resources and budget for activities to be managed;
  - clarify risk plan as relevant for planned activities;
  - develop plans for communications, human resources and quality.

- Executing:

  - appoint and set up the Project Management Team, including external resources;

- manage communications for change.

- Monitoring and controlling:

  – assess acceptance of changes;
  – review and modify scope of changes, activities and variations from the baseline.

- Closing:

  – identify, plan and execute actions required to release changes relevant to corporate business;
  – close the project with the relevant affordability plan.

Activities inherent in the Change Management effort can also be referred to the knowledge areas of Project Management. This is, however, beyond the scope of the current discussion.

In support of an overall view of Change Management in its broad sense, essential points can be summarized taking into account the comprehensive context of Project Management in its extended and strengthened characterization of processes, competences, tools and techniques, which aim to produce expected project/programme benefits:

1. To provide sufficient resources (primarily schedule, people and budget) to support and strengthen project deliverables, including organizational concepts, development policies and cultural changes.

2. To involve parties interested in (or affected by) the changes to ensure the most complete and flexible solution (Stakeholder Engagement)

3. To prepare provisions against the risks of hostility or lack of acceptance towards changes by devising stakeholder management plans and communication management plans, while carefully monitoring hostile or disinterested signals.

4. To enhance Project Management flexibility, to ensure identification of adaptation needs both in the Project Management plan and possibly at the programme management level.

5.   To plan and assess the proceeding of acceptance and approval of project changes with respect to the resulting performance.

6.   To strengthen the affordability of benefits expected from project changes by devising carefully planned and measurable efforts aiming at the transition of project deliverables to the operation stage.

The 'Narrow Sense' of Change Management

This complementary view of Change Management is somewhat different; it considers changes that occur within projects.

In this case, Change Requests (CRs) can be issued in order to deviate from the current project plans.

In the Project Plan there must be provisions to manage CRs, including, for example:

- identification of Change Request;

- classification;

- assessment;

- approval/disapproval;

- execution;

- appraisal of all contractual implications, if any.

Appropriate Configuration Management and Change Management systems should be in place to ensure the likelihood of successful project performance as well as of achieved Project Management maturity for the organization. These systems should incorporate rules and procedures aimed at defining, identifying, accounting and progressively controlling the components of project products/outputs, in order for the functional, technical and physical specifications to be successfully met.

Change Management, in its more specific connotation of management of changes, must be conceived to keep under constant control all modifications required throughout the project lifetime, ensuring consistency, integration, coordination and control in each of its elements.

Accordingly, Project Management systems must incorporate and apply appropriate 'Change Management systems' to implement defined processes for CRs, authorizations, executions and appraisals, in line with the stipulated roles, responsibilities and procedures.

In addition, such systems must ensure that products/services released through project deliverables be maintained under appropriate configuration management.

Configuration is defined as a certain status of the product/service resulting from the project effort; the 'Configuration Item' will be each element of the configuration that is being managed.

Configuration management systems must:

- identify and cross-correlate the different configuration items;

- keep track of the different item versions ('versioning');

- manage information on their applicability, procedures, documentation and authorization processes.

Project Change Control Systems

In order to put in place the systems that have been discussed, it is essential to adopt an appropriate Change Control Process. This is a key pre-requisite to achieve project requirements, while ensuring that every modification that has been introduced in the project context be adequately defined, assessed and approved before being executed.

Change Control will be incorporated into the project on the basis of five key formal processes:

- submittal and receipt of modification requests;

- review and acknowledgement of modification requests;

- assessment of modification request feasibility;

- approval of modification requests;

- execution and closure of modification requests;

These processes will be explored in more detail below.

SUBMITTAL AND RECEIPT OF MODIFICATION REQUESTS

This process provides for the opportunity of project modification requests being submitted by any member of the project team. It is the standard procedure by which requestors identify requirements for changing any of the project connotations (scope, deliverables, schedule, budget, expenditures, organization, etc.).

Requestors must submit CRs to the Change Manager. CRs are sheets providing a summary of the request for change, its description, rationale, benefits, costs and impacts, along with support documentation.

REVIEW AND ACKNOWLEDGEMENT OF MODIFICATION REQUESTS

This process allows the Change Manager to review the CR and determine the requirement for a comprehensive feasibility study to be executed by the Change Control Board (CCB) in order for an exhaustive assessment of the impact of CR to be carried out.

Key decision drivers will be the number and complexity of change options that are requested. The Change Manager will open a CR in the 'Change Log'.

ASSESSMENT OF MODIFICATION REQUEST FEASIBILITY

This process requires a comprehensive feasibility study of the CR. Included in the study will be the definition and evaluation of:

- requirements;

- options;

- costs and benefits;

- risks and issues;

- impact;

- the action plan.

The quality of feasibility studies is reviewed to ensure that they will have been executed in line with stipulated requirements; the CCB will receive the final product after approval. The Change Manager will collect the documentation and submit it to the CCB for final review.

This documentation will include:

- the original CR;

- the approved feasibility study;

- the supporting documentation.

APPROVAL OF MODIFICATION REQUESTS

This process requires formal review of CRs by the CCB, with the possibility of selecting one of the following judgements:

- reject modification;

- request further information;

- approve the change as it is;

- approve the change subject to certain conditions (technical, administrative, legal, contractual, etc.).

CCB decisions will be primarily based on the following criteria:

- risk for the project in incorporating the change;

- risk for the project in *not* incorporating the change;

- impact to the project in incorporating the change (schedule, resource, finance and quality).

EXECUTION AND CLOSURE OF MODIFICATION REQUESTS

This process requires that the CR be completely implemented and includes:

- identification of the change schedule (the date for the implementation of the change);

- test/simulation of the change prior to implementation;

- change implementation;

- checking of successful change implementation;

- communication of successful change implementation;

- closure annotated on the Change Log.

This process must be accompanied by an accurate definition of the corporate functions involved, which must be clarified and known by all stakeholders as the essential requirement for the proposed change to be successful in line with schedule, cost and performance expectations. The following responsibilities are assigned to the corporate functions:

1. The requestor identifies the need for change and formally addresses the need to the Change Manager. Responsibilities range from identifying the project change needs to formally documenting this need through the submission of a stipulated change request form to be reviewed by the Change Manager.

2. The Change Manager is in charge of receiving, recording, monitoring and controlling the progress of all the changes in a project, as well as being responsible for:

   - acknowledging all CRs to be annotated on the Change Log;
   - categorizing all acknowledged CRs and prioritizing them;
   - reviewing all CRs to obtain further information to be submitted to the CCB;
   - initiating the feasibility study;
   - monitoring the progress of all CRs.

It is also part of the Change Manager's tasks to prioritize all issues and define risks, as well as to convey feedback from the CCB.

3. Various responsibilities are vested in the Feasibility Study Group, including the exploration of possible options for CRs, costs, benefits and miscellaneous impacts. All the results will be documented in a feasibility report to be submitted to the CCB.

4. It is up to the CCB to determine authorizations for all CRs and also to:

   - review all CRs forwarded by the Change Manager;
   - acknowledge all documentation supporting CRs and determine approval/rejection;
   - resolve conflicts among intersecting changes;
   - determine implementation dates for approved requests.

5. It is up to the implementation group to implement and review all project changes and also to:

   - establish change schedules;
   - implement all project changes;
   - test all changes prior to their release to operation;
   - review the degree of satisfaction – quantitative and qualitative – of changes that have been implemented;
   - close requests with annotations on the Change Log, which contains all CRs acknowledged and monitored until they are resolved.

Implementation and Critical Success Factors (CSFs)

Following our insight into the process through which CRs are managed in projects, the next step is the exploration of the key elements to be considered by the Project Manager in addressing the above-mentioned process.

CRITICAL SUCCESS FACTORS

Factors that are critical to the success of a project are as follows:

- the Change Manager must be of a necessary level of seniority as well as possessing the necessary skills;

- appropriate criteria should be used in selecting the Change Management system to be adopted, especially if ICT-based systems (software) are envisaged;

- the process must be periodically reviewed in line with a stipulated plan.

Adequate authority must be vested in CCB members in order to enable them to carry out evaluations and formulate subsequent judgements.

COSTS

Major costs resulting from the implementation of Change Management are related to personnel and tools.

Additional cost elements are:

- new personnel recruiting costs;

- optional initial data entry costs;

- workplace costs;

- software tool costs in support of Change Management;

- costs for purchasing hardware, set-up, licences, etc.;

- costs for initial training and follow-up sessions;

- initial and follow-up consultancy costs.

METRICS

Process performance can be measured by means of certain metrics, some of which are listed below:

- the percentage of unsuccessful CRs out of the monthly total of approved CRs, as a measure of the effectiveness in appraising risks in the Change Management process;

- the percentage of rejected CRs out of the monthly total, as a measure of the initial discrimination capability in the Change Management process;

- the number of monthly unauthorized CR implementations in order to ascertain if the process has been bypassed;

- the presence/number of backlogs of unprocessed CRs in order to compare actual workloads to available resources;

- the percentage of CRs generating implementation problems out of the total and the monthly amounts, as a lesson learned for subsequent planning actions;

- the percentage of CRs having an 'urgent' priority status over the monthly total in order to ensure that priority allocation methods are applied correctly.

Stakeholder Communication Management

One of the implications of effective Change Management is communication strategy. It is worth recalling the general principles of Communications Management in the broader category of projects; accordingly, the specific case of Project Change Management will be discussed.

Communications Management drives the inter-relationships among all parties that are interested in a project in order to ensure that necessary and appropriate information is directly conveyed to the right destination(s) at the right time, using the right mechanisms and at the right cost. Knowing how to communicate is a skill of paramount importance to Project Managers, since they – as asserted in specialized reports – spend more than 80 per cent of their work time in project communications. Knowing how to 'communicate the change' is a facet of accurate project communication management.

Whenever communication management is incorrect, this is a major contributor to project failure and, accordingly, communication problems should be identified, analysed and judiciously solved.

In order for the exchange of communications to be correctly understood, it is necessary to make a selection of the communication procedure (the 'communicative approach') and its mechanisms, as well as to be particularly careful in doing this. If the change is not clearly identifiable in the communicative approach, how can a Project Manager lead a project for change? Would a 'new' communicative approach not be the best example of a change?

Frequently Project Managers are presented with general rules that they will have to customize on a case-by-case basis and in line with their personal experience as well as with the recurring support of expert advice:

1.   select the right communicative approach;

2.   select the right communicative mechanism;

3.   communicate effectively.

Effective and efficient communications derive from a Communication Plan describing the purpose to be achieved, the mechanisms to be used, the procedures and the exact duration of each communication. Broadly speaking, Communication Plans should include the definition and description of:

- the requirements, categorization and characteristics of information to be exchanged;

- the methods and technologies to be applied;

- the frequency of communications;

- responsibilities and destinations;

- criteria for plan update;

- the content of exchanged reports.

All of this information must be conveyed in line with the details required by the different stakeholders; therefore, their identification, classification and regular management are key factors in order for projects – especially projects for change – to be successful.

References and Further Reading

Archibald, R.D. and Archibald, S.C. 2013. *Leading & Managing Innovation: What Every Executive Team Must Know about Project, Program & Portfolio Management.* West Conshohocken: Infinity Publishing.

Turner, J.R. (ed.) 2007. *Gower Handbook of Project Management*, 4th edn. Farnham: Gower Publishing.

Chapter 12

Project Closeout and Lessons Learned

CARMINE RUSSO

Purpose

The purpose of Project or Phase Closeout is to evaluate the project performance and draw out any lessons learned so that best practices can be applied to future projects and most importantly to create a formal ending to the planned work.

Many Project Managers don't realize that just as it is important to formally kick off a project when the overall planning phase is completed, it is also important to successfully close the project or phase.

The value of having a planned project or phase closure is in leveraging all of the information and experience gathered throughout the project or phase. If the planned result is implemented and the team is immediately released, there is no opportunity to perform staff evaluations or document key lessons learned. We also know that a project can end unsuccessfully as well. Even in this case, the Project Manager will realize that there are key lessons learned, team evaluations and other important activities in order to learn as much as possible from what happened during the project. In both cases, the responsibility of the Project Manager to build project closure activities into the project schedule. These activities should be seen as vital parts of the project, not as an afterthought as the team is being disbanded. The project is not considered complete until the closure activities are performed – just as it would not be complete without the implementation activities being finished.

According to the PMBOK, 5th edn, paragraph 3.7, Closing Process Group:

the Closing Process Group consists of those processes performed to conclude all activities across all Project Management Process Groups to formally complete the project, phase or contractual obligations. This Process Group, when completed, verifies that the defined processes are completed within all Process Groups to close the project or project phase, as appropriate, and formally establishes that the project or project phase is complete. This Process Group also formally establishes the premature closure of the project. Prematurely closed projects may include for example: aborted projects, cancelled projects, projects in a critical situation. In specific cases when some contracts cannot be formally closed (e.g. claims, ending clauses etc.) or some activities are to be transferred to other organizational units, specific hand-over procedure may be arranged and finalized. At project or phase closure the following may occur: Obtain acceptance by the customer or the sponsor to formally close the project or phase, Conduct post project or phase-end review, Record impacts of tailoring to any process, Document lesson learned.

The purpose of this chapter is to adopt a practical approach for the Phase or Project Closeout. The Project Closeout process begins with a Post-implementation Review. The review may start with a survey designed to ask for feedback on the project from the Project Team, customers, and internal and external stakeholders. Once feedback has been collected and evaluated, an assessment meeting is conducted to glean best practices and formulate lessons learned to inform the management for future efforts. If possible, the best practices and lessons learned should be stored in a centralized organizational repository, the Project Management Information System (PMIS). It could be a dedicated system, a specific folder on a server or cloud, etc. A facilitating access and retrieval option by managers and Project Managers of future projects should be provided.

Project Closeout ends with administrative closeout – providing feedback on Project Team members, updating the skills inventory, capturing key project metrics and filing all pertinent project materials in the project repository.

List of Processes

This phase consists of the following processes:

- Conduct Post-implementation Review, where the Project Manager assesses the results of the project by soliciting feedback from team members, customers and other stakeholders through the use of a survey to gather together lessons learned, best practices and performance patterns or trends, and communicating these results in the form of a Post-implementation Report.

- Perform Administrative Closeout, where the Project Manager formally closes the project by providing performance feedback to team members and archiving all project information.

- Document Lessons Learned, after obtaining the agreement of the customer or the sponsor to formally close the project or phase, conducting post project or phase-end review, recording impacts of tailoring to any process. The Project Manager at this stage will document lessons learned, to be shared for future projects.

List of Roles

The following roles are involved in carrying out the processes of this phase:

- Performing Organization Management.

- Project Sponsor.

- Project Manager.

- Project Team Member.

- Internal stakeholders.

- External stakeholders.

- Customer.

List of Deliverables

The major outcome of this phase is the Post-implementation Report, which formalizes the feedback received from all involved parties, and identifies best practices and lessons learned.

The output from the tasks performed as part of conducting a Post-implementation Review serves as the building blocks for the report.

Of even more importance is the transfer of lessons learned and best practices from the Post-implementation Report to an organizational repository of Project Management data.

The final deliverable of this phase is the Archived Project Repository. Figure 12.1 lists all Project Closeout processes, tasks and their deliverables.

Process	Task	Deliverables
Conduct Solicit Feedback Post-Implementation Survey	Conduct Solicit Feedback	Post-Implementation Survey
	Conduct Project Assessment	Project Assessment Meeting
	Prepare Post-Implementation Report	Post-Implementation Report
Perform Administrative Closeout	Update Skills Inventory and Provide Performance Feedback	Update Skills Inventory Performance Feedback
	Archive Project Information	Archived Project Repository
Lessons Learned	Document Lessons Learned	Archived Lessons Learned in the Project Repository so best practices could be applied to future projects

Figure 12.1   Process – tasks – deliverables

Conduct Post-implementation Review

PURPOSE

A project is considered complete when it has been effectively completed and sent to the Performing Organization and approved from the Project Sponsor. At this point in the Project Management life cycle, the responsibilities of the Project Manager are to assess how closely the project met the customer's needs, to highlight what worked well, learn from mistakes made during the project, identify patterns and trends, work out ways to improve upon processes executed throughout the project and, most importantly, communicate results.

The purpose of 'Conduct Post-implementation Review' is to gather the information together required to meet these responsibilities and to present it in a Post-implementation Report.

ROLES

The following roles are involved in the Post-implementation Review:

- Project Sponsor.

- Project Manager.

- Project Team members.

- Customers.

TASKS

The tasks executed in support of Conduct Post-implementation Review are:

- solicit feedback;

- conduct project assessment;

- prepare Post-implementation Report.

SOLICIT FEEDBACK

It is very important to solicit feedback from the Project Team. Because they have a different point of view from that of customers and consumers, Project Team members provide a 'close look' at the way in which the project was executed. They are also an important resource for communicating lessons learned and best practices.

The most important measures of the success of a project are whether the product was developed and delivered successfully and how well the needs of the customers have been met. The most effective way to determine these measures is to solicit feedback. The Project Manager should gather feedback using a survey appropriate to the project. Depending on the size and type of the project and the structure of the Performing Organization, different surveys may be required for different stakeholder groups, and surveys will need to be distributed to the appropriate individuals. At a minimum, feedback should be solicited from the Project Sponsor and Project Team members who performed the tasks in the Project Schedule. The Project Manager should determine whether surveys should also be given to customer representatives, consumers or other stakeholders in order to collect sufficient information for assessing the success of the project in meeting its goals and their needs. The survey must also assess the outcome of the project and the performance of the Project Team and the Performing Organization. The Project Manager must stress to all survey participants the importance of their honest feedback as one of the primary mechanisms for assessing the project's performance.

The written survey should be distributed, in either electronic or hardcopy form, with a specific due date for its completion. The Project Manager should follow up if the survey is not returned on time. If distribution is extensive, it may be helpful to keep a list of to whom and when the survey was sent and returned.

The Project Manager also has the option of conducting a survey in person or over the phone. An interview survey can often be more effective than a written one. While those responding to a written survey are limited to answering the questions as they are written, an intuitive Project Manager will be able to expand upon the verbal responses of the survey participant, gathering information that might otherwise not be forthcoming. In some cases, however, participants may be reluctant to disclose information as honestly in person. In addition, the Project Manager may not be the appropriate person to administer the survey interview to some stakeholder groups.

It is also important to obtain feedback on the performance of the Project Manager. The Project Manager's immediate supervisor, or an assigned resource with a similar capacity, needs to take responsibility for obtaining straightforward feedback from the Project Sponsor, the customer and the Project Team.

POST-IMPLEMENTATION SURVEY EXAMPLE

Since every group involved in the project experiences it from a different perspective, survey questions should be tailored to the particular expectations of key groups identified in Project Roles and Responsibilities. These evaluations should apply not only to the execution of the project, but also to satisfaction with the project's product (or service), and with the support the Performing Organization provided to the Project Team.

The following survey is intended as a guideline and provides sample questions that may be asked as part of soliciting feedback. The Project Manager should review the questions to determine which to include for the selected target audience. The respondents should be encouraged to provide not only a numerical rating (with 1 = not at all or poor, 2 = adequate or satisfactory and 3= to a great extent or excellent), but also their comments as to what worked well, what could have been done better and recommendations for conducting future projects.

GENERAL INFORMATION

Project name: _____ Date: _____

Your name: _____Your Performing Organization: _____

Your role on the project: _____

Dates of your involvement: _____

Questions	Rating (1–3)	Comments (What worked well? What could have been done better? What recommendations do you have for future projects?)
Product effectiveness		
How well does the product or service of the Performing Organization work?		
How well does the product or service of the project meet your needs?		
When initially implemented, how well did the product or service of the project meet the stated needs of the Performing Organization?		
When initially implemented, how well did the product or service of the project meet the stated needs of the Performing Organization?		
What is your overall assessment of the outcome of this project?		

Taking the previous example, once the survey feedback has been completed and collected, the Project Manager must review, analyse and summarize the results for subsequent presentation at the Project Assessment Meeting. The following is an example of suggested list of categories to use when collecting survey information on the project:

- Project Team performance.

- Performance of Performing Organization.

- CSSQ management (Cost, Scope, Schedule, and Quality).

- Risk management.

- Communications management.

- Product effectiveness.

- Acceptance management.

- Organizational change management.

- Issues management.

- Project implementation and transition.

The feedback, once summarized, will be used during the Project Assessment Meeting as a starting point for identifying lessons learned and best practices to use in future projects. It will also be included in the Post-implementation Report created at the end of Project Closeout. Customer satisfaction should be a primary concern. It is important for a Project Manager to know that a project may finish on time, on budget and meeting all defined quality standards, and every deliverable may have been fully error-free and perfectly compliant with the project scope, but if the customer is not satisfied with the product or service delivered, the project cannot be considered to be a success!

CONDUCT PROJECT ASSESSMENT

The Project Manager's goal for this task is to meet with selected members of the Project Team and the stakeholder community to present the summarized results of the feedback surveys, discuss all other aspects of the completed project, gain consensus on what was successful and what was not, and work out best practices and lessons learned.

In addition to the Project Team, the Project Manager should consider inviting Project Managers from the Performing Organization with experience on similar projects. Based on experience and prior knowledge, other Project Managers can provide information and insight on the assessment process. It is a good idea for the Project Manager to distribute the summarized survey results to each participant in advance of the Project Assessment Meeting so as to allow them to come prepared to address the contents. In order to provide the best possible products and services to customers, Performing Organization management must strive to continuously improve the way in which projects are managed and products are delivered. During the course of the assessment meeting, participants will consider the summarized feedback results and the experience of the Project Managers in attendance to discuss and assess the performance of the project. Based upon these discussions, the group will identify and agree upon lessons learned. These lessons will not only provide benefits to the current Project Team, but will also help managers and team members of similar projects. The lessons may be positive or negative. Lessons learned must not simply be identified during the meeting. It is also important to document each one and develop an action plan describing when and how they might be implemented within the Performing Organization. During the course of the project, the Project Manager, the customer and the Project Team members most likely recognized certain procedures that, when exercised, improved the production of a deliverable, streamlined a process or suggested ways to improve standardized templates. Best practices are documented as part of the Project Assessment Meeting and are later shared with other Project Managers so that they can be repeated. In some cases, the outstanding 'successes' might be translated into new procedures to be followed by future projects.

PREPARE THE POST-IMPLEMENTATION REPORT

After the Project Assessment Meeting, the Project Manager prepares the Post-implementation Report. In the report, the Project Manager distils information gleaned from the discussion and organizes it according to the feedback categories described above, adding information on key project metrics. The report documents the effectiveness of the product in meeting the needs of the customer, the effectiveness of the management of the project and the Project Team, how well the Performing Organization supported the project, lessons learned, best practices to be used in future projects and the key project metrics that will enable the Performing Organization to compare success measures across projects. It also contains recommendations for improvements to be used by other projects of similar size and scope. During Perform Administrative Closeout, the report is archived in the project repository.

The Project Manager must present or distribute the Post-implementation Report to members of the Performing Organization. In Performing Organizations that undertake many projects, it is most effective to assign an individual or agency unit to take ownership of collecting and organizing the information, teaching the lessons learned and implementing the best practices throughout the organization.

A proactive approach to be taken is to suggest your Organization Management to have a central repository, which is owned and maintained by someone within your company's Performing Organization, in order to provide a place where lessons learned and best practices can be archived for use by all Project Managers in the company. After a while, as more and more information is added to this repository, it will become part of a very valuable knowledge base that, when leveraged, will translate into remarkable improvements on all organization projects.

PROJECT POST-IMPLEMENTATION REPORT EXAMPLE

Company name
Project Post-implementation Report

Project identification

Projectname:_____ Date:_____

Sponsor name: _____ Project Manager: _____

Report prepared by: _____

For each of the following, summarize its effectiveness within the context of this project.

Highlight significant responsibilities and the effectiveness in accomplishing them.

Identify and discuss 'outliers' – specific stakeholder groups dissatisfied with the performance or those wildly enthusiastic about it.

Identify and discuss specific issues.

Project effectiveness
CSSQ Management (Cost, Scope, Schedule and Quality)
Risk management
Communications
Acceptance management
Organizational Change Management
Issues management
Project implementation and transition
Performance of Performing Organization
Performance of Project Team
Key metrics
<div align="center">**Cost** **Schedule** **Scope** **Quality**</div>

For the above Key Project Metrics (quadruple constraints), describe:

COST

Percentage difference between the final cost, the final approved baseline cost estimate and the original cost estimate.

Number of approved changes made to the original budget.

Number of 're-baselined' budget estimates performed.

SCHEDULE

Number of milestones in the baseline schedule.

Number of baseline milestones delivered on time (according to the last baseline schedule).

Difference between elapsed time of original schedule and final actual schedule.

Difference between elapsed time of final baseline and final actual schedule.

SCOPE

Number of baseline deliverables.

Number of deliverables delivered at project completion.

Number of scope changes in the post-planning phases.

QUALITY

> Number of defects/quality issues identified after delivery.
>
> Number of success measures identified in the Business Case that were satisfied or achieved at project completion.

Perform Administrative Closeout

The purpose of 'Perform Administrative Closeout' is to perform all administrative tasks required to bring the project to an official close. The resources involved in this role are:

- the Project Manager; and

- the Team Leader.

During the course of the project, Project Team members most likely enhanced their current skills or obtained new ones. The investment made in improving individual skills should not be lost. In order to leverage skills on future projects and to facilitate and encourage individual growth, the Project Manager should maintain a record of the skills developed and used on the project. If a skills inventory exists within the Performing Organization, the Project Manager or Team Leader must be sure each Project Team member takes the time to update it with any newly developed skills and any new project roles that were assumed. An up-to-date inventory will become invaluable to future Project Managers when attempting to appropriately staff their projects. It can also be used as input for an individual's immediate supervisor when providing performance feedback.

'Perform Administrative Closeout' involves the execution of the following tasks:

- update skills inventory and provide performance feedback;

- archive project information.

UPDATE SKILLS INVENTORY AND PROVIDE PERFORMANCE FEEDBACK

If no skills inventory exists within a Performing Organization, the Project Manager should encourage the Performing Organization to implement one. The inventory can be as simple as a hardcopy list or as sophisticated as an electronic skills database, depending upon the needs and desires of the organization.

The Project Manager and/or Team Leader must also take the time to document his or her feedback on the accomplishments and performance of each Project Team member. As the person most aware of the day-to-day activities performed by the Project Team, the Project Manager or Team Leader is the most appropriate person to provide honest and accurate feedback. Feedback documentation should be prepared and reviewed with the individual team members first. Following this performance discussion, the documentation is submitted promptly to each Project Team member's immediate supervisor to be used as input for performance appraisals.

The performance feedback mechanisms (appraisal forms, project exit interviews, etc.) specific to the Performing Organization should be used.

ELECTRONIC SKILLS DATABASE EXAMPLE

For example, the Organizational Electronic Skills Database may contain the following information:

Personal information:

First name:	Last name:	Date of birth:	SSN:
Home address:	Sex: M/F	Hiring date:	Dismissal date:
Home phone no.:	Mobile phone no.:	Email:	Other:

Information about the employee position within the organization:

Company name
ID number
Division
Project
Years of experience within the organization
Total years of experience
Job title
Manager's name
Other

Educational information:

Title	Date	Description	Average mark
High School Diploma			
BS Degree			
Master's Degree			

Certifications:

CAPM
PMP
PRINCE2 Foundation
PRINCE2 Practitioner
IPMA Level D or others
ITILv3
Other

Other courses taken	Date	Title	Duration (days/months)
Entrepreneurship			
Intro to finance			
Other			

Languages	Level (fluent, proficient, only spoken)
English	
French	
Spanish	
Italian	
Other	

Employee company location	Country	From	To	Room	Floor	Phone

Employee experience:

Insert Row	Period	Organization	Role	Account	Client
	From 01/01/201x to 31/12/201x	ABCD Corporation	Quality Control Manager – Control Division	Quality Monitoring and Control	XYZ
	Description of Project/Area				
	Tools – Languages – Methodologies				

From 01/01/201x to 31/12/201x	ABCD Corporation	Project Leader	Implementation of Organization Quality System	XYZ
Description of Project/Area				
Tools – Languages – Methodologies				

Employee evaluation card:

Insert Row	Initial Evaluation Validity	End Evaluation Validity	Points Scored	Description of Obtained Evaluation	Consideration from Employee	Efficacy of Formation	Notes
	01/01/201x	31/12/201x	Enter here the Score Points (Use Organiza-tional scoring method to de-fine final score points)			Yes/No	
	Training Needed		(example: Needs to take advanced class on Quality and Project Management).				
	Integrative Final Notes From Evaluator						
	Note from the Director of Human Resources						
	01/01/201x	31/05/201x				Yes/No	
	Training Needed		(example: Needs to take a course ITILv3 – Service Management).				
	Integrative Final Notes From Evaluator						
	Note from the Director of Human Resources						
	01/01/201x	31/05/201x	Enter here the Score Points (Use Organiza-tional scoring method to de-fine final score points)			Yes/No	Taken Project Management Course
	Training Needed		Suggest to take the PMP Exam				
	Integrative Final Notes From Evaluator						
	Note from the Director of Human Resources						

Insert Row	Group	Area	Know How	Utilizes it	Autonomous	Specialist	Other
	Other Knowledge	QUALITY	PROCESS ANALYSIS		✓		
	Other Knowledge	QUALITY	INTERNAL AUDIT	✓			
	Other Knowledge	QUALITY	REFERENCE NORMS		✓		
	Other Knowledge	QUALITY	WORK FLOW		✓		
	Information System Knowledge	PROGRAMMING LANGUAGES	COBOL		✓		
	Information System Knowledge	PROGRAMMING LANGUAGES	FORTRAN		✓		
	Information System Knowledge	PROGRAMMING LANGUAGES	JAVA	✓			
	Information System Knowledge	PROGRAMMING LANGUAGES	JAVA2 EE	✓			
	Information System Knowledge	PROGRAMMING LANGUAGES	ORACLE FORMS	✓			
	Information System Knowledge	PROGRAMMING LANGUAGES	ORACLE PL/SQL	✓			
	Information System Knowledge	PROGRAMMING LANGUAGES	ORACLE REPORT	✓			
	Information System Knowledge	PROGRAMMING LANGUAGES	SQL SERVER		✓		
	Information System Knowledge	DATABASE	ACCESS	✓			
	Information System Knowledge	DATABASE	IDS2		✓		
	Information System Knowledge	DATABASE	ORACLE		✓		
	Information System Knowledge	TECHNICAL ANALYSIS	DATA FLOW DIAGRAM		✓		
	Information System Knowledge	TECHNICAL ANALYSIS	ENTITY RELATIONSHIP		✓		

Insert Row	Group	Area	Know How	Utilizes it	Autonomous	Specialist	Other
	Information System Knowledge	TECHNICAL ANALYSIS	OOA OBJECT ORIENTED ANALISYS	✓			
	Information System Knowledge	OPERATING SYSTEMS	DOS	✓			
	Information System Knowledge	OPERATING SYSTEMS	GCOS		✓		
	Information System Knowledge	OPERATING SYSTEMS	WINDOWS 200x		✓		
	Information System Knowledge	OPERATING SYSTEMS	WINDOWS 95/98/ME/XP		✓		
	Information System Knowledge	OTHER	ABC FLOW CHART		✓		
	Information System Knowledge	OTHER	EXCEL		✓		
	Information System Knowledge	OTHER	POWER POINT				
	Information System Knowledge	OTHER	PROJECT			✓	
	Information System Knowledge	OTHER	WORD		✓		
	OTHER	OTHER	OTHER				

ARCHIVE PROJECT INFORMATION

Throughout the course of the project, the Project Manager maintains a project repository. As the project progresses, the purpose of the repository is to create a central point of reference for all project materials to be used by anyone involved in the project. Once the project comes to an official close, the repository provides an audit trail documenting the history and evolution of the project. During Project Closeout, the Project Manager should examine the repository to ensure that all relevant project-related material, documents produced, decisions made, issues raised and correspondence exchanged have been captured. In addition, the Post-implementation Report should be included. When the project is officially closed, the project repository should include the following materials (consider also a scanned version in PDF format):

- Project-supporting documentation, including the Business Case and the Project Proposal.

- Project description/definition documents such as the Project Charter and the Project Plan.

- Any working documents or informal documents defining the cost, scope, schedule and quality of the project.

- Project schedules – retain all copies electronically, but only include the baseline and final schedule in the hardcopy repository.

- Financial details of the project.

- Project scope changes and requests log.

- Project status reports.

- Team member progress reports and timesheets.

- Issues log and details (open and resolved).

- Project acceptance log by deliverable.

- Project Deliverable Approval Forms, with original signatures.

- Risk Management Worksheets.

- Audit results, if relevant.

- Correspondence, including any decision-making memos, letters, emails, meeting notes, etc.

- The Final Project Acceptance Form, with original signatures.

- The Post-implementation Report.

A hardcopy repository should be archived in a designated documentation area. It may be made available electronically at the discretion of the Project Sponsor in accordance with organizational records management policies.

The expected delivery is an Archived Project Repository, that is a collection of all project related materials, documents produced, decisions made, issues raised and correspondence exchanged, providing the history and evolution of the project.

PROJECT REPOSITORY TABLE OF CONTENTS EXAMPLE

Company name
Project Post-implementation Report

Project identification

Projectname:_____Date:_____

Sponsor name: _____ Project Manager: _____

---

*The following is a suggested **Table of Contents** for your project repository (a repository example could be Microsoft SharePoint or something similar where you could insert index fields and metadata in order to find document information more easily). Of course, the organization and content of your actual repository may differ depending on the scope and type of project and your personal preference.*

- Project Proposal.
- Business Case.
- Project Charter.
- Project Scope Statement.
- Contract Document References.
- Organization Guideline References.
- Project Schedule.
- Quality Management Plan.
- Audit Summary Report.
- Budget Estimate.
- EV Report.
- List of Risks/Risk.
- Description of Stakeholder and their Involvement.
- Communications Plan.

- Post-implementation Survey(s).
- Post-implementation Report.
- Change Control Forms.
- Signed Approval Forms.
- Meeting Notes/Minutes/Correspondence.
- Project Status Reports.
- Progress Reports.
- Project Work Products/Deliverables.
- End of Phase Checklists, etc.

DOCUMENT LESSONS LEARNED

All lessons learned gathered from running the previous project phases should be documented so that best practices can be applied to future projects.

References and Further Reading

PMI® 2013. *The Guide to the Project Management Body of Knowledge*, 5th edn. Newtown Square: Project Management Institute.

Chapter 13

Human Factors in Project Life Cycle Economics

BARBARA BOCCASINI

Project Life Cycle and Project Phasing

The life cycle of projects is composed of a sequence of activities that are very different from one another, as well as being of varying levels of significance from an economic perspective. These activities are generally assigned to divisions in organizations, in line with their roles, which may often be completely differentiated. Projects require continuous and constant scrutiny through their entire life cycle and specific work teams are generally appointed by companies to monitor the various phases of projects (for instance, teams in charge of audits).

An example is provided by the project phasing adopted in the publications issued by the European Cooperation for Space Standardization (ECSS) and described in ECSS-M-ST-10C Rev. 1, which is a standard Project Management document for aerospace applications (see also Chapter 3 of this volume). Table 13.1 summarizes the main tasks of project phases.

Table 13.1   Project tasks of ECSS-M-ST-10C

Phases	Typical tasks
0 – Mission analysis and needs identification	• elaborate the mission statement (needs, expected performance, physical and environmental constraints) • identify possible mission concepts • perform the preliminary assessment (market and economic studies)
A – Feasibility	• assess the technical and economic feasibility • identify critical technologies • elaborate the risk assessment

Table 13.1   Continued

Phases	Typical tasks
B – Preliminary definition	• elaborate the Project Management, engineering and product assurance plans and the verification programme • elaborate the baseline master schedule and the baseline cost at completion • finalize the product tree, the work breakdown structure and the business agreement documents
C – Detailed definition	• completion of the detailed design definition of the system at all levels in the customer–supplier chain • detailed definition of internal and external interfaces
D – Qualification and production	• complete qualification testing and associated verification activities • complete manufacturing, assembly and testing • prepare acceptance data package
E – Utilization	• perform all activities in order to prepare the launch • perform verification, commissioning and support activities
F – Disposal	• implement the disposal plan

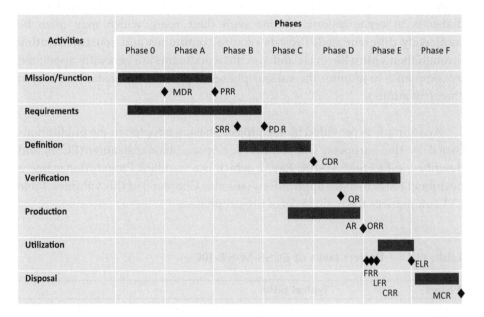

Figure 13.1   Project phases of ECSS-M-ST-10C

A typical arrangement of a project life cycle, in accordance with the ECSS standard mentioned above, follows a Plan-Do-Check-Act approach, including project reviews at scheduled intervals (Figure 13.1):

- Mission Definition Review (MDR) at the completion of Phase 0.

- Preliminary Requirements Review (PRR) at the completion of Phase A.

- System Requirements Review (SRR) before the completion of Phase B.

- Preliminary Design Review (PDR) at the completion of Phase B.

- Critical Design Review (CDR) at the completion of Phase C.

- Qualification Review (QR) before the completion of Phase D.

- Acceptance Review (AR) and Operational Readiness Review (ORR) at the completion of Phase D.

- Flight Readiness Review (FRR), Launch Readiness Review (LRR) and Commissioning Result Review (CRR) before the completion of Phase E.

- End-of-Life Review (ELR) at the completion of Phase E.

- Mission Closeout Review (MCR) at the completion of Phase F.

Project life cycle reviews typically take place in meetings that involve all company divisions contributing to a specific project stage. These meetings are formalized in reports that include not only the outcomes of monitoring actions performed, but especially action plans to resolve any criticalities and achieve expected improvements.

The Importance of Project Team Members

In compliance with guidelines of project effectiveness, team activities should never be self-verified and/or self-validated. This simple independence principle serves as a basis to ensure that the activities planned in the various project stages are accurately controlled.

Team members are generally selected from different company divisions in accordance with the range of their backgrounds. This differentiation of experiences and professional cultures will enable team members to enrich their verification skills and particularly to improve the effectiveness and extent of tasks to be performed.

This preamble provides a clear demonstration that communication is a primary factor for achieving cost-effectiveness and final success in projects as well as in any of their activities. If it is considered that, in most cases, the output elements of a certain project stage become the input elements of a subsequent stage, this provides a good justification of the significance of clear and accurate information exchanges among different organizations and company divisions, which also contribute to ensuring that project cost and schedule objectives are met.

Furthermore, project tasks are usually cooperative tasks, whereas at the corporate level, responsibilities are usually individual (organization leaders or team leaders). Appropriate selection criteria should therefore be envisaged to identify qualified personnel for team leader functions on the basis of specific interviews.

By and large, soft skills are representative of personal attitudes encouraging teamwork, as well as positive individual contributions within the organization. This sort of ability is much more difficult to achieve than technical competence.

This chapter will discuss how communication and leadership – from the perspective of a project team – should not be excluded from the totality of factors influencing project life cycle economics; however, as a matter of introduction, some general examples are provided for a better insight to the concept of soft skill:

- Decision-making aptitude – be decision-oriented, able to consider a range of opinions and alternatives, and aware of the consequences of choices.

- Ready acceptance of commitments – be reliable, enthusiastic and motivated.

- Flexibility – be capable of keeping pace with developments and changes taking place in the organization and of accepting innovative roles with a positive and self-confident attitude.

- Capability to manage your schedule – be ready to prioritize tasks, especially as project key events are approaching, to achieve best results with minimum effort and to work on different projects in the same timeframe.

- Creativity and problem-solving capability – be able to apply logic as well as imagination and to perceive problems and solutions simultaneously.

- Aptitude to teamwork – be able to keep an eye on project objectives, to aim at achieving objectives cooperatively, to show openness and integrity, and to provide your team with constructive contributions.

- Awareness of responsibilities – be proud of your actions, conscious of your responsibilities and respectful of the errors of others as well as your own.

- Capability to work under pressure – maintain a focus on your duties even under over-pressurized conditions, when time is lacking and decisions are required quickly yet judiciously.

Introduction to Communication

Good communication skills are certainly crucial to ensure harmony at work and, consequently, to improve project performance and effectiveness. Typically, these personal characteristics go hand in hand, for example, with the capability to express opinions without being aggressive, to resolve conflicts easily and to persuade the audience, while accepting constructive criticism.

It is especially customary in consulting companies to encourage the participation of employees in periodic courses providing awareness of the importance of soft skills and their implementation. The reason for this in a consultancy environment is the importance of being ready to familiarize oneself with a range of different organizations and to realize their needs in order for the employee to be soon considered as dependable. There are situations in which 'quick win' business approaches are adopted or *ad hoc* change management proposals are formulated and supported during their implementation by expert teams, such as when a company is totally or partially transferred to a different owner, while maintaining its activities.

Communication processes are not intended solely as information exchanges, since they imply that interacting parties are mutually influenced; these processes should always be analysed by considering their specific contexts and the rationale for their initiation.

For this reason, it is important to define the dimensions of the context in which communication processes are realized:

- Physical dimension – the place where parties communicate (the meaning of technical terms is lost if they are used in unexpected contexts).

- Time dimension – the moment at which the communication process occurs (information is received at defined times).

- Historical dimension – the relationship between communicating parties (on the basis of how much they know each other, especially in terms of communicating with the manager).

- Psychological dimension – the level of empathy (non-verbal communication).

- Relational dimension – communication practice (communication in the workplace is different from communication in families).

It is important to understand that good communication or bad communication does not exist: communication reflects a relational scheme. Every communication instance can be broken down into two elements:

- The content (what is being said): sharing information (referential function); letting somebody believe something or do something (conative function).

- The relationship: how something is said.

A typical percentage composition of communication is: seven per cent verbal (words); 38 per cent para-verbal (volume and expressivity of voice, celerity of speech, pauses, breaths, etc.); 55 per cent gesture (body language).

Communication always has a purpose: we may wish to have some people take a certain action or to stimulate consciousness in somebody.

A few principles are relevant in communication processes:

- feedback is used to ensure that an objective is accurately met;

- the focus is on other people;

- if somebody misunderstands, the error is mine.

Communication is not merely informing somebody: the context is important, but the primary goal is to understand to what extent the intended message is maintained.

In order for communication to be practical and effective, it is important to be conscious of our ability to communicate with other people in a verbal or para-verbal form. In the context of communication, sociologists also use the term 'proxemics' to define the spatial interactions of humans (that is, studying the individual attitude to move to a greater or shorter distance while interacting with other people). Intra-psychic communication (emotion, behaviour and willingness) should also be part of our good consciousness.

An additional element of interest in communication is the representation system that is used, i.e. how information is organized:

- visual (creating mental images) – 'clear as day', 'I've had a light bulb moment';

- aural – 'tell me', 'listen', 'this idea sounds good';

- kinaesthetic (creating sensations around things) – 'I've grasped this concept', 'this project seems solid'.

Non-verbal communication is determined, for example, by moving facial muscles, by looking at different distances and directions when speaking, by gesture, by tone of voice and by personal look (formal or informal attire).

Communication goes through three sequential steps:

- Interaction – knowing one another and socializing (Asset Management, for example, uses socialization techniques among team members).

- Information – sharing knowledge and work methodologies.

- Transformation – being creative and able to make changes on the basis of lessons learned at work (skills, abilities, etc.).

The main communication styles are as follows:

- Aggressive – arrogant tone of voice, obstinacy in enforcing personal opinions without accepting objections, lack of interest in listening to other speakers, persistent interruptions of speeches, verbal aggression and disrespect, persistent invasions of someone else's space, disregard of different opinions, pointing fingers at someone else, etc.

- Passive – hesitation in expressing personal ideas, fear of being judged, fearful or submissive tone of voice, lack of self-confidence, self-blame for underperformances, sense of inferiority, the need to feel approved, etc.

- Assertive – showing interest in listening to other speakers, inclined to asking questions to confirm understanding, determination in asking politely and firmly to continue speaking if interrupted, openness to exchange of ideas, affirmation of personal opinions without underrating or overpraising other attendees, loyalty, tolerance, comprehension, etc.

In a number of companies, meetings are held to analyse and discuss the different communication styles and to provide employees with guidelines to learn about the assertive style. This is a simple summary of guidelines for assertive communication:

- Message listening and receptiveness – focusing on speakers while paying less attention to personal ideas and acknowledging what is being said without criticism and prejudgment.

- Message processing – making constant efforts to understand various opinions and focus on requests received from someone else, showing interest in others for their feelings and their approachability (encouragement/disbelief, confidence/pessimism) as well as their intended position within the team.

- Responsiveness to messages – being able to avoid aggressive and/or threatening responses, being aware of explanations required and testing the level of receptiveness by summarizing the message as has been understood.

- Aptitude to capture attention – being able to identify major topics for discussion, avoiding lengthy reports, using plain language and a clear voice, leaning forward, beginning with a concise list of contents and ending a long presentation with a final summary (visual support is helpful).

- Clear identification of purpose – being aware of how to contribute to the team.

- Openness to dialogue – creating a friendly environment, willingness to listen, loyalty in interactions and consideration of others to ensure that personal ideas can be expressed and contributions allowed from colleagues.

- Support of personal position – being able to present objective information, avoiding subjective opinions, while focusing on the relevant topic and reducing digressions.

- Ability to avoid personal criticism – the focus of criticism should be on behaviours rather than on individuals. Constructive proposals should be directed towards improving performance instead of criticizing others for the methods they use.

Further insights into the concepts of communication and leadership will be discussed later in this chapter. Meanwhile, an introduction to the 'Maslow Pyramid' is provided to represent human needs in such a way as to analyse relationships among individuals and working group dynamics (Figure 13.2). In 1954, Maslow, an American psychologist, proposed a hierarchy of needs in which every need must be satisfied before considering higher-level needs.

The hierarchy of needs, as envisaged by Maslow (Figure 13.2), includes the following:

- Physiological needs (breathing, food, water, sleep, procreation, etc.) are at the bottom level of the pyramid, since they are basic needs related to survival.

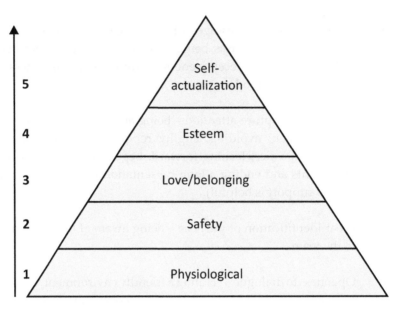

Figure 13.2   Maslow Pyramid

- Safety needs (security of body, employment, resources, morality, family, health, property, etc.) are one level higher, since they are expected to ensure a degree of safeguard and stability to individuals.

- Love/belonging needs appear at the next level to represent the social interactions of individuals, their quest for making friends, loving and being loved, as well as belonging to a group to cooperate with others for a common purpose.

- Esteem needs, at the next level up, are concerned with self-esteem, confidence, achievement, respect of others and respect by others so as to feel approved of and efficient.

- Self-actualization needs, at the top level, refer to morality, creativity, spontaneity, problem-solving ability, lack of prejudice and acceptance of facts.

Effectiveness of Team Communication

In order for communication to be effective, the following attributes are required:

- Targeted – communication should be intended to support specific activities related to decision making, to the development of alternatives for problem solving and to the management of interactions.

- Pragmatic – collection and analysis of data and facts should be privileged by using all possible interpretations for the benefit of understanding a certain problem.

- Transparent – completeness in communication is essential to ensure that information from each team member is made available to the rest of the team.

- Situational – communication should be consistent with the circumstance and the current stage of the team's work. The commitment of each team member is required for harmonization with the needs and professional culture of other members.

Problem-solving techniques are cognitive mechanisms that are used in training sessions in order for personnel to become familiar with methods to manage difficult situations and select the best possible alternatives. An example of experiment that provided major results is discussed below.

Mayo's Hawthorne Experiments

In the 1920s, certain experiments were carried out for organization development in terms of human relations. In particular, George Elton Mayo, an industrial, sociologist and organization theorist, was in charge of an experiment at the Hawthorne works of the General Electric Company in Chicago between 1924 and 1927.

The experiment was about fatigue and monotony effects on job productivity, and it was carried out acting on variables such as rest breaks and working hours. Mayo's research findings revolutionized both management theory and practice and contributed to motivation theory.

Mayo conducted this experiment on six women: he took them from the assembly line and segregated them from the rest of the factory. During the entire experiment, this little group worked under the eye of a supervisor who was more a friendly observer than a disciplinarian. Each time he introduced changes to their working conditions, Mayo discussed them with and explained them to the women in advance. The group was employed in assembling relays: the women had to put together 40 separate parts and then drop the completed mechanism into a chute. The relays were mechanically counted as they slipped down the chute. They calculated the production rate under normal conditions (48 hours per week, including Saturdays and no rest pauses), which was 2,400 relays a week for each woman. Starting from this basic rate, Mayo began introducing various changes, each of which was continued for a test period that could vary from a minimum of four to a maximum of 12 weeks. Throughout these variation periods, an observer was present during working hours: he noted all that went on and kept the women informed about the experiment. In addition, he asked for information and listened to their complaints. Changes in production rate were measured by increased or decreased relay production in each experiment period:

- Normal conditions: output went down.

- Two five-minute rest pauses: output went down.

- Two 10-minute rest pauses: output went down sharply.

- Six five-minute pauses: output fell slightly and the women complained that their work rhythm was broken by frequent pauses.

- Two rest pauses, the first with a hot meal supplied by the company free of charge: output went down.

- The women were dismissed at 4:30 pm instead of 5:00 pm: output went down.

- The women were dismissed at 4:00 pm: output remained the same.

- Back to normal conditions: output was the highest ever recorded, averaging 3,000 relays a week.

The conclusions of the experiment were as follows:

- The social world of adults is patterned about work activity and work is a group activity.

- Workers' morale and productivity is more important than physical work conditions: need for recognition, security and sense of belonging.

- A complaint is commonly a symptom manifesting disturbance of an individual's status within a company.

- Social demands from inside and outside the work plant can both condition the attitude and effectiveness of workers.

- Informal groups at work exercise strong social control over the work habits and attitudes of individuals.

- Group collaboration must be planned and developed – it does not occur by accident.

The most important conclusion of these experiments was that if group collaboration is achieved, human relations may reach a level of cohesion which resists the disrupting effects of an adaptive society.

Elton Mayo discovered a general improvement in production that was completely independent of any change he introduced, demonstrating that the current theory (advocated by Frederick W. Taylor) of workers being motivated solely by self-interest was not correct. It did not make sense that productivity would continue rising gradually, so Mayo began looking around and realized that the women had formed a social environment.

What happened during the experiments was that six individuals became a team that committed itself wholeheartedly and spontaneously to cooperation: they felt themselves to be participating freely and without afterthoughts. These six women were consciously working without coercion from above or limitation from below, so they could feel satisfied in working under less pressure than ever before. In fact, regular medical checks showed no sign of cumulative fatigue and absence from work declined by 80 per cent. The women were not pushed around or bossed about by anyone and under these conditions they developed an increased sense of responsibility so that discipline and authority came from within the group itself.

Workplaces are social environments that are able to carry social values and within them, people are motivated by much more than economic self-interest. Observations about these experiments demonstrated that:

- being singled out from the rest of the factory workers raised self-esteem in the individual forming the group;

- being allowed to have a friendly relationship with their supervisor increased the women's happiness at work;

- discussing changes in advance with the supervisor helped the women feel part of a team.

The supervisor behaviour secured group cooperation and loyalty, and for this reason productivity rose even when rest breaks were taken away. This phenomenon has been called the Hawthorne effect and has been described as the reward you reap when you pay attention to people: the mere act of showing people that you are concerned about them usually spurs them on to better job performances.

For example, suppose you have taken management trainees and have given them specialized training in management skills that they do not possess at the moment: this act gives the trainees the feeling that they are so valuable to the organization that time and money are being spent on developing their skills; they feel that they are on a track to the top and this motivates them to work harder and better. The motivation is independent of any particular skills or knowledge they may have gained from the training session.

The Hawthorne effect has also been called the 'somebody upstairs cares' syndrome: when people spend a large amount of their time at work, they must have a sense of belonging, of being part of a team: when they do so, they produce better results.

Leadership

Social psychology refers to studies of individual attitudes within groups; it is especially applicable in project teamwork. Social studies have demonstrated that in every working group there is an individual who tends towards dominant behaviour: this is the definition of leadership.

Several observations have confirmed that individuals who make the most use of their influence on the rest of the team tend to become leaders for others. Leaders are team members who make the most decisive choices; leadership is the connotation of the most prominent role in a group.

In the relatively recent past, leadership was referred to individuals having a certain personality, whatever group they belonged to. Current studies on social psychology applied to communication and leadership provide opposing interpretations. Assertiveness in communication is certainly a primary factor, but – as already emphasized – communication is a bilateral action.

Therefore, leaders are required to:

- be familiar with the topics addressed by the team, with the actions to be undertaken and the goals to be achieved;

- recognize and select attitudes that are preferable in the different situations;

- be persuasive.

Leaders must be goal-oriented as well as capable of creating an appropriate environment in the team in order for team tasks to be successfully accomplished. Leadership practices may belong to one of three categories:

- Authoritarian leaders – these leaders tend to centralize the decision-making power, to minimize delegation of authority to other team members and to be always the hub of the communication network. Their control is predominant; they constrain the behaviour of other team members. This sort of leadership is not the worst one because the behaviour of these leaders is always dictated by situations that occur; in stressful and challenging situations, these leaders are able to ensure that the team goal is achieved in a short time. On the other hand, however, team morale is negatively influenced in the medium to long term.

- Democratic (cooperative) leaders – these leaders ensure that their teams operate through an optimum balance of efficiency and satisfaction. Team members are constantly encouraged to make decisions and are aware of their share of responsibility both in terms of contributing to team decisions and in addressing team goals. This style of delegation enhances the performance of decision-making processes, in which the full range of team capabilities is involved; while these processes become more complex, and possibly burdensome and extended, they result in better outputs, both at the team level and at the individual level. Efforts made at the outset to establish the appropriate environment in the team increase its stability as well as the durability of the results achieved.

- *Laissez-faire* leaders – these leaders are somewhat confident in team members. Their low interest in the tasks to be executed results in less efficient performance as well as in less team satisfaction. Their decisions become compulsory for the team and their attitude towards responsibilities is elusive.

In summary, leadership is a context-sensitive phenomenon. It can be addressed both ways: top-down (leaders manage groups) and bottom-up (leaders, being an integral part of their teams, try to understand the dynamic among and needs of team members). The willingness of team members to become leaders and the willingness to elect a team leader establish a circular relationship.

Conclusions

To conclude this brief discussion of human factors, we will now list and describe the 28 soft skills proposed by Lei Han, a Stanford engineer recognized as a top career success expert, which are the results of a famous piece of research:

1. Empowered mindset – looking at any situation, especially a difficult one, as an opportunity to learn and grow, focusing your attention on improving yourself instead of changing others.

2. Self-awareness – knowing and understanding what motivates and inspires you, being able to observe yourself and understand how your perceptions are driving your actions.

3. Emotion regulation – being able to manage your emotions, especially negative ones, at work in order to think clearly and objectively, and act accordingly.

4. Self-confidence – believing in yourself and your ability to accomplish anything.

5. Stress management – being able to stay calm and balanced in challenging situations. Knowing how to reduce your stress level will increase your productivity and prepare you for new challenges.

6.   Resilience – being able to bounce back after a disappointment.

7.   Ability to forgive and forget – being able to forgive yourself for making a mistake and forgive others who have wronged you so that you can focus your mental energy on your career goals.

8.   Persistence and perseverance – being able to maintain the same energy and dedication in your effort to learn, do and achieve in your career despite difficulties, failures and oppositions.

9.   Patience – being able to take a step back in a seemingly rushed or crisis situation.

10.   Perceptiveness – giving attention to and understanding the unspoken cues and underlying nuance of communication and actions of other people.

11.   Communication skills – being able to actively listen to others and articulate your ideas.

12.   Teamwork skills – being able to work effectively with people presenting different skill sets, personalities or work styles.

13.   Interpersonal relationship skills – having the empathy and capacity to build good relationships with people at work and in your network.

14.   Presentation skills – effectively presenting your work results and ideas formally to an audience.

15.   Meeting management skills – possessing the capacity to lead a meeting in order to reach productive results.

16.   Facilitating skills – being able to coordinate and solicit well-represented opinions and feedback from a group with diverse perspectives to reach the best solution.

17.   Selling skills – building buy-in to an idea, decision, action, product or service.

18.   Management skills – creating and motivating a high-performing team.

19.   Leadership skills – defining and communicating visions and ideas that inspire others to follow with commitment and dedication.

20.   Mentoring/coaching skills – providing constructive wisdom, guidance and feedback that can help others to further their career development.

21.   Managing upwards – proactively arranging your relationship with your top management, their expectations of your work and their perception of your performance.

22.   Self-promotion skills – proactively and subtly promoting your skills and work results to influential or powerful people in your organization and network.

23.   Skills in dealing with difficult personalities – being able to still achieve the work result needed while working with someone whom you find difficult.

24.   Skills in dealing with difficult/unexpected situations – being able to stay calm and still effective when faced with an unexpected or difficult situation.

25.   Savvy in handling office politics – being able to understand and proactively deal with the unspoken nuances of office and people dynamics in order to protect yourself from unfairness as well as furthering your career.

26.   Influence/persuasion skills – being able to influence perspectives or decision making while allowing the people you influence to believe that they made up their own minds.

27.   Negotiation skills – being able to understand the counterpart motivations and reach a resolution that satisfies both sides while maintaining good relationships for future interactions.

28.   Networking skills – being able to be interesting and interested in business conversations that motivate people to want to be in your network.

References and Further Reading

European Cooperation for Space Standardization 2009. *ECSS-M-ST-10C Rev. 1. Space Project Management. Project Planning and Implementation.* Noordwijk: ECSS.

Lewis, J.P. 2002. *Project Leadership.* New York: McGraw-Hill.

PART II

Project Cost and Value for Constructions and Facilities: Introduction to Part II

MASSIMO PICA

When we mean to build,
We first survey the plot, then draw the model;
And when we see the figure of the house,
Then must we rate the cost of the erection.

William Shakespeare, *Henry IV* – II, i, 3

Cost-effective construction processes depend on the achievement of continuously evolving technical skills, as well as on lessons learned in the different theatres of operations of construction specialists. Bringing projects to their completion requires careful consideration of the sequence of design stages of the project life cycle, in parallel with the procurement processes leading, to the greatest possible extent, to a successful outcome; this also applies to the processes of renovation of existing assets.

Learning how to design constructions to be subsequently built and maintained requires a lengthy training process.

New professional competences (such as construction control experts, project validators, safety experts and facility managers) are involved in the management of specific sections of design and construction processes. The 'know how' and 'can do' connotations of design and construction specialists are valuable competitiveness drivers, especially in the more strategic evolution areas of construction (environmental and social sustainability, additional baseline building performances, process re-engineering and technological innovations, and management practices).

Design processes along with project implementation processes take into consideration a whole series of factors influencing the project life cycle and its economic appraisal from the project scope formulation through to the asset use and maintenance.

Construction sites can be managed at best by the application of convenient scheduling techniques to the identification, analysis and implementation of individual stages of construction processes (or perhaps, in specific cases, repair/renovation processes).

The definition of lists of activities to be scheduled is subject to three conditions:

- identification of process details, creation of a hierarchy among individual activities, which are expected to be differentiated and classified as macro-activities and micro-activities and subsequently listed in homogeneous groups;

- determination of activity durations depending on how construction processes are arranged; and

- definition of dependencies among activities, from both technical and organizational points of view and also taking into consideration the site configuration.

In the course of the project life cycle, all stakeholders are expected to be in possession of convenient skills to ensure that each project action and documentation item is properly understood, interpreted and communicated. In the early design stages, it is necessary to manage a combination of information items (dimensional, constructional, environmental, physical, technical and morphological) to be coordinated and represented in design documents and subsequently decoded, verified and integrated prior to the conclusion of the whole design process, ensuring the most efficient project implementation in accordance with the stated requirements. Both technical expertise and management expertise are therefore needed in all the project stages to support a cost-effective evolution from the initial design through to – and beyond – the commissioning of the asset.

Concerning software tools considered as a solution to enable the development of Project Management practices, and specifically looking at the construction sector, the following key findings are reported by construction software users:

- Users of construction estimating software produce faster and more accurate bids. Companies that use construction estimating software underestimate and overestimate projects less often than spreadsheet users. They also have shorter bid turnaround times.

- Construction estimating software users report fewer challenges with their system. Specifically, in over 70 per cent of reported occurrences, construction estimating software users have found that their system rarely makes bidding on projects difficult. On the other hand, about half of spreadsheet users report that their system often makes bidding on projects difficult.

- These results were more pronounced among medium- and large-sized companies (namely, those with an annual revenue of more than £0.5 million). There is therefore a greater opportunity for specialized construction estimating software to improve efficiency at larger companies. Conversely, for smaller companies, simple tools such as spreadsheets can prove to be satisfactory for cost estimating.

On the basis of these considerations, it is deemed convenient to comparatively analyse the effectiveness of spreadsheets and specialized construction estimating software for corresponding applications.

Medium-sized and large companies are – allegedly – most concerned with how well construction estimating software meets their requirements. Smaller companies may be less satisfied with construction estimating software because they are not bidding on the same volume, or complexity, of jobs that larger companies bid on. In some cases, the functionality in construction estimating software, more than a small company needs, tends to make them less efficient and therefore less satisfied with the fit of their system.

The three most difficult costs to estimate are financing, equipment and materials costs. Overlooking costs (for example, scaffolding) will very or somewhat often lead to an estimating error; the second and third most frequent causes of estimating errors are reported to be miscalculating transportation and contingency costs.

Construction estimating users are most satisfied with how quickly and accurately they are able to create bids with their software system. The better the estimating processes are standardized, the more important the benefits of construction estimating software; in most cases, including spreadsheet users, process standardization appears to be a top challenge to estimating.

The mechanisms and processes involved in the life cycle of construction projects, through to their completion, under the conditions of open competitiveness are also strongly associated with the internationalization of the economy and on the resulting demand for equitable regulatory practices. Taking into account the European Directives no. 17 of 2004 on procurement procedures and No. 18 of 2004 on procedures for the award of public works contracts, public supply contracts and public service contracts – and also considering the new stakeholders acting in the procurement scenario – economic operators at the national level are committed to facing the new challenges of international competitiveness.

Chapter 14

Planning for the Project Life Cycle of Constructions and Facilities

MASSIMO PICA

Introduction to Project Management for Built Assets

According to Turner (2009: 2): 'A project is a temporary organization to which resources are assigned to do work to deliver beneficial change'.

While in the construction area and among construction operators, the notion of project has been very well known for centuries, at the same time there is a strong perception of conditions of uncertainty underlying in construction activities and of the risk inherent in their objectives. On the other hand, except for occasional circumstances, no systematic effort has been expended in recording, analysing and assessing the influence of these unwanted occurrences.

In the construction environment, the concepts of project and uncertainty go hand in hand at an increasing rate, taking as a typical definition of uncertainty the variation from a situation of routine to the condition in which knowledge of technology is limited, known methods may lead to unclear outcomes and the degree of discrepancy is high.

Construction Project Management can essentially be seen from two points of view: (1) the methodologies and procedures adopted for the planning and monitoring of individual projects; (2) the technical and communication skills of Project Managers. At a corporate level, the assessment of Project Management capabilities is based on the specific strengths and weaknesses revealed in the aforementioned areas.

Companies operating in the construction area represent a peculiar case among manufacturing companies. Their finished products are neither divisible nor transportable; they are formed by elements that, although being physically distinguishable, can hardly be separated into parts being independently operated: residential buildings can be partitioned into flats with no loss in their functionality, whereas hospitals cannot be operational except in their entirety. Transportability is also excluded, due to the inherent nature and size of constructions.

Construction companies are also expected to reconcile different – and sometimes conflicting – needs: functional specializations and small- to medium-sized business, centralized control and operational independence of construction sites, accurate work planning and flexibility of operations.

Each activity – as defined in common Project Management mechanisms (work breakdown structures (WBSs), bar charts and network techniques (CPM, PERT)) – is associated with some appropriate assignment of resources and a corresponding economic value, showing a non-linear behaviour of the cost-time curve – the so-called 'S-curve'. The problem of resource levelling is also inherent in this context.

Scheduling and control efforts are directed towards assessing the economic and financial performance of construction works through the elements of cost accounting (fixed and variable costs, direct and indirect costs) and the accrual accounting system.

Accounting procedures are inherent in the project life cycle to ensure – along with other specific procedures – that stakeholder requirements are constantly met and that a high-quality level is preserved. When the built asset is ready for final acceptance tests prior to its release, contractual documents are reviewed along with accounting documents and work orders to ascertain the compliance of the asset to contract agreements, project specifications and other applicable rules.

When assembly systems in construction sites grow in terms of complexity – diverging from standard deterministic practices – process vulnerability (that is, exposure to risks) becomes higher and successful outcomes become more difficult to achieve. Interface, interdependency and novelty related to people, products and processes are deemed to be among the key characteristics of complex projects.

In construction projects, uncertainty conditions are particularly remarkable and strong in their correlation to such factors as:

- the variability (non-repeatability) and complexity of construction projects;

- the separation between the project definition process and the construction process; and

- the high complexity of organization processes, requiring an extremely variable number of participants.

As a consequence of the variability of parties interacting in the construction process, organizational complexity becomes a key issue of the process, whereas – for example – the technological approach can be considered a more traditional element.

Construction projects present certain specific connotations. For example, they require a high degree of strategic coordination among the different levels of contractors and subcontractors; furthermore, from project to project, the structure of participating enterprises is subject to variations.

Second, construction projects include a number of sub-processes:

- Design, concluded by the definition of quality, cost and time objectives to be reflected in the project execution.

- Preparation and negotiation of the project proposal, concluded by the assignment of responsibility for the execution of the project to construction companies.

- Site preparation, concluded by the review of construction criteria, methodologies, procedures and schedules selected to comply with project objectives.

- Construction works on the designated site in accordance with project specifications.

The definition of project objectives requires a careful review of project details, taking into account the high degree of irreversibility of every project; therefore, mistakes or omissions will be irrevocably harmful.

Project objectives are subsequently apportioned to a hierarchy of sub-projects covering the individual construction lots. At the lowest level of this hierarchy, each executable task is assigned to internal and/or external parties mutually interacting, as described in the contractual documents.

Afterwards, the overall project event schedule is defined. Key dates and other schedule constraints will be tailored to the project; this is essential for the entire project planning exercise (including the cost estimating exercise), especially when project durations are short.

Activity networks are addressed next, identifying project activities, their duration, their execution constraints, their resources and their organizational details. This is an extremely complicated effort when the number of activities is high and/or activities are strongly inter-related.

Activity networks are the basic operational structures for using PERT or CPM procedures in exploring different options to arrive at an optimum value which will lead to the definition of a baseline plan.

Necessarily, construction Project Management will include the final assurance that project objectives at a certain time are met, on the basis of variances identified between the baseline and the actual situation of the project.

The Project Life Cycle Perspective for Constructions and Facilities

Cleland and King (1988) provide their personal example of construction project life cycle arranged in four stages:

- Feasibility – technical hypothesis formulation, project and feasibility study. This stage is concluded by the judgement on the project's feasibility.

- Planning – overall estimation of timelines, costs, contract conditions, milestones and description of activities. This stage is concluded by subcontract signatures.

- Construction – this is the project key stage, in which the asset is built.

- Start-up – the built asset is delivered.

Projects encompassed in the construction business are sometimes of a large size and are usually characterized by a low degree of repetitiveness. In fact, while individual operations denote a certain amount of uniformity, this is no longer true for a project in its entirety. Therefore, if the uniqueness of individual projects is considered in its real significance, lessons learned from previous projects cannot be accounted for in practice.

Contractual agreements – broadly speaking – require that construction companies remain in line with schedules, costs and specifications that have been mutually established. As a consequence, prior to any firm commitment, it is mandatory that risks associated with the implementation of a project be carefully scrutinized.

Accordingly, in frequent cases, planning efforts can reduce unpredictability boundaries inherent in construction projects to ensure that contractors are able to develop their undertakings more effectively and efficiently. The importance of planning processes for the successful management and performance of construction activities cannot be overemphasized, also taking into account the involvement of top-level managers in the efficiency of construction processes and, usually, the commitment of resources in contract execution (in terms of funds and time), which may be challenging both at a process level and at an organizational level.

The outputs of construction projects frequently result from the application of simple but heterogeneous technologies, relevant to the different components of built assets (for instance, utilities, electrical, mechanical, electronic and hydraulic). Project planning for constructions is therefore a combined and specialized effort, which is expected to be efficiently coordinated and integrated, especially when the project size requires the concurrent involvement of contractors and a number of subcontractors. Project planning is inherently a unique effort due to the limited degree of standardization of construction products and processes.

In addition to this preamble, showing to which extent construction planning processes can be affected by peculiar conditions and complexity factors, there is evidence that bringing projects to completion frequently involves massive cash flows, with misalignments between inflows and outflows generating potential difficulties that may be financially critical for small-sized companies or whenever the company has been exposed to pre-existing debts. Project schedule and cost planning must therefore be concurrent, so that any schedule variation will be consistent with the corresponding economic variation.

The planning stage initially includes a detailed analysis of the project and of its implementation process, along with the evaluation of contracts, procurement documents, design factors (architectural, structural, facilities, etc.) and siting factors. Arrangements for the construction site are set up (as will be discussed below), including any subcontracting provisions, as well as for materials supply and availability of personnel. All systematic analyses of project elements and organizational details will be completely explored.

Subsequently, a detailed schedule of project implementation is envisaged. Documents from the planning stage are used as inputs: a project breakdown identifies all the lower-level components and an analysis of operations on these components is carried out, including their cost estimates. It is worth noting that the project implementation documents are also used as contractual interfaces between the contractor and the client. Once more, at this stage of the process, the project budget and the schedule (and also the project WBS) must be checked for their consistency with the established plans for cost, time and performance baseline management.

Clearly, in every construction process, from an efficient management perspective, specific attention should be addressed to project execution and concurrent project control, including convenient feedback mechanisms. The elements under control will especially be the following: resource management, coordination of contractor and subcontractor efforts on the site, quality of materials/operations and compliance with safety regulations. Control actions should be as immediate as possible in the event of variances from the planned baseline: taking into consideration the project progress, more exactly in initial stages, it should be emphasized that any delay in activating corrective measures could compromise the successful outcome of the entire project and its compliance with contract requirements.

Finally, every project culminates in a certain amount of lessons learned. As the project is completed, all issues generated and all mistakes incurred are reviewed *ex post* and, of course, the profitability of the project initiative is scrutinized. In current practices, there is evidence that this final review is sometimes overlooked, whereas it should always be considered as an essential pre-condition for the development of organizational culture. Certainly, conducting critical reviews of projects and their implementation ensures that the probability of errors in future project initiatives will be lower and also induces changes in organizations in favour of their survival or, possibly, their growth potential.

While the initial stages of projects are typically characterized by uncertain perspectives in terms of schedule, cost and adherence to performance expectations, the degree of uncertainty is clearly lower in the later project stages; on the other hand, alleviating the consequences of delays occurring in the final stages of the project becomes more difficult and expensive. Criticality is also higher in early stages of the project, since the impact of early decisions on the project's evolution and its successful outcome is stronger.

As already noted, construction projects are characterized by the heavy influence of cost and schedule factors (for example, their durations are frequently longer than a year), and their management (including project outputs and processes) is faced with the uniqueness of project efforts, or – in more favourable cases – a low degree of repetitiveness. Therefore, it is frequently the case that no dependable reference elements – in terms of schedule, cost and performance – can be used, except for specific project areas; planning for each project initiative requires that specific reference elements be evaluated.

Economic, schedule and technical/quality elements involved in project implementation may also be strongly interdependent: for example, delays in project activities may generate considerably higher costs to complete the project, whereas cost reductions may derive from improved planning provisions leading, for example, to shorter work durations.

In many cases, construction companies operate in multi-project environments, characterized by projects competing with one another in the use of corporate resources and/or in being managed by the same individual. Under these conditions, resource requirements and project priority issues have to be defined, both in the short term and, especially, in the long term. This means that an insightful planning practice is essential and that dependable predictions are necessary to forecast resource requirements and timelines across the project life.

Interdependences between projects may be seen from two complementary points of view:

- At the level of individual activities, when there are finish-to-start constraints between two activities requiring the use of the same single piece of equipment that is available.

- At the whole project level, when available resources (for example, carpenters) are not sufficient to meet the resource requirements of concurrent projects.

There is – in theory – an obvious solution to these kinds of conflicts, which is project prioritization based on specific criteria, such as the following:

- delivery dates;

- risks of penalties;

- technical risks;

- project profitability;

- expected cash flow;

- impact on other projects.

Carrying forward a project across its life cycle essentially involves a sequence of processes beginning with individual intentions and continuing until completion when all external inputs deriving from the multiplicity of needs, and from economic and regulatory factors, are satisfactorily reconciled. Therefore, during and after the design stage of a project, its growing complexity may require interdisciplinary and differentiated efforts.

The management of a project – and more precisely the cost-effective management of its life cycle – requires appropriate personal and professional abilities which are dependent on the inherent nature of the project, besides the knowledge of a number of concepts and the capability to adopt stipulated procedures in order to enable a complete assessment of problems related to the project life cycle.

Any project, leading to a new and unique output, presents an obvious level of uncertainty. The usual arrangement of projects in stages, across their lifetimes, provides a mechanism to effectively control the project evolution. The key element of each of the project stages is the production of one or more deliverables, representing tangible and verifiable outputs, such as a feasibility study, a detailed project or a structural component.

At the conclusion of each stage, a project review (more exactly, a Design Review) takes place to appraise the deliverables produced and the project performance data (cost and schedule) at that time.

Planning processes are not exclusively connected to the initiation of a certain project, but they are continuously invoked whenever a discrepancy is reported between the project plan and its actual performance.

Preliminary plans are formulated before the initiation of the project, including the definition of all the activities, the resource requirements, the assignment of responsibilities, the schedule of activities and their cost estimation. Execution plans can be seen as instances of preliminary plans. For example, if the preliminary plan states that for a certain activity, two person-months of a carpenter are required, the execution plan will define the carpenter's name for the two-month assignment, or two names, both for a one-month assignment. Similarly, the dates defined in a 'relative' way – with respect to the project initiation – in the preliminary plan become 'absolute' in the execution plan.

SCOPE PLANNING

Project scope planning is the detailed definition of activities included in the project mission or excluded from it. The project is divided into a number of elementary activities, which are usually large and variable from project to project; 'elementary' means that a more detailed definition is not mandatory.

RISK MANAGEMENT PLANNING

Risk management includes all actions required to address possible unforeseen events that may influence the performance of the project. For example, risks may arise when a required construction permit is delayed, so that the project requiring this permit becomes delayed as well, or when human resources in the project are limited, so that the illness of an operator creates a risk to the project.

Risk management usually involves two separate planning processes: risk management planning and risk factor response planning.

SCHEDULE DEFINITION

Project schedules, based on the WBS properly defined for each project, are planned taking primarily into account activity durations and precedence constraints.

COST PLANNING

Activity execution costs are deemed to be the most obvious cost items in a project, whether they are internal costs or external costs (subcontracts).

In addition to execution costs, consideration should also be given, for example, to:

- initial costs relating to the analysis of owner needs and to the preparation of preliminary plans;

- management and control costs relating to the definition of execution plans, review of requirements, assessment of deliverables, running of meetings, preparation of project reports, etc.;

- coordination costs relating to other project labour expenses not accounted for in previous cost categories (for example, travel and subsistence).

Effective Planning for the Construction Site Installation

The usual practice of establishing calendar durations and relations (start-finish, start-start, finish-finish) between expected site operations is certainly and typically appropriate as the first step of the site installation process. The next step begins with a specific question: to what extent are we confident that the logical process and the sequence of operations are really optimized and that we have attained the threshold in the given context?

First of all, it is advisable to consider available volumes and to confirm that storage areas and internal pathways are adequately designed in the Site Installation Plan (or a similar document). This is a significant factor, since constraints are posed on subcontractors concerning their procurement processes, the quantity of material to be installed on-site, and the design of site safety and of collective protection systems. Second, consideration should be given to the number of devices needed to lift the materials to be installed on-site by subcontractors.

Elements and variables that have to be considered for a comprehensive discussion are so numerous that it is necessary to adopt a step-by-step approach. Our primary target is the optimization of site design, of operational sequence and of interfaces among work teams in order to derive a quantitative indication of how to maximize the output-to-effort ratio.

A good site installation schedule should take into account the compliance to planned safety requirements in order to ensure that safety hazards are minimized. As an example, the following operational steps are suggested:

- divide the building in individual elementary work cells (EWCs);

- resource scheduling and identification of the work breakdown element (WBE) having the maximum duration (no crashing);

- schedule drafting and review of the WBE to eliminate interferences and inactivity.

The design of the EWC considers the number of separate workplaces that are employed by individual operations carried out by one team at a time. The maximum number of workplaces will depend on the size of the individual EWC: the smaller the cells are, the lower the operational effectiveness and the resulting benefits will be.

Resource scheduling is based on the appraisal of WBEs that are present in each EWC (the WBE is defined as an element at a certain level of the WBS for the entire project). The WBE having the maximum duration is identified, imposing a 'no crashing' condition, so that this maximum duration will also usually influence the timing of the subsequent operations in other workplaces. Concrete casting is a typical case in which this condition applies.

The third step in the above list consists of the WBE apportionment in EWCs belonging to the building and of the schedule drafting (for example, a Gantt chart). The schedule should ensure that in every cell considered, the work should be continuous and uninterrupted to the maximum possible extent.

Organization of Construction Sites

The growing trend of uncertainty and competitiveness in the present-day construction trade has led to an increased focus on organizational problems, which also derives from the effectiveness and economic benefits of innovative organizational approaches.

The organizational details of construction sites are essentially defined on the basis of the most efficient configuration of the construction process, so that each activity is associated with one or more operators in charge of it, and each operator has specific assignments, responsibilities and hierarchical connections. In addition, for each activity, it will be necessary to define operational procedures, control procedures, conflict resolution methods, information systems and information flows.

More precisely, it is convenient to optimize the differentiation and integration of tasks and responsibilities, providing for any required aggregation of tasks or their transfer to a different operator, ensuring that responsibilities are clearly and firmly allocated and that control and conflict resolution procedures are effectively implemented.

The final organization layout will be composed of block diagrams, flow charts, precedence diagrams and a more detailed and descriptive list of activities.

All these information sets will be used to delineate a baseline schedule. Subsequently, the following steps will be performed:

- definition of organizational structures for individual subsystems/ operators and for site operations;

- development of organization plans;

- information and training sessions for site operators.

Business Elements of Construction Projects

In terms of 'business', the development of the Business Case and the Business Plan are tangible and objective provisions to help determine whether the initial formulation of a project takes into account, as a minimum:

- the needs that are supposed to be fulfilled by the project initiative and what the intended project target is;

- the content (the 'core concept') of the initiative, in terms of users, information and products;

- the environmental context of the initiative and its interfaces.

- the human, financial and material resources required to initiate the project;

- the analysis of the project feasibility and of its SWOT (Strengths, Weaknesses, Opportunities and Threats).

To clarify the last point above, SWOT analysis is a common technique widely applied to support decisions, especially in the initial stages of a project, by identifying and listing all possible project benefits and shortcomings. The following list describes this in more detail:

- Strengths – these can include skills, experience, behaviour, enthusiasm, supportiveness of team members and, in addition, from an organizational point of view, economic stability, which is an enabler against unforeseen circumstances, and the proficiency of external relationships.

- Weaknesses – these may refer to the antonyms of the strength factors mentioned above. Analysing weaknesses places emphasis on their potential improvements or, on the other hand, on having to treat them as constraints.

- Opportunities – these are favourable events that, whenever they occur, realize the expectations of the project success in terms of meeting schedule and cost targets as well as expectations of the benefits accrued after the project is actually executed.

- Threats – these may be the consequences of weaknesses or external influences, namely from the market, from the regulations or from other relevant factors.

The final result is the input of relevant information to fill up the boxes shown in the upper half of Figure 14.1.

Not only does the opportunity-risk analysis integrate the descriptive information provided by the SWOT analysis, but it also combines the scores assigned both to the opportunities dimension and to the risks/uncertainties dimension of the graph in the lower half of Figure 14.1, so that the opportunity–risk inter-relationship can be identified by a point in one of the quadrants of the graph.

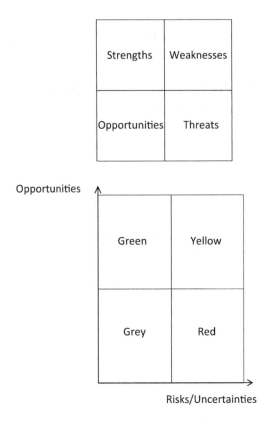

Figure 14.1   SWOT analysis and opportunities/risks assessment

In colours, usually the upper-left quadrant is shown in green, representing a favourable combination between high opportunities and low risks. The top-right quadrant is yellow, expressing a precautionary notice of high risks tied with high opportunities. The bottom-right quadrant is red, denoting the dominance of risks over opportunities. The bottom-left quadrant bears a neutral colour, usually grey, to signify low project risk related to low opportunities, that is, a scarcely appealing condition suggesting no urgency to proceed if there are more attractive solutions.

Comparing the SWOT analysis with the opportunity–risk analysis, the latter quantifies the relative weight of project elements (such as the expected project profitability or the importance of the project as an added value included in opportunities; the vagueness of the project scope or constraints on project feasibility, schedule and cost, among risks) and the rating of each element on a scale from one to five, so that each element has a relative value of its weight multiplied by its rating. In addition, while SWOT analyses tend to accommodate specific one-time projects, opportunity–risk analyses appear to be adaptable to recurring projects and convenient for comparisons between them.

References and Further Reading

Azim, S.W. 2010. *Understanding and Managing Project Complexity*. Manchester: University of Manchester Press.

BCIS. 2008. *Standardized Method of Life Cycle Costing for Construction Procurement*. London: Building Cost Information Service.

BS ISO. 2008. *BS ISO 15686–5:2008 Buildings and Constructed Assets – Service Life Planning; Part 5 – Life Cycle Costing*. London: British Standards Institution.

Cleland, D.I. and King, W.R. (eds) 1988. *Project Management Handbook*. Englewood Cliffs: Prentice Hall.

Turner, J.R. 2009. *The Handbook of Project Based Management: Leading Strategic Changes in Organizations*. New York: McGraw-Hill.

Chapter 15

Fundamentals of Construction Economics

MASSIMO PICA

Basic Elements of Cost-Effective Construction Project Management

THE ROLE OF CONSTRUCTION ECONOMICS IN PROJECT LIFE CYCLE MANAGEMENT

Buildings are, inherently, very expensive assets. Basically, costs may arise from the time and the amount of physical resources that have been expended; data from US practice report that the construction process of a standard building requires about one-fifteenth of the work life of an individual, whereas a skyscraper may require a number of work lives ranging from 50 to 100, and several work lives for annual maintenance.

After the completion of the design stage, cost-effectiveness factors begin to influence the construction process. Working indoors is preferable, where ideal conditions subsist and mechanized processes are possible. Consideration should be given to accurate work organization, procurement of materials from qualified vendors at reasonable prices and careful schedules of material inflows.

With regard to the professional role of specialists in Construction Economics (CE), the following remarkable assertion is provided by de Valence in his book (2011: 1):

> Perhaps there is no definitive answer to the 'What is CE?' question, or perhaps the answer depends on the reason for asking the question in the first place. Reflecting the different views of CE there are two approaches to the debate over the future development of CE.

Subsequently, de Valence emphasizes:

> *the gap between the practice of CE, by quantity surveyors, cost consultants and consulting economists who do life-cycle costing, investment appraisal and cost–benefit analyses, and CE research done mainly by academics. It would be fair to say that the debate over future development of CE and its theoretical foundations is not a major concern for practitioners. But is it really a concern for CE academics? If it is, what is being done about it, and if not why not?*

This chapter tries to explain some of the challenges that the professional practice of CE is increasingly facing in its application to the life cycle management of current and future construction projects.

CONSTRUCTION COSTS AND PROFITS

> *Underlying the construction process, from conception to demolition, is a lot of useful economics. (Myers 2008: 1)*

As noted by Myers, profit is the component included in construction costs to pay for the services of contractor companies. More specifically, normal profit (or normal Rate of Return) can be identified as the minimum level of remuneration required to ensure that existing companies are able to remain in their present area of production.

Profit can be obtained by subtracting total costs from total revenues – which, in turn, are calculated by multiplying quantities sold by their prices.

Myers' main message – and a clear message as well – is that construction economics, implicitly referred to in the life cycle of projects, in accordance with his statement above, embraces the three perspectives of an overview of the economy, a study of industrial sector and an analysis of construction market.

An accurate insight into construction costs (Myers 2008) would require that certain typical economic elements be taken into consideration: the opportunity cost of capital and of labour, the relationship between output and inputs of the company production processes, the concepts of diminishing marginal returns, the short-run fixed and variable costs, the project costs, the long-run costs and the economies of scale.

IMPACT OF COST ESTIMATING AND BUDGETING IN CONSTRUCTION PROCESSES

The Total Cost Management Framework, published by the Association for the Advancement of Cost Engineering – International (AACEI), provides the following definitions (Hollmann 2006: 50):

> *Cost estimating is the predictive process used to quantify, cost, and price the resources required by the scope of an investment option, activity, or project. Budgeting is a sub-process within estimating used for allocating the estimated cost of resources into cost accounts (the budget) against which asset cost performance will be measured and assessed.*

And, subsequently (Hollmann 2006: 139):

> *Cost estimating is a process used to predict uncertain future costs. In that regard, a goal of cost estimating is to minimize the uncertainty of the estimate given the level and quality of scope definition. The outcome of cost estimating ideally includes both an expected cost and a probabilistic cost distribution. As a predictive process, historical reference cost data (where applicable) improve the reliability of cost estimating. Cost estimating, by providing the basis for budgets, also shares a goal with cost control of maximizing the probability of the actual cost outcome being the same as predicted.*

While it must be considered that projects starting with poor estimates are doomed to failure, there is no question that estimating work is difficult.

BILLS OF QUANTITIES

A Bill of Quantities (BOQ) can be completed in different ways, in accordance with its purpose. If, for example, a certain structural element is composed of simpler sub-elements, straight pipes, curved pipes and other specific components, all having the same size, different criteria can be followed for a quantitative analysis of this structural element:

- Mass – the BOQ in this case will identify the corresponding class of work element and indicate its mass, or a quantity expressed in a relevant unit of measure. An additional distinction will be made between, say, a rectilinear pipe and a more complex sketch, taking into account the percentage rate of special pieces (such as curves or connectors). This will make workload calculations and subsequent work time analyses possible.

- Length – the same pipe sketch can be identified by the pipe length, or a conventional length in case of special elements (this frequently occurs in price books).

- Basic constituent elements – detailed lists can be used for materials to be purchased, in accordance with the relevant Bills of Materials.

Schedule and Cost Analysis for Budget Preparation

ENGINEERING DATA AND CONSTRUCTION TIMESCALES

On the basis of engineering data, two key information groups are collected to ensure that a schedule analysis can be carried out:

- the quantity to be assembled for each class (and sub-class) of work elements, from which workloads, timescales and personnel requirements can be calculated;

- the logical constraints of operations sequences, to be established also in accordance with construction expertise.

Activity networks are drafted in line with operations sequences; experience and good practice may suggest tentative values for activity durations, also taking into consideration potential resources and project organization.

It is already possible at an early stage to identify the critical path and the consistency of the construction schedule with the overall project schedule constraints.

As soon as the BOQ is issued, workload estimates can be formulated; this will normally occur at the Level 4 or Level 5 of the WBS, that is, a greater level of detail than is used in the network analysis.

When workloads are known, it will be possible to establish resource requirements (person-months) and their allocation in order to carry out further refinements in accordance with usual analytical/graphical methods.

CONSTRUCTION COSTS AND PARAMETRIC BUDGETS

Budget preparation criteria may follow an analytical approach, based on the detailed analysis of all the cost elements of the work to be estimated. This will be discussed later in this chapter. Conversely, parametric budgets are based on the identification of one or more parameters representing the work, to be used as references for the estimate.

It should be emphasized that the degree of project definition, the budget accuracy and the budget preparation effort are strongly correlated. By analogy to process industry practices, five different levels of budget classification can be envisaged (AACEI 2011), as shown in Table 15.1. The budget preparation effort in this table is measured by statistical criteria in which the value 1 is assigned to 0.005 per cent of project cost – inclusive of the engineering and construction costs, the cost of capital and other costs attributable to the owner – so that the maximum value of 100 will correspond to 0.5 per cent of the project cost.

Nevertheless, this is only one of the existing criteria. In Chapter 17 of this volume, the AACEI classification system (AACEI 2011) will be compared with similar classifications, issued in the UK by ACostE and RICS.

Table 15.1   Classification of budgets

Level	Method	Degree of project definition	Accuracy of budget	Budget preparation effort
V	Analogy	Less than 2 per cent	-20 to 50 per cent +30 to 100 per cent	1
IV	Parametric	From 1 to 15 per cent	-15 to 30 per cent +20 to 50 per cent	2 to 4
III	Preliminary cost estimates, short list of materials	From 10 to 40 per cent	-10 to 20 per cent +10 to 30 per cent	3 to 10
II	Detailed unit costs, extended list of materials	From 30 to 70 per cent	-5 to 15 per cent +5 to 20 per cent	4 to 20
I	Detailed unit costs, detailed list of materials	From 50 to 100 per cent	-3 to 10 per cent +3 to 15 per cent	5 to 100

The criteria on which parametric budgets are based are commonly in use, in addition to being – broadly speaking – the only available information during the initial project concept stage and the subsequent feasibility study. Parametric methods, for example, will be applied to early calculations of construction costs based on the average cost per unit volume (whether used or not) or of the cost of a railway section based on its length.

In summary, with reference to the AACE International classification system, Class 5 estimates (order of magnitude) are convenient in the absence of detailed engineering data, while at the other end, Class 1 estimates (part of definitive estimates) are possible in a detailed engineering scenario.

ANALYTICAL BUDGETS

The analytical approach to budget estimates requires an outline definition of the project plan and schedule as well as a BOQ, in accordance with levels IV and V of the AACE International classification.

Costs will be budgeted in adherence to the Cost Breakdown Structure of the project, with a distinction between direct costs and indirect costs.

Labour costs will be derived from an estimate of reference productivity data for the company or from bibliographical sources, selecting a suitable efficiency factor for the real operational conditions.

Material costs and subcontract costs will be estimated from company data and updated by considering more recently available proposals where relevant.

Budget estimates may be refined in subsequent steps as a result of the progress of engineering efforts and of consultations with owners, leading to a definitive budget which will be the basis for the final proposal and the contract negotiation.

Definitive budgets, usually corresponding to AACEI level V, will describe in detail:

- the total of high level direct and indirect costs required for the calculation of the expected contribution margin or the expected net profit margin;

- contingencies on direct costs (for quantity variations, as determined by engineering uncertainties) and on indirect costs (for unexpected circumstances related to project uniqueness, project location and other factors determined by the Project Manager).

With a certain degree of simplification, the total project cost C – to be estimated by the contractor as part of the project proposal – may be approximated by the sum of three components:

- a fixed amount C_0, including non-capitalized investment costs for site set-up and shut-down;

- a quantity related component, unit cost (p) times quantity (Q);

- a time-related component, unit cost (s) times duration (T).

In turn, from the owner side, consideration will be given to the entire range of life cycle costs and profits.

Risk analysis is required through the construction budgeting process, implying a convenient economic appraisal of risk contingency, subject to the Project Manager's determination and authority. In conclusion:

- an accurate level of engineering detail is required to assess both costs and durations; budgets may not be justifiable when the engineering effort is still in a preliminary phase or is poorly executed;

- a cost and schedule control system must be in place;

- cost and schedule risks must account for an initially stochastic scenario and for an incomplete transition to a deterministic scenario at a later stage;

- in complex project environments – that is, in most cases – effective integration must be in place between specialized project professionals and generalist professionals.

The Economic Evaluation of Construction Projects

CASH FLOWS

Any project is characterized by cash initially flowing out to pay for the costs of engineering, procurement, construction and commissioning. Once the construction begins its operating stage, revenues begin to flow into the owner company.

The rate at which the owner organization spends money during the design and construction phase of a project is usually determined by the terms of the contract that they have with an Engineering, Procurement and Construction (EPC) company.

Usually, the additional money needed above what it cost to build the asset, to commission it and to keep it running is accounted for as working capital. Working capital is best thought of as the money that is tied up in asset operation.

Cash flows at the end of the project are frequently neglected in profitability analysis, since their timing is uncertain and they are often far enough in the future that they have a minor impact on any of the measures of profitability.

Project cash flows will be addressed in more detail in the next section.

PROJECT FINANCING

The financial management of the construction life cycle may require large amounts of capital. Construction owners must raise the finances to support such investments. The way in which funds are raised to finance construction projects determines the cost of capital for the owner, and therefore sets the expected financial rate of return that the projects must achieve. As such, the construction Project Management should have an awareness of this subject to carry out economic analyses and optimization of the design.

All debt contracts require payment of interest on the loan and repayment of the principal. Interest payments are fixed costs, and if a company defaults on these payments, then its ability to borrow money will be drastically reduced. Since interest is deducted from earnings, the greater the leverage of the company and the higher the risk to future earnings, and hence to future cash flows and to the financial solvency of the company. Finance managers are therefore committed to ensuring that the cost of servicing the debt (the interest payments) does not cause problems to the company.

The overall cost of capital sets the interest rate that is used in economic evaluation of projects. The total portfolio of projects funded by a company must meet or exceed this interest rate if the company is to achieve its targeted return on equity and hence satisfy the expectations of its owners.

TAXES AND DEPRECIATION

Taxes can have a significant influence on the cash flows from projects. The construction Project Management should consider the effects of taxation and tax allowances such as depreciation in order to make an economic evaluation of the project.

Incentives may be provided by governments to encourage companies to make capital investments, which will create employment, generate taxation revenue and provide other benefits to politicians and the communities they represent. The most common incentives used are tax allowances: some form of depreciation charge is introduced as a tax allowance, by which the fixed capital investment can be deducted from taxable income over a period of time.

Depreciation is a non-cash charge, which reduces income for taxation purposes. There is no cash outlay for depreciation and no money is transferred to any fund or account, so the depreciation charge is added back to the net income after taxes to give the total cash flow from operations.

SENSITIVITY ANALYSIS

Economic analyses of projects can only be based on the best estimates that can be made of the investment required and the cash flows. A sensitivity analysis is a way of examining the effects of uncertainties in the forecasts on the viability of a project, since the actual cash flows achieved in any year will be affected by uncertainty factors.

The purpose of sensitivity analysis is to identify those parameters that have a significant influence on the viability of a project over the expected range of variation of each of these parameters.

To carry out the analysis, the investment and cash flows are first calculated using the most probable values that are considered for the various factors; this establishes the base case for analysis. Various parameters in the cost model are then adjusted, assuming a range of error for each factor in turn. This will show how sensitive the cash flows and economic criteria are to errors in the forecast figures. A sensitivity analysis gives some idea of the degree of risk involved in making judgments on the forecast performance of the project.

Project Schedule and Cash Flows

The project schedule establishes the timeline of project resource utilization and the project cash flows, which are essential both to the owner and to the contractor:

- the owner is enabled to predict time-phased payments in accordance with the progress of the project work packages;

- the contractor is able to predict time-related variations of the difference between costs incurred and profits earned during project execution.

The management of construction projects across their execution is characterized by peculiarities deriving from a number of factors:

- the phasing of the execution process;

- the procurement procedure, including the contractual clauses that are applicable to the schedule of payments;

- the divergence between the cost estimate included in the project proposal and the actual costs incurred by the contractor in the project execution;

- cash flows are negative up to a certain point of the project timeline and may influence the contractor's aptitude to sustain the expected progress of work packages.

By means of the cash flow budget, the financial plan of the project is quantified and tailored to the project schedule. Frequently, contractors have to incur costs in advance of payments received in accordance with project progress – for example, to pay salaries to workers. This requires that contractors must either temporarily borrow a certain amount of money or draw it from their own financial resources.

Contractual conditions and owners attitudes regarding project payments have a marked influence on the financial situation of the construction site. Contractual conditions are expected to control certain aspects, such as:

- appraisal of executed work packages and subsequent payment;

- the duties and responsibilities of operators in the payment procedure;

- the maximum allowed duration of each step of the procedure.

Economic Appraisal of Projects

FUNDAMENTALS OF PROJECT ECONOMIC ANALYSIS

As will be seen below, the investment payback time is one of the simple economic measures that can be estimated quickly if the project investment and cash flows are known. It can be derived from the ratio of the total investment to the average annual cash flow. It assumes that all the investment is made in year zero and revenues begin immediately. The simple payback time is, strictly speaking, based on a cash flow, but for the sake of simplicity, taxes and depreciation are often neglected and the average annual income is used instead of cash flow.

Another simple measure of economic performance is the Return on Investment (ROI). The ROI is an average value over the entire project that is obtained by dividing the cumulative net profit by the product of the asset life and the initial investment.

APPRAISAL OF PRIVATE PROJECTS

Private projects are evaluated on the basis of cost, value and profitability, which are taken into consideration for the entire project duration of, for example, N years.

First, the total cost LCC across the project life cycle can be expressed as a function of the annual direct costs C_{dn}, the annual indirect costs C_{in} and the discount factor i, for each generic year n across the project life cycle:

$$LCC = \sum_{n=1}^{N} \left\{ (C_{dn} + C_{in}) * \left[\frac{1}{(1+i)} \right]^n \right\}$$

Second, concerning project value, this can be considered from two different perspectives:

- the 'asset view' – emphasizing the direct effect of project execution on the value of the asset involved in the project;

- the 'revenue view' – evaluating the indirect effect on the revenue.

The difference between the two approaches is that in the 'asset view', there is no influence of time on the value of property, whereas the 'revenue view' takes into consideration the timeframe in which the project is located.

In terms of Net Present Value (NPV), each of the alternatives mentioned above can be represented quantitatively, respectively:

$$NPV = V_m - V_{m0}$$

where V_m is the market value of the property 'after the project' and V_{m0} is the market value 'without the project', and

$$NPV = \sum_{n=1}^{N} \left[(R - R_0) * \frac{1}{(1+i)^n} \right]$$

where R is the owner's revenue 'after the project' and R_0 is the revenue 'without the project'. The latter equation, for an infinite value of N, becomes:

$$NPV = \sum_{n=1}^{\infty} \left[(R - R_0) * \frac{1}{i} \right]$$

Third, appraisals of project profitability are influenced by the owner's characteristics, especially risk attitudes, and by the identifiable technical and economic alternatives. More precisely, investors may prefer either projects that are likely to ensure an increase of the value of their assets in a short period of time or projects that may increase owner revenue.

In terms of values, projects may be profitable if the following condition is met:

$$V - V_0 > C$$

where:

V_0 = property value before the project

V = property value after the project

C = cost of project execution

In terms of revenues, projects may be profitable if the increase of revenue after the project is higher than the cost of invested capital:

$$R - R_0 > C^* i$$

A 'relative' profitability criterion is provided by the project rate of return (ROR – or, more precisely, Return on Project (ROP)):

$$r = (R - R_0) * \frac{1}{C}$$

which is to be compared to other similar values applicable to alternative investments in order to ensure that the project having the highest ROR is selected.

Another expeditious profitability indicator is the payback period:

$$T_{pb} = \frac{C}{R}$$

which, albeit apparently simplistic, covers both project profitability and project risk. In fact, whenever the owner can successfully recover the invested capital C in a short period of time, the project will be economically of interest as well as moderately sensitive to economic fluctuations, inflation rate changes and other sources of risk.

All the profitability indicators mentioned above, however, present a significant shortcoming. In fact, they only account for a short-term perspective in which – ideally – value increases (compared to costs) or revenue increases (compared to costs of capital) and costs materialize immediately between the before-project situation and the post-project situation.

Actually, this is only correct when the project execution and the increases of value and/or revenue occur in a very limited period of time. Conversely, if durations are longer – as is nearly always the case – the classical models described cannot be considered consistent in the way they express reliable profitability judgments; therefore, time-related models should be used.

Models based on project NPV are among these models, as previously discussed: profitable conditions, in this case, are increasingly ensured whenever the NPV tends towards higher values.

The discounted income-to-cost ratio provides a second profitability indicator:

$$\text{Income/cost} = \frac{\sum_{n=1}^{N} \left[R * \frac{1}{(1 + i)^n} \right]}{\sum_{n=1}^{N} \left[R * \frac{1}{(1 + i)^n} \right]}$$

A third time-related indicator is the internal ROR, that is, the value of i which equates the discounted sum of incomes to the discounted sum of costs. The internal ROR is calculated by an iterative procedure; the higher the value, the more profitable the project investment.

Profitability indicators for project execution can be used either individually or in combination. For example, the payback period method could be used in a preliminary stage, while – at later stages – other better indicators would provide more accurate insights into the profitability of the project.

APPRAISAL OF PUBLIC PROJECTS

Cost-Benefit Analyses (CBAs) identify public projects presenting, for a community, economic feasibility conditions for their execution. The focus of CBAs is on the implementation of quantitative economic criteria as the basis for project appraisal.

CBAs are prepared by considering the transition from a 'financial analysis' to an 'economic analysis'. These approaches are specifically different because:

- some costs and benefits are only applicable to the community that is interested in the project and not to the entities in charge of project execution (that is, these are external and/or indirect costs);

- while in financial analysis, properties and services are accounted for at market prices, economic analysis reflects opportunity costs and prices related to values accrued to the community.

Benefits and costs (both across the project life cycle) can be defined as:

- direct benefits and costs accrued by the party that executes the project and undertakes the asset life cycle management;

- indirect benefits and costs accrued by other parties not involved in the execution of the project.

Both investment costs and follow-up life cycle costs are inclusive of the execution of the project and of the other works required for the asset functionality.

A key problem of CBAs is that the timelines of costs and benefits are misaligned. Therefore, the two project lifetime cash flows, for comparative purposes, must be scaled to the same point in time by discounting at a given rate.

This is made by considering the 'economic life' of the construction, that is, the period of time beyond which the net marginal annual benefit, discounted to time zero, provides negligible increases to the economic NPV.

Whatever the economic life (for example, 25 years or otherwise), the next problem is the definition of the proper discounting rate. From a financial point of view, this value is to be obtained by comparison to the revenues from alternative investments (bonds or otherwise). On the other hand, from an economic point of view, there is no such convergence of opinions on how to define a convenient discounting rate.

The following are the most usual project selection criteria derived from CBAs:

- the discounted benefit-to-cost (B/C) ratio;

- the discounted value of the difference between incomes and costs, that is, project net benefits measured by the NPV;

- the internal ROR of the project investment.

Usually, criteria using the NPV and the internal ROR are equivalent. As a rule, the NPV criterion, albeit affected by monetary values, is deemed more reliable than the internal ROR, which in turn is dimensionless. Comparable project information is obtained from these criteria whenever the discount rate in NPV calculations is the same as that used to establish if an internal ROR is 'high' or 'low'.

Common applications of CBAs to alternative (mutually exclusive) projects lead to the selection of the project having the highest B/C value. However, in some cases, this method gives an incorrect result. The following example provides more details:

Project	P1	P2	P3
Annual benefit (k£)	750	920	1,000
Annual cost (k£)	300	400	500
B/C ratio	2.50	2.30	2.00

Using the highest B/C criterion, P1 would be selected. Now, suppose that the last row is replaced by the net annual value, that is, B-C:

Project	P1	P2	P3
Annual benefit (k£)	750	920	1,000
Annual cost (k£)	300	400	500
Net annual value	450	520	500

Accordingly, P2 appears preferable, having the highest net annual benefit. Nevertheless, the higher annual cost of P2 compared to P1 (£100,000 more) leads to questioning whether the difference of net annual values (£70,000 in favour of P2) provides enough justification for P2 to be selected. This question can be answered by considering the B/C ratio calculated on the 'difference' between P2 and P1:

$$\text{P2 minus P1} \Rightarrow \text{B/C} = \frac{920{,}000 - 750{,}000}{400{,}000 - 300{,}000} = \frac{170{,}000}{100{,}000} = 1.7 > 1$$

This means that, for each additional investment of £1 in P2, compared to P1, a benefit of £1.70 is achieved. Hence, P2 is preferable to P1.

Comparing, now, P3 and P2:

$$\text{P3 minus P2} \Rightarrow \text{B/C} = \frac{1{,}000{,}000 - 920{,}000}{500{,}000 - 400{,}000} = \frac{80{,}000}{100{,}000} = 0.8 < 1$$

As a consequence, for each additional investment of £1 in P3 compared to P2, a benefit of £0.80 is achieved. Accordingly, P2 is the preferred solution: its benefit for the total project expenditure is the greatest, despite the fact that its B/C ratio is lower than P1.

This result will be more clearly understood if P2 costs and benefits are split into two parts. First, we consider £750,000 of benefits along with £300,000 of costs: the resulting B/C = 2.50 equates to the value for P1. The remaining P2 benefits (£170,000) and costs (£100,000) yield B/C = 1.70, which is in favour of P2.

Deeper insights into the BCA for construction projects are provided in the comprehensive book by C.S. Park (2002).

The Balance of Project Returns and Costs across a Project Life Cycle

The economic justification of projects, that is, the appraisal of an investment for a project, is certainly a primary concern for organizations wishing to pursue the initiative of a project. Current discussions on the Return on Investment (ROI) from projects and on how to calculate it sometimes miss the fact that the ROI is essentially related to the profitability of the entire organization, deriving from the ratio of its operating income to the value of investments (more generally, the ROI should be calculated from the operating income divided by the Earnings Before Interests and Taxes (EBIT)). Where an individual project is concerned, the ROP is a more appropriate concept.

Before going into more detail on this, two preliminary explanations are necessary. First, a usual situation is that returns and investments related to the project have to be estimated around the time of its initiation when relevant information on the project is vague; however, the project costs and incomes can be taken into account in a sort of business case based on a simulation that will allow the organization to appraise the relative impact of the different situations, bearing in mind the underlying degree of uncertainty in this approach.

The second preamble derives from the cost categories to be considered. As far as a ROI is concerned, no comparison with the costs incurred can be made before the final output of the project has begun its operating cycle, at which moment, however, costs will have reached a certain figure, whereas returns are still around zero or negative. On the other hand, if the assumptions supporting the business case become true, as the project output is operated, the subsequent economic benefit (that is, a higher profit and/or a lower cost) leads to a growing

ROI. At the same time, operating costs are incurred as a result of the resources expended (personnel, material, energy, etc.).

Following these clarifications, it is now possible to see how the ROP can be estimated in practice; numerical values of project costs and benefits in the example are purely indicative.

Project benefits here refer to reduced resource needs and less expensive processes; they are estimated from the first year of operation and maintenance stage, following the project set-up stage. On the other hand, fixed (investment) costs are charged in the set-up period, while subsequently annual operating and maintenance costs are incurred; clearly, in the set-up period and in the initial phase of the five-year operating and maintenance period, costs are expected to be higher than benefits.

	SET UP	YEAR I	YEAR 2	YEAR 3	YEAR 4	YEAR 5	TOTAL
Benefits	0	42,000	68,000	76,000	83,000	78,000	347,000
Investment costs	23,000	0	0	0	0	0	23,000
Operating costs	0	32,000	43,000	51,800	51,800	51,700	230,300
Maintenance costs	0	4,800	7,000	6,400	5,800	4,300	28,300
Difference	-23,000	5,200	18,000	17,800	25,400	22,000	65,400
Cumulated difference	-23,000	-17,800	200	18,000	43,400	65,400	0
Undiscounted ROP							23.22%

Table 15.2   Example of ROP calculation

The ROP is calculated as the ratio of the annual difference between benefits and costs divided by the total costs across the five years.

From these data, some sensitivity analysis may provide further insight into how the ROP can be influenced by variations of values. For example, if investment costs decrease from 23,000 currency units to 21,200, the resulting ROP will be 24.02 per cent – that is, a very slight increase – but if higher investment costs (30,000 currency units instead of 23,000) produce a 10 per cent reduction in operating and maintenance costs, the resulting ROP will be as high as 32.12 per cent.

From a general perspective, the following conclusion can be drawn: the return on a project should be balanced not only against initial (investment) costs, but also against operating and maintenance costs incurred subsequently. This implies considering an average lifetime for the project output, during which operating and maintenance costs typically overcome project set-up costs to a great extent.

References and Further Reading

AACEI, 2009a. Recommended Practice No. 31R-03. *Reviewing, Validating, and Documenting the Estimate*. Morgantown: AACE International.

AACEI, 2009b. Recommended Practice No. 36R-08. *Development of Cost Estimate Plans – As Applied in Engineering, Procurement, and Construction for the Process Industries*. Morgantown: AACE International.

AACEI, 2010. Recommended Practice No. 34R-05. *Basis of Estimate*. Morgantown: AACE International.

AACEI, 2011. Recommended Practice No. 18R-97. *Cost Estimate Classification System – As Applied in Engineering, Procurement, and Construction for the Process Industries*. Morgantown: AACE International.

Arizona State University/Alliance for Construction Excellence, 2002. *Job Order Contracting for Novices*. Tempe: Arizona State University.

Brent, R.J. 1996. *Applied Cost-Benefit Analysis*. Cheltenham: Edward Elgar.

De Valence, G. 2011. *Modern Construction Economics*. Abingdon: Spon Press.

HM Treasury, 2011. *The Green Book. Appraisal and Evaluation in Central Government*. London: The Stationery Office.

Hollmann, J.K. (ed.) 2006. *Total Cost Management Framework. An Integrated Approach to Portfolio, Program, and Project Management*. Morgantown: AACE International.

Humphreys, K.K. 1991. *Jelen's Cost and Optimization Engineering*, 3rd edn. New York: McGraw-Hill.

Humphreys, K.K. 2005. *Project and Cost Engineers' Handbook*, 4th edn. Morgantown: AACE International.

Myers, D. 2008. *Construction Economics: A New Approach*, 2nd edn. Abingdon: Taylor & Francis.

Park, C.S. 2002. *Contemporary Engineering Economics*, 3rd edn. Upper Saddle River: Prentice Hall.

Pilcher, R. 1993. *Principles of Construction Management*. London: McGraw-Hill.

Prieto, B. 2012. Comparison of Design Bid Build and Design Build Finance Operate Maintain Project Delivery. *PM World Journal*, I(V), December 2012.

Shim, J.K. and Henteleff, N. 1995. *What Every Engineer Should Know about Accounting and Finance*. New York: Marcel Dekker.

Spiro, H.T. 1996. *Finance for the Nonfinancial Manager*, 4th edn. New York: John Wiley & Sons, Inc.

Chapter 16

Identifying Cost and Life Expectancy Information

DAVID CHURCHER

The Role of Cost and Life Cycle Information

Cost and life expectancy information are fundamental to the calculation of life cycle costs, irrespective of whether this calculation is carried out in advance of initial construction so as to select the best economic solution or during the operating life of the asset so as to optimize the remaining value in the asset. While cost and life expectancy may be related, as it is usual but not guaranteed for more expensive materials and components to last longer, these two groups of information are usually obtained from different sources and thus represent two distinct information collection tasks.

The precision of the information that it is possible to collect will, naturally, affect the precision of the overall Life Cycle Cost (LCC) calculation. It is important to recognize that there are other factors affecting LCC precision as well, but these will not be covered in this chapter.

The collection of cost and life cycle information may be the most time-consuming and therefore the most expensive task within an LCC study. In this chapter, we will look at some of the information sources that are available and will consider the practical problems that this information poses for the LCC analyst and what strategies can be used to overcome those problems.

Structuring Cost and Life Expectancy Information

If an LCC study is an analysis of all the costs and benefits associated with a project during its lifetime, then it is clear that each activity or event that contributes to that LCC has to have a cost or benefit associated with it. It is usual, therefore, for an LCC model to be, in its simplest form, a list of activities or events occurring during the life cycle. This list is often going to be lengthy and therefore needs to be structured. The concept of a work breakdown structure is covered elsewhere in this book (see Chapter 6), but this is usually confined to a breakdown of the tasks associated with initial construction. While this is helpful for categorizing life cycle costs, it is not sufficient and a more extensive breakdown of costs is needed.

One useful structure within which to organize all the costs associated with the life cycle of an asset is that given in the UK supplement to ISO 15686–5. This is based on the ISO definition of what is contained within both a whole life cost and a life cycle cost, and this is best illustrated diagrammatically. Figure 16.1, adapted from ISO 15686–5, shows the breakdown of cost elements within the Whole Life Cost (WLC) and the LCC. This version shows occupation costs as a sub-category of life cycle cost, whereas the ISO includes occupation costs within non-construction costs.

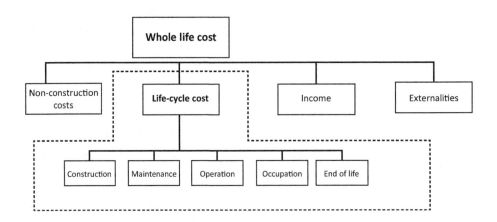

Figure 16.1   Distinction between the WLC and the LCC
Source: Adapted from ISO 15686–5.

The five broad categories identified as part of a life cycle cost are broken down into more detail in the UK supplement to ISO 15686–5. Some examples of these more detailed sub-categories are shown in Table 16.1. For a specific asset or project, these sub-categories can be reduced or expanded as appropriate.

Table 16.1   Cost categories and sub-categories

Cost category	Example sub-categories
Construction	Design costs Licences, certificates and compliance checks Works costs Fit-out costs
Maintenance	Planned major replacement costs Planned minor replacement costs Planned repair costs Unplanned replacement and repair costs Redecoration costs Adaptation costs
Operation	Utilities (gas, electricity, oil, water, waste) Cleaning Asset management, administration and survey costs Insurance and property taxes
Occupation	Furniture and fittings Security, helpdesk, reception, switchboard Catering, vending, hospitality
End-of-life	Demolition Inspections Dilapidations (reinstatement at end of lease)

Cost categories appropriate for any given LCC study will be selected, primarily taking into account the following elements:

- the nature of the study that is carried out;

- the brief received from the client commissioning the study;

- the time and budget available for certain cost elements to be included and others to be excluded;

- other practical case-specific issues.

Analysts should be careful not to build in any bias to the study by following the client's wishes without question.

Information about the life expectancy of the different materials, components or assemblies being included in an LCC study will need to be obtained to determine the replacement dates for all items. Clearly, items will only need to be replaced if their life expectancy falls within the period covered by the study, known as the 'study period'. Items with short life expectancies, when compared to the study period, may need to be replaced more than once and the life cycle cost model must take account of this.

In considering the impact of life expectancy on an LCC study, it is important to differentiate between a study that starts with initial construction, when it is assumed that all materials and components start as new, and a study that models the life cycle cost of an existing building, system or product. In the latter case, the data collection phase of the study must include a survey of the existing items to gauge their condition and therefore their remaining life expectancy. As part of this exercise, it is helpful to know when each item was installed – this may have been at the time of initial construction at some date in the past or of a more recent replacement. In addition, it is necessary to know what the expected life expectancy of each item is so that its next replacement date and any subsequent replacement dates can be estimated as accurately as possible.

Sources of Cost Information

The cost information necessary for an LCC study can come from a variety of sources. These include both public and private sources, and these have their own advantages and disadvantages.

Public sources of cost information are often known as price books, although now they are more likely to be in database form or available as online subscription services. One of the best-known price books in the UK is the series published by E&F Spon, which has been published in varying forms since 1873 and now covers architecture and building, mechanical and electrical services, external works and landscape, and civil engineering and highway works. Even though this price book is now published as four separate volumes, it suffers from the same disadvantage as all public price books, namely that the range of activities included is limited. The limit is either set by the practicalities of publication, although that is not a problem for electronic databases, or by the breadth of information that is available to the compilers. The information contained within the Spon's price books is edited by Davis Langdon, a large and well-known firm of quantity surveyors, and it is believed that this company draws on the wide range of construction contracts it is involved in each year, as well as the expertise of its in-house surveyors. Another source of price information is the BCIS subscription service that is operated as a subsidiary of the Royal Institution of Chartered Surveyors. Although the compilers of any price book will have built up a large database of the most commonly used materials, components and systems, there will always be some items that are too specialist to allow a general cost to be calculated, or are recent innovations where the experience of calculating a cost has not had time to become established.

Price books typically present most of their costs as unit build-ups incorporating a material element and a labour element. For example, the price of carpet floor covering will be quoted in terms of a unit of measurement, in this case square metres, and with a material cost, say £5.50, and a labour requirement, say 0.2 hours. An overall labour cost will be applied throughout the whole price book, say £12.50/hour. The material cost and labour requirement are then used to calculate the overall unit rate, in this example £8.00/m^2. Prices for different quality carpets can be obtained by altering the material element of the price on the basis that a cheap carpet takes the same time to lay as an expensive carpet.

While public price books have the disadvantage of limited content, they do have the advantage of transparency. This means that the cost information used in an LCC study can be cross-checked by auditors or reviewers.

The alternative to public sources of cost information is for an organization to collect and manage its own database of cost information. Clearly this has an overhead cost associated with it, but this may be worthwhile if the organization has a limited number of cost elements to maintain. It may also be necessary if the organization needs costs for elements that are too specialist to be included in the public price books. This approach also means that the organization really needs to be the owner or operator of a large estate, so that the range of items likely to be needed for future projects is already covered by existing buildings or infrastructure. A good example of this in the UK is the Property Services Agency (PSA), which used to manage and maintain property for central government departments. This diversity of buildings gave the PSA a ready source of cost information for the kinds of buildings that the government was likely to need, and it compiled and published schedules of rates for different types of construction work. When the PSA was closed down, the price books continued to be maintained by a private sector organization (Carillion plc) and published.

In reality, it is unlikely that using only public sources of information or only private sources of information will be sufficient. For many practical LCC studies, some combination of the two is going to be necessary. One of the implications of this mixed approach is the difficulty of making sure that all cost data is equally precise. This is discussed in more detail in the discussion on practical issues below.

Sources of Life Expectancy Information

Life expectancy information is needed for every physical material, component or system included within an LCC study. As stated earlier, this is so that the replacement costs can be scheduled correctly during the study period and therefore that the correct net present values of those replacement activities can be calculated.

Obtaining life expectancy information is as challenging as - and sometimes even more challenging than - obtaining cost information. In many cases this is because life expectancy information is seen as less immediately relevant to building and infrastructure owners than cost information which can be used to estimate departmental budgets for capital projects and for ongoing maintenance and utility costs. In addition, materials producers and equipment manufacturers have a vested interest in establishing that their product is perceived to have the maximum life expectancy, without necessarily providing the warranties or guarantees that would expose them to financial liabilities in cases of premature failure.

Like cost information, life expectancy information can be obtained from public and private sources, with many of the same advantages and disadvantages. While public sources are simple to obtain or to access, they are not as comprehensive as public price books. This is to be expected, since many similar materials or products would have the same basic life expectancy. The public sources of information are also not updated as regularly as the price books. Again, this is to be expected, since while prices change from year to year, and even from month to month, life expectancy is much more closely linked to production methods and underlying technologies which may stay the same for many years. The outcome of these situations is that life expectancy information is not as financially lucrative to compile and to publish, and the effect of this is to limit the availability of life expectancy information to irregular research activities or to specific areas of construction activity.

The most significant disadvantage of public life expectancy information is that most of the published information is the result of expert assessment of the average life expectancy of a given material or type of component rather than the systematic measurement of the actual life of materials and components in real projects. While this second approach would be much preferred, from the perspective of independence and transparency, the costs associated with collecting and analysing such information mean that it is almost always uneconomical to carry out.

Because public life expectancy information is usually a view of the average life of a material or component, it almost certainly will not apply in every respect to any given project. For some types of LCC study, this is not a problem. In particular, when an LCC study is being carried out on a design that is still in its concept stage, the extra precision obtained from modelling the project scenario more accurately is not warranted. Also, in a study comparing different technical designs, the contextual information about how the project as a whole differs from the average situation is likely to have a similar impact on each separate LCC model and therefore will not affect the relative difference in calculated LCC between the alternatives.

Private sources of life expectancy information are even more dependent on the scale of the owner or operator's estate than cost information. Public life expectancy information comes directly from recording actual installation and replacement dates for materials and equipment, and so this is only possible if there is a significant history of estate management to draw on. In the case of small estate owners, the only practical way for such organizations to obtain private life expectancy information is to collaborate with like-minded organizations through a network or association. But even then, the challenges of relating each particular piece of information to the location, usage, original specification and maintenance philosophy in place at each site will remain.

One example of a group-wide collection of life expectancy information is the database of building services component life coordinated by the American Society of Heating, Refrigerating and Air-Conditioning Engineers (ASHRAE). This started as an internal research project engaging ASHRAE members, but has been continued. The online database is free to access and the data set can also be downloaded in spreadsheet format. Of course, this database only covers US buildings and focuses on the equipment types and specifications that are used in the US. But even with this caveat, the data can provide a useful cross-check of information from other sources for projects and applications outside of the US.

Practical Issues with Cost and Life Expectancy Information

One of the most significant practical issues with using publicly available cost and life expectancy information is that the published data for a given component or construction activity tends to be a single figure representing the average cost or average life expectancy. While this may be good enough for early stage studies where only very approximate figures are required, it may not be good enough for more detailed studies where more precision is needed.

There are, however, methods available to translate a generic average cost or life expectancy into a project-specific figure, and these are summarized below.

To tailor a generic cost to a project-specific one, the usual approach is to apply correction factors either to the whole cost or to the principal components of the cost – the material element and the labour element. Correction factors for the whole cost are of two types: price indexation and geographical correction. Price indexation is the way of updating a published cost figure, which will have been correct at the date of compilation, for any changes in prices due to inflation or deflation that have occurred between that date and the date for which the price is required. This is particularly an issue with published price books where editions are usually published annually. However, actual prices change continuously. The published prices will be related back to a price index and the publishers of the price book will usually make available a monthly update to the price index, which users can apply to the published figures to bring them up to date. For example, a price book published in January 2014 may be referenced to a price index of 234, based on an index that started in January 1990 with a value of 100. For a project being costed in July 2014, the index may have increased to 237, so every price in the book can be multiplied by the ratio 237/234 to bring it up to date.

Geographical indexation is a general correction to allow for the fact that construction work has different prices in different parts of a country. The price book will be based on prices at a particular location or on a country-wide average. The publishers will include index figures for different regions based on their analysis of regional costs. For example, a UK-average price may be quoted in the price book, with an index of 100. But for a project in London, the price index may be 115, meaning that all prices should be multiplied by 115/100 to give a local price. For a project in Wales, the price index may be 92, so the local price will be 92/100 of the national price.

As well as applying indexation to the whole cost, an index may be applied just to the material or labour element, or even different indices to each. This allows for differences in price that reflect local labour rates or different materials costs based on geographical distance.

A different form of indexation is to account for the nature of the project or the site. For example, sites with very high security measures, such as defence establishments, or sites with particular access constraints, such as inner-city sites, may apply a special cost index to allow for the additional overhead of gaining access and other activities that reduce the effective working day.

To tailor a generic life expectancy to a project-specific one, the recommended approach is to apply a series of correction factors to allow for different aspects of the material or component installation, exposure and use. A set of correction factors is included within ISO 15686, and these are summarized in Table 16.2. This also includes some considerations for deciding an appropriate level of each correction factor.

Table 16.2   Life expectancy correction factors

ISO 15686 factors			Example considerations
Installed quality	A	Quality of components	Manufacture, materials, protective coatings
	B	Design level	Design standards, sheltering by rest of structure
	C	Work execution	Site management, standard of workmanship, weather conditions during installation
Environment	D	Indoor environment	Ventilation, condensation risk, aggressive atmosphere
	E	Outdoor environment	Coastal or inland site, traffic emissions, elevation of the building/asset, temperature fluctuations
Operational conditions	F	In-use conditions	Adherence to designed use-periods, type of user/wear and tear
	G	Maintenance	Quality and frequency of maintenance, ease of access

Each of these factors can be assessed for each material or component being used in an LCC study. To apply the factors, the circumstances of the project or study are used to estimate a set of factors for each material or component, with the default value being 1.0, lower figures being used for factors where the life expectancy would be lower than average and higher figures being used for factors where the life expectancy would be higher than average.

For example, to estimate the design life of a concrete wall in a harsh coastal environment, the following factors may be selected by the analyst:

A) Quality of components   0.9

B) Design level   0.9

C) Work execution   0.8 (bad weather during construction)

D) Indoor environment   1.0 (does not apply to this component)

E) Outdoor environment   0.6 (salt-spray, strong winds, heavy rain)

F) In-use conditions   1.0 (no particular user impact)

G) Maintenance   0.7 (local authority cannot afford to follow recommended maintenance regime)

So if a standard concrete wall has an expected life of 100 years, this particular wall would have an estimated life of 100 * 0.9 * 0.9 * 0.8 * 1.0 * 0.6 * 1.0 * 0.7, or 27 years. If this wall was part of an LCC study with a 60-year study period, then instead of not needing to be replaced at all during the study period, the wall now needs to be replaced twice, at years 27 and 54.

A practical issue with published life expectancy information is the difference in life expectancy according to different sources for the same or similar items. This issue mainly applies to equipment and components rather than materials. Some analysis was carried out by the Building Services Research and Information Association (BSRIA) in the UK to compare life expectancies for a range of building services components from a variety of sources. This analysis showed the very wide range of life expectancy figures that could be obtained from public sources. For example, fans were given life expectancies of anywhere from five years up to 30 years. The fact that such wide discrepancies exist strengthens the argument for an organization to maintain or collect its own life expectancy information.

Another practical issue with published life expectancy information is the type of information that is provided. Some sources provide a single figure, which represents an average life expectancy. Other sources give a range between upper and lower bounds. Others give a frequency distribution. Each has its own advantages and disadvantages, which are summarized below.

Single figures are the easiest to interpret and use in life cycle cost models and calculations. But they give no information about the spread of possible life expectancies either above or below the average figure. An example of this kind of information is the life expectancy information contained in CIBSE Guide M for mechanical and electrical equipment.

Simple ranges show the extent of variance between low and high life expectancy, but do not give any information about the shape of the distribution between these two extremes. As simple life cycle cost calculations require a single figure from which to calculate replacement dates, this is usually achieved by taking the mid-point of the range as a simple average.

Frequency distributions show both the extent and the shape of the life expectancy. Mean and median figures can be calculated, as well as standard deviations. However, these distributions need data sets of actual life expectancies and these are not available for all types of component or material. In a simple life cycle cost calculation, the mean or median figure can be used, but the full distribution can be used if more sophisticated modelling using Monte Carlo simulation is required.

Conclusion

The practical issues that apply to the use of cost and life expectancy information affect the precision of the LCC study. These issues, as well as other reasons, mean that there are practical limits to the precision with which any life cycle cost can be calculated. In practical applications, even with the best information, it is unlikely that an LCC study can be given a precision better than ±five per cent. In cases where the information is not as good, the precision will be worse, with early stage studies giving life cycle costs which may be as much as ±30 per cent.

The reliance of LCC studies on the information and data that are used to populate the life cycle models means that all sources of information should be carefully documented. This will not only help the analyst address any questions raised by the client or others, but will also help those using the study in later years understand where the costs and life expectancies came from.

References and Further Reading

ASHRAE 2014. Component Life Expectancy Database. Available at: http://xp20.ashrae.org/publicdatabase/service_life.asp.

BCIS 2008. *Standardized Method of Life Cycle Costing for Construction Procurement.* London: Building Cost Information Service.

BS ISO 2008. *BS ISO 15686–5:2008 Buildings and Constructed Assets – Service Life Planning; Part 5 – Life Cycle Costing.* London: British Standards Institution.

Churcher, D. 2008. *Whole-Life Costing Analysis.* Bracknell: BSRIA.

CIBSE 2008. *CIBSE Guide M – Maintenance Engineering and Management.* London: Chartered Institution of Building Services Engineers.

Langdon, D. (ed.) 2014. *Spon's Architects' and Builders' Price Book.* Abingdon: Spon Press.

TSO 2011. *PSA Schedule of Rates for Mechanical Services,* 6th edn. Wolverhampton: Carillion Services.

Chapter 17

The Evolution of Construction Cost Estimation and Project Management

MASSIMO PICA

The greatest of all gifts is the power to estimate things at their true worth.

François de la Rochefoucauld (Paris, 1613–80)

Basic Requirements of Project Delivery Systems

In order for construction projects – either new projects or renovation, repair or sustainability projects – to be successful, it is essential that cost estimates be accurate, timely and justifiable. The construction delivery method is deemed essential as well. Prieto (Prieto 2012), in comparing the two project delivery approaches of Design Bid Build (DBB) and Design Build Finance Operate Maintain (DBFOM), states that:

> under DBB, the owner retains significant interface risk between the designer and builder and in multi-prime projects also retains integration risk across the primes.

Whereas:

> a DBFOM project delivery approach significantly modifies the risk profile of the owner as the DBFOM contractor now assumes both this interface risk as well as the integration risk across all project elements … The Owner holds risks associated with his contract with the DBFOM contractor. These risks may include any shared risks or owner retained risks as they have negotiated.

Newer, cooperative construction delivery methods as well as construction cost estimating and project delivery software technology are both seen as significant developments for the purposes of collaboration, transparency and better information.

Popular overseas is a form of Integrated Project Delivery (IPD) developed about 25 years ago: Job Order Contracting (JOC), which is a competitively negotiated, fixed-unit price and indefinite quantity contract construction project procurement method. Among other benefits asserted in favour of the JOC system, emphasis is placed on lower administration and procurement costs and mitigated design costs – technical specifications being defined and included as part of the basic JOC agreement.

Life Cycle Management and Life Cycle Cost Management

Metaphorically, the life cycle of projects can be compared to a segment having the length of a metre, encompassing a concept stage, a construction stage, a utilization stage and a number of often unavoidable changes of functional destination, until the end of life is reached. The two first centimetres of this segment may represent the period from the initial idea from the completion of design, followed by three centimetres covering the construction effort and, from the fifth to at least the ninetieth centimetres, the utilization and modification period; at the ninetieth centimetre, the asset begins to lose its functionality, anticipating the end of its 'biological' cycle through the last centimetres.

Methods have been devised to quantify the functionality of constructions along their life cycle, against an ideal situation that can be identified by the construction as newly built. The current degree of functionality can be expressed by the 'distance' D between the actual and the optimal conditions of functionality, representing the effort that would be required to restore optimal conditions. This can only be assessed accurately whenever an analysis of the individual elements included in the construction is possible. Structures, vertical walls, roofs, floors, stairs, lifts and equipment are scored in accordance with their status (0 for an optimal condition not requiring refurbishment, 1 for a totally bad condition requiring complete refurbishment) and each element is ranked in accordance with the ratio p of its cost to the cost of the entire construction (for example, in reinforced concrete constructions, 0.25 for structures, 0.15 for vertical walls, etc.). Multiplying the status score by the ratio p, the product will be indicative of refurbishment cost for the element and the sum of these products will be indicative of the total refurbishment cost on a scale from 0 to 1.

Table 17.1 provides an example of the calculation for D on the basis of status scores and values of ratio p. The status score of 0.2 indicates good conditions, 0.2–0.6 mediocre conditions, 0.6–0.8 bad conditions and 0.8–1 extremely bad conditions.

Table 17.1   Status of construction based on status of elements

Construction elements	Cost ratio p	Status score				
		0.0	0.2	0.6	0.8	I
Foundations	0.05	0.0				
Vertical structures	0.10		0.2			
Horizontal structures	0.15			0.6		
Outer frameworks	0.35			0.6		
Partitions	0.10				0.8	
Stairs and lifts	0.10			0.6		
Equipment	0.15				0.8	
Total	1.00	D = 0.58				

The values in Table 17.1 are applicable when information is available for the entire range of construction elements; otherwise, if the assessment is made exclusively on visible elements – which is often the case – the values in Table 17.2 below will be applicable.

Table 17.2   Status of construction based on status of visible elements

Construction elements (visible only)	Cost ratio p	Status score				
		0.0	0.2	0.6	0.8	I
Painted walls	0.05					I
Plastered walls	0.10				0.8	
Roofs	0.35		0.2			
Railings, gutters, other finishings	0.05				0.8	
Outer frameworks	0.25			0.6		
Lobbies and stairs	0.15			0.6		
Lifts	0.05					I
Total	1.00	D = 0.53				

Cost Considerations in Engineering and Construction Projects

The dominating connotation of engineering and construction projects is the uniqueness of project costs, which is reflected in the relevant Cost Breakdown Structure.

A distinction is made between direct costs and indirect costs. Direct costs are those varying in relation to production factors. Indirect costs are arranged in first-level indirect costs (company overhead costs) and second-level indirect costs (project-specific overhead costs).

The following terms are used in project cost accounting:

- gross margin = the difference between sales revenue and direct costs;

- net margin = the difference between gross margin and indirect costs (second level);

- project profit = the difference between gross margin and project-specific indirect costs (first level – prorated).

Direct costs are functions of installed quantities, while indirect costs can be one-time (fixed) or proportional to a time variation. Direct costs can be also arranged at two levels: the first for materials and labour, and the second for support costs (equipment and its operating personnel and consumables).

Contingency reserves must always be accounted for in relation to unexpected cost impacts generating potential risks. Contingency reserves on direct costs may be correlated to technical factors (quantity variations in fixed price contracts and other unexpected circumstances) or economic factors (efficiency variations). Contingency reserves on indirect costs are, in turn, associated with economic risks (for example, project extension) or financial risks (charges for delayed payments, currency exchange risks, etc.).

Usual values for contingency reserves range from 3 to 15 per cent of costs, depending on the degree of budget estimate accuracy and of project definition; should this contingency element be neglected, the contribution margin would be affected.

Exogenous factors causing unexpected costs can be represented by accidental events or *force majeure*; these can be turned into costs through insurance contracts. Endogenous factors are inherent to the project and correspond to operational, technical, economic and financial causes.

Costs in Construction Sites

Cost accounting in construction sites is not a simple operation, especially in the case of multiple contracts converging on a single site. The different cost categories that exist in a certain site have to be treated differently and are related to different production factors.

According to their nature, costs may be classified in internal costs and external costs. Examples of internal cost elements are labour, logistics, equipment, utilities and overheads. Examples of external cost elements are subcontracts and incorporated materials. The re-arrangement of these cost items in accordance with their destination leads to the following classification:

- costs for site management and supervision;

- costs for site support;

- costs for site logistics;

- costs for site set-up and shutdown;

- costs for lodgings set-up and shutdown;

- costs for on-site construction works (civil, mechanical, electrical, etc.).

SITE MANAGEMENT AND SUPERVISION

Management cost elements are primarily related to administrative and planning duties, as well as to site security and quality, that are apportioned on the basis of site manufacturing costs. Supervision costs account for indirect personnel (site engineers, surveyors, inspectors, etc.); these costs must be accounted separately when supervision is undertaken by subcontractors on their own.

SITE SUPPORT

Included in this category are costs for caretakers, housekeepers, porters, etc. Also included are costs for support personnel and for the depreciation of support equipment. The basis of the apportionment for all these costs is represented by on-site construction costs.

SITE LOGISTICS

This category includes all living expenses for personnel as well as depreciation of lodgings and field equipment, consumables, etc. Costs in this category are apportioned on the basis of actual personnel attendance.

SITE SET-UP AND SHUTDOWN

Costs for labour and materials (for example, concrete from conglomerate mixers) are accounted for in line with site set-up and shutdown procedures. When analytical data are not available, site shutdown costs may be estimated as 50 per cent of site set-up costs.

LODGINGS SET-UP AND SHUTDOWN

Costs for labour, materials, depreciations, etc. are accounted for in compliance with lodgings set-up and shutdown procedures. When analytical data are not available, lodgings shutdown costs may be estimated as 50 per cent of lodgings set-up costs.

ON-SITE CONSTRUCTION WORKS

Institutional site costs are accounted for. These are arranged in macro-activities (civil, mechanical, electrical works, etc.); their basis of apportionment is represented by direct hours expended in each macro-activity.

For each individual site and each individual macro-activity, average costs per manufacturing hour will be calculated as follows:

- the amount of monthly manufacturing hours will be derived from site statistics;

- cost allocation will be made on the basis of the amount of monthly manufacturing hours multiplied by the respective standard cost;

- an average cost per manufacturing hour will be determined for each cost centre and cost balances will be accounted for.

The Importance of Cost Management in Construction Projects

Efficient cost management practices are primarily based on well-structured accounting information and cost documentation systems (especially Bills of Quantities, Scope Statements, Statements of Work, etc.), whose benefits can be summarized as follows:

- increased proficiency of project execution;

- better guidance and substantiation of administrative work;

- encouragement to undertake teamwork;

- easier identification of any deficiency and related corrective actions;

- improvement of services; and

- reduced costs and increased profits.

Project cost estimating, across the entire life cycle, requires knowledge of all elements of cost from project conception to completion. This includes: direct material and labour costs, indirect costs, general administration costs, profit, finance cost, owner costs and start-up costs. This may also include operation and maintenance costs for selection of project alternatives.

As asserted in the AACEI *Total Cost Management Framework* publication:

> *The cost estimating process is typically performed concurrent to or iteratively with the asset and project planning and evaluation processes.*

The AACEI classification system (AACEI 2011) is compared with similar classifications, issued in the UK by ACostE and RICS, in Table 17.3. This also provides a demonstration of the fact that whenever the detail of the engineering definition is insufficient, the resulting budgets will not be accurate, nor will they consider contingencies as is required to efficiently manage unpredictable circumstances that may occur across the project execution.

Table 17.3 Comparison of classification systems

AACE International	Association of Cost Engineers	Royal Institute of Chartered Surveyors
Class 5	Order of magnitude estimate – Class 4 -30/+30 per cent	Feasibility study – Order of magnitude estimate -25/+50 per cent
Class 4	Study estimate – Class 3 -20/+20 per cent	Conceptual design – Appropriation estimate -15/+25 per cent
Class 3	Budget estimate – Class 2 -10/+10 per cent	Preliminary design – Budget estimate -10/+20 per cent
Class 2 Class 1	Definitive estimate – Class 1 -5/+5 per cent	Detail design – Definitive estimate -5/+10 per cent

Trade-offs between Project Duration and Project Cost

Taking into consideration that project activity duration is (also) related to the greater or lesser allocation of resources, activity durations can be shortened if ensuing costs can be supported. Therefore, activity durations can be considered decision variables, to be correlated with the project (life cycle) cost.

Typically, in the activity duration estimating exercise, 'nominal' activity durations are determined; whenever a cost increase can be accepted, durations can be shortened (this is called 'crashing'; see Chapter 8). Shorter activity durations might be required when any existing project deadline constraints would be infringed by activities at their nominal duration. Deadline constraints for the entire project or parts of it will determine optimum activity durations, trading off increased activity costs against shorter durations.

It may be recognized that the complexity of this effort is essentially related to how the crashing cost is quantitatively influenced by shorter durations: the cases of linear costs, convex costs and concave costs will be discussed below.

LINEAR COSTS

In the simplest case, activity cost is a linear function of activity duration. Suppose that extreme values are known for the duration of activity i:

- the maximum duration u_i (that is, the 'nominal' duration) for a standard resource allocation;

- the minimum duration l_i (that is, the 'crash time') that cannot be further shortened whatever additional resources are allocated.

The linear model assumes that activity durations may have any value between l_i and u_i, and that costs vary accordingly.

Figure 17.1 depicts the variation of cost for activity i against its duration. The notion of 'marginal crashing cost' can be introduced, representing the cost of making the duration of activity i shorter by one time unit (for example, one day).

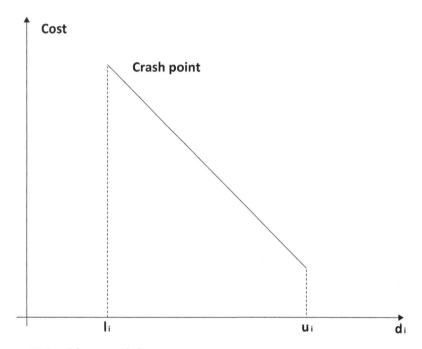

Figure 17.1   Linear activity cost

CONVEX COSTS

In more general cases, the crashing cost for activity i may be a convex function of the duration decrease y_i, as expressed by the functional relationship $c_i(y_i)$. This situation occurs, with some frequency, when an incremental effort is needed to further reduce the duration of an activity; if costs are convex for all of the activities, the total cost function, that is, the sum of activity costs, will also be convex.

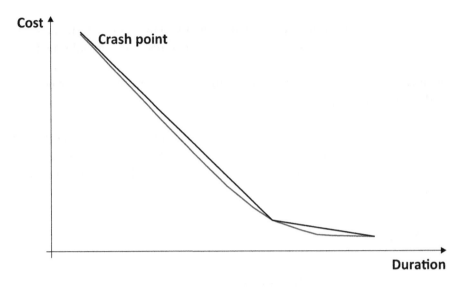

Figure 17.2　Approximation of convex costs

The continuous cost curve can be conveniently approximated by a sequence of linear segments (Figure 17.2), representing the situation in which the marginal cost of duration decrease is, for example, 10 for the first x weeks, 20 for weeks $x + 1$ through y and 25 beyond week y.

CONCAVE COSTS

Crashing costs are said to be concave when the effort to reduce activity durations is decreasing. This is a comparatively less frequent case, although its occurrence is possible.

For example, suppose that a complex assembly of components, to be placed in sequential holes, would require a carpenter for five days, at the cost of five person-days. If only four days are scheduled, a second carpenter is hired and the cost becomes eight person-days. The more carpenters are hired, the shorter the total duration, but higher the total cost.

Again, as in the case of convex costs, the continuous cost curve can be conveniently approximated by a sequence of linear segments representing marginal costs (Figure 17.3).

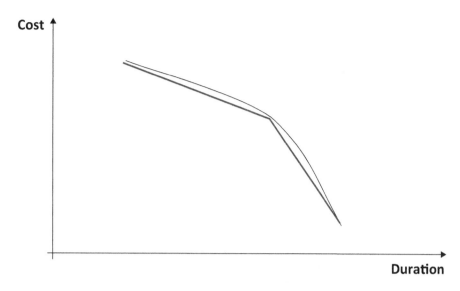

Figure 17.3   Approximation of concave costs

Fundamentals of LCC Management of Constructed Assets

The LCC is the sum of the initial project costs, the operating costs, the maintenance costs and eventually – whenever relevant – the disposal costs of the project output at the end of its period of use. This is a primary term for a careful assessment of the overall cost/benefit ratio for the intended investment.

The concept of LCC, as discussed in earlier chapters of this book, has different connotations in the case of constructions. Prior to the publication of ISO 15686–5:2008 *Buildings and Constructed Assets – Service Life Planning; Part 5 – Life Cycle Costing* in 2006, the European Commission had tasked the British company Davis Langdon Management Consulting with developing a common European methodology for the evaluation of the LCC in constructions. The title of this research work was 'Life Cycle Costing (LCC) as a Contribution to Sustainable Construction: A Common Methodology' – No. 30-CE-0043513/00–47; it began in January 2006 and was completed with a draft methodology ('A Common European Methodology for Life Cycle Costing') and its supporting documentation.

Already in November 1997, the European Commission had issued a communication on the subject of 'The Competitiveness of the Construction Industry', including a discussion on the construction process. The Commission identified the requirement to improve competitiveness in the construction sector, specifically by introducing the mechanisms of LCC analysis along with convenient application criteria in the different stages of the construction process. The intention was to ensure that final users would be able to assess exhaustively both investment costs and follow-up whole life costs in order to determine what solution could be best suited to their needs, as well as in accordance with environmental constraints deriving from the strategic principles stated by the Commission in 2004.

Davis Langdon pursued the following objectives:

- to enhance the competitiveness of the construction industry;

- to improve the consciousness of the extent to which environmental factors affect Life Cycle Costs;

- to increase process effectiveness throughout the construction life cycle;

- to optimize long-term costs and formulate more accurate estimates; and

- to enhance data management, risk management and procurement practices.

One of the conclusions reached was the confirmation that LCC evaluation procedures are essentially iterative. Construction projects follow step-by-step evolutions, involving decision gates which require the selection of products, components and materials, and lead to a progressive definition of the LCC of the project while it approaches its completion step by step.

The LCC of a construction is defined by the ISO standard 15686–5 as part of the Whole Life Cost (WLC). According to the BSI/BCIS publication *Standardized Method of Life Cycle Costing for Construction Procurement*, the WLC also encompasses non-construction costs (land and enabling works, finance costs, rental costs, user support costs, taxes and miscellaneous costs) in addition to case-specific costs of externalities defined as:

> *costs associated with the asset, which are not necessarily reflected in the transaction costs between provider and consumer.*

All these costs are subtracted from the income elements mentioned in the publication. Accordingly, the following cost elements included in the LCC can be identified: construction costs, maintenance costs, operation costs, occupancy costs and end-of-life costs. The latter includes, as lower-level cost elements, disposal inspection costs, demolition costs, costs of reinstatement to meet the contractual requirements and any further end-of-life cost items included at the client's request.

Davis Langdon issued in May 2007 its 'Final Methodology – Life Cycle Costing (LCC) as a Contribution to Sustainable Construction: A Common Methodology', providing details of the following 15 steps included in its procedure:

Step 1: identify the main purpose of the LCC analysis.

Step 2: identify the initial scope of the LCC analysis.

Step 3: identify the extent to which sustainability – and specifically environmental – analysis relates to LCC.

Step 4: identify the period of analysis and methods of economic evaluation.

Step 5: identify the need for additional analyses (risk/uncertainty and sensitivity analyses).

Step 6: identify project and/or asset requirements – confirm key parameters.

Step 7: identify options to be included in the LCC exercise.

Step 8: assemble cost and time data to be used in LCC analysis.

Step 9: verify values of financial parameters and the period of analysis.

Step 10 (optional): review risk strategy and carry out preliminary uncertainty/risk assessment.

Step 11: perform the required economic evaluation.

Step 12: carry out detailed risk/uncertainty analysis (if required).

Step 13: carry out sensitivity analysis (if required).

Step 14: interpret and present initial results in required format.

Step 15: present final results in the required format and prepare a final report.

The outcomes that can be expected on completion of each of the steps in the methodology will be examined later.

The Utilization of LCC Techniques

LCC techniques are used to estimate the total cost of ownership of constructions. They ensure that comparative cost assessments can be made over a specific period of time, taking into consideration a number of economic factors that are relevant across a project life cycle, including initial capital costs and future operational and asset replacement costs.

While in European countries procurement procedures are not required to consider Life Cycle Costs (which, however, have been introduced in concept by the IEC standard 60300–3-3:2004 'Dependability Management Part 3-3: Application Guide – Life Cycle Costing'), they are involved to some extent in public procurement directives regarding the assessment of the most economically advantageous tender (MEAT) for construction works and services.

Concerning the aforementioned Davis Langdon findings that resulted from the request of the European Commission, the steps of the procedures are listed below, along with the expected output(s) for each of them.

STEP 1: IDENTIFY THE MAIN PURPOSE OF THE LCC ANALYSIS

A statement of purpose of analysis and an understanding of appropriate application of LCC and its related outcomes.

STEP 2: IDENTIFY THE INITIAL SCOPE OF THE LCC ANALYSIS

Understanding of:

- the scale of application of the LCC exercise;

- the stages over which it will be applied;

- issues and information likely to be relevant;

- specific client reporting requirements.

STEP 3: IDENTIFY THE EXTENT TO WHICH SUSTAINABILITY – AND SPECIFICALLY ENVIRONMENTAL – ANALYSIS RELATES TO LCC

Understanding of:

- the relationship between sustainability assessment and LCC;

- the extent to which the outputs from a sustainability assessment will form inputs into the LCC process;

- the extent to which the outputs of the LCC exercise will feed into a sustainability assessment.

STEP 4: IDENTIFY THE PERIOD OF ANALYSIS AND METHODS OF ECONOMIC EVALUATION

- Identification of the period of analysis and what governs its choice.

- Identification of appropriate techniques for assessing investment options.

STEP 5: IDENTIFY THE NEED FOR ADDITIONAL ANALYSES (RISK/ UNCERTAINTY AND SENSITIVITY ANALYSES)

- Completion of preliminary assessment of risks/uncertainties.

- Assessment of whether a formal risk management plan and/or register is required.

- Decision on which risk assessment procedures should be applied.

STEP 6: IDENTIFY PROJECT AND/OR ASSET REQUIREMENTS – CONFIRM KEY PARAMETERS

- Definition of the scope of the project and the key features of the asset.

- Statement of project constraints.

- Definitions of relevant performance and quality requirements.

- Confirmation of project budget and timescales.

- Incorporation of LCC timing into the overall project plan.

STEP 7: IDENTIFY OPTIONS TO BE INCLUDED IN THE LCC EXERCISE

- Identification of those elements of an asset that are to be subject to LCC analysis.

- Selection of one or more options for each element to be analysed.

- Identification of cost items to be included.

STEP 8: ASSEMBLE COST AND TIME DATA TO BE USED IN LCC ANALYSIS

Identification of:

- all costs relevant to the LCC exercise;

- the value of each cost;

- any add-on costs to be applied;

- time-related data (for example, service life/maintenance data).

STEP 9: VERIFY VALUES OF FINANCIAL PARAMETERS AND THE PERIOD OF ANALYSIS

- The period of analysis is confirmed.

- Appropriate values for the financial parameters are confirmed.

- Taxation issues are considered.

- The application of financial parameters within the Cost Breakdown Structure is decided upon.

STEP 10 (OPTIONAL): REVIEW RISK STRATEGY AND CARRY OUT PRELIMINARY UNCERTAINTY/RISK ASSESSMENT

- The schedule of identified risks is verified.

- A qualitative risk analysis is undertaken and the risk register is updated.

- The scope and extent of quantitative risk assessment are confirmed.

STEP 11: PERFORM REQUIRED ECONOMIC EVALUATION

- The LCC analysis is performed and the results are recorded for use in step 14 below.

STEP 12: CARRY OUT DETAILED RISK/UNCERTAINTY ANALYSIS (IF REQUIRED)

- Quantitative risk assessments are undertaken and the results interpreted.

STEP 13: CARRY OUT SENSITIVITY ANALYSIS (IF REQUIRED)

- Sensitivity analyses are undertaken and the results interpreted.

STEP 14: INTERPRET AND PRESENT INITIAL RESULTS IN REQUIRED FORMAT

- Initial results are reviewed and interpreted.

- Results are presented using the appropriate formats.

- The need for further iterations of LCC exercise is identified.

STEP 15: PRESENT FINAL RESULTS IN THE REQUIRED FORMAT AND PREPARE A FINAL REPORT

- The final report is issued in accordance with an agreed scope and format.

- A complete set of records is prepared in line with ISO 15686–3 *Building and Constructed Assets – Service Life Planning: Part 3 – Performance Audits and Reviews.*

References and Further Reading

Ashworth, A. 2004. *Cost Studies of Buildings.* Harlow: Pearson Education.

BS ISO 2008. *BS ISO 15686–5:2008 Buildings and Constructed Assets – Service Life Planning; Part 5 – Life Cycle Costing.* London: British Standards Institution.

Bull, J.W. (ed.), 1993. *Life Cycle Costing for Construction.* Glasgow: Blackie Academic & Professional.

Davis Langdon Management Consulting, 2007a. *Final Guidance. Life Cycle Costing (LCC) as a Contribution to Sustainable Construction. Guidance on the Use of the LCC Methodology and its Application in Public Procurement.* London: Davis Langdon.

Davis Langdon Management Consulting, 2007b. *Final Review. Life Cycle Costing (LCC) as a Contribution to Sustainable Construction: A Common Methodology. Literature Review.* London: Davis Langdon.

Davis Langdon Management Consulting, 2007c. *Final Specification. Life Cycle Costing (LCC) as a Contribution to Sustainable Construction: Specification Framework for Software Development.* London: Davis Langdon.

Davis Langdon Management Consulting, 2007d. *Final Review. Life Cycle Costing (LCC) as a Contribution to Sustainable Construction: A Common Methodology. Final Report.* London: Davis Langdon.

Davis Langdon Management Consulting, 2007e. *Life Cycle Costing (LCC) as a Contribution to Sustainable Construction: A Common Methodology. Final Report Summary.* London: Davis Langdon.

Davis Langdon Management Consulting, 2007f. *Final Methodology. Life Cycle Costing (LCC) as a Contribution to Sustainable Construction: A Common Methodology.* London: Davis Langdon.

Davis Langdon Management Consulting, 2010. *Development of a Promotional Campaign for Life Cycle Costing in Construction. Final Report.* London: Davis Langdon.

Fabrycky, W.J. and Blanchard, B.S. 1991. *Life-Cycle Cost and Economic Analysis.* Englewood Cliffs: Prentice Hall.

IEC, 2004. IEC 60300–3-3:2004. *Dependability Management Part 3–3: Application Guide – Life Cycle Costing.*

Prieto, B. 2012. 'Comparison of Design Bid Build and Design Build Finance Operate Maintain Project Delivery'. *PM World Journal,* I(V), 1–7.

Seeley, I.H. 1995. *Building Economics,* 4th edn. Basingstoke: Palgrave Macmillan.

Chapter 18

Environmental Impact and Lifetime Cost-Effective Sustainability of Constructed Assets

MASSIMO PICA

Life Cycle Assessment, Life Cycle Design and Environmental Sustainability

Since the final years of the twentieth century, the quantitative methodology of *Life Cycle Assessment* (LCA) has been adopted to analyse, evaluate and recognize the environmental impact of products, especially those used in constructions and concerning the processes executed in their life cycle.

LCA essentially relates to the interactions between products and their environment, including the extraction and production of materials and their subsequent utilization until final disposal. The elements taken into consideration are the environmental impacts of the asset being assessed, from the perspectives of ecosystem health, human health and resource depletion.

The objectives and scope of the assessment are defined initially. As part of this effort:

- the rationale for LCA to be developed and the utilization of its results are clarified;

- the details of the scope are provided, in terms of the output and its boundaries (this process may be repeated later, as required);

- the expected performance of products/services is defined across the entire duration of their life cycles;

- the quality of the data relevant to LCA is defined (quality level and assessment criteria).

The subsequent stage is the Life Cycle Inventory (LCI). This stage consists of the definition of the asset and its boundaries, of the process flow chart and of the data management, the latter including:

- data collection;

- definition of calculation procedures;

- preparation of inventory tables;

- analysis of sensitivity, data variability and uncertainty; and

- definition of deliberate omissions.

The third stage of LCA is the assessment of impact. This includes: a classification of environmental effects on human health, environment and resource depletion; a characterization of environmental impacts on the basis of quantitative units (for weight, energy, etc.); a normalization of different environmental effects based on a certain common scale; and a weighted appraisal of the contributions from different impact categories.

The final stage of LCA is the interpretation of results. The inventory stage and the assessment stage are reviewed against the objectives and scope of the assessment that were established at the inception of LCA; subsequent conclusions and recommendations may be formulated, for example, to revisit objectives and scope or – more essentially – to explore the integration with economic, technical and socio-political factors.

Following the same approach as that taken by LCA, sustainable development will have to embrace all product life cycle stages, including production, distribution, operation and maintenance and final disposal as a whole. This leads to a product-system design concept, involving all accompanying processes that occur along its life cycle.

The principles of Life Cycle Design (LCD) provide methodological solutions to achieve the objectives of environmental impact reduction by analysing all the product-system life cycle stages. At the same time, step by step, the environmental perspective becomes integrated into all the life cycle processes, including design, management and commercial processes, and all material and energy inputs, as well as impacts of emission and waste, are minimized qualitatively and quantitatively.

The LCD approach can be implemented in one of three possible cases:

- design for the entire system and for the entire life cycle stages;

- design for products that will be part of a system;

- design for products to be partially or totally controlled by other parties.

Any of these solutions will support an easier identification of environmental impacts so that they will be effectively reduced without further postponements until the subsequent life cycle stages.

The relevant environmental strategies will address the following technical and economic factors:

- minimization of resources – careful use of materials and energy;

- selection of resources having a lifetime low environmental impact – evaluation of materials, processes and energy sources for their eco-compatibility;

- optimization of product life – design for long lifetime and intensive utilization;

- extension of material life – design for better value of disposed materials;

- easier disassembly – design for separable parts and materials.

Regarding Environmental Impact Assessment (EIA), Chen, Li and Turner (Chen et al. 2007: 494) provide the following statement:

> *Environmental Impact Assessment (EIA) is used to identify the environmental, social and economic impacts of a project during initiation.*

And subsequently:

> *By using EIA both environmental and economic benefits can be achieved, such as reduced cost and time of project implementation and design, avoided treatment/clean-up costs and impacts of laws and regulations.*

As pointed out by the same authors, initial accomplishments included in an EIA are the identification of key issues and concerns of interested parties ('scoping') and the decision as to whether an EIA is required on the basis of information collected ('screening').

The scoping stage takes into consideration the following elements:

- identification of the project to be realized;

- preliminary design characteristics;

- interfaces with existing planning and scheduling mechanisms;

- identification of sites of interest;

- alternatives to be reviewed;

- intended methods for impact analysis and prevention;

- components, factors and types of data to be used;

- a summary estimation of environmental impacts and especially the most critical impacts;

- opportunities for impact mitigation or removal;

- relevant specific requirements;

- provision for authorizations required to realize the project.

The project screening stage is essentially based on the review of project elements, size, use of resources, sensitivity to potentially harmful environmental effects and risks of accidents.

Whenever an EIA is required, as a result of the above stages, it includes further insights into the programmatic context and the project development context, along with their interactions with the concurrent environmental context.

From the programmatic perspective, for example, the degree of consistency between the proposed project and the objectives of harmonization to existing plans is considered, along with an estimated schedule of individual project phases and an appraisal of the degree of project feasibility on the basis of its quantification.

The following elements are taken into consideration in the project development environment:

- the rationale of the project proposal and its affordability (including, where relevant, the results of a cost/benefit analysis);

- the identification of interactions between the project proposal and the existing infrastructures;

- the comparison to the 'no-action' alternative, in terms of the benefits accrued from the project implementation;

- the evaluation of alternative locations;

- the description of the technical specifications of the project, along with its operational requirements;

- the definition of environmental sustainability factors influencing the project solution, both during the construction stage and the subsequent operational management stage;

- the description of siting arrangements.

Cost Sources and Cost Categories in the LCA Approach

Significant costs are sometimes created by the adoption of a LCA approach, whenever an EIA is undertaken, which may require lengthy authorization procedures. As stated by Chen et al. (2007):

> *Costs can arise from:*
> - *drawing up the case, including the preparation of an EIA;*
> - *the holding of an enquiry, including legal fees, attendance, inspection, etc.;*
> - *idleness of the project team between the completion of design (required for the consent) and commencement of work (after consent has been obtained) – errors of communication can arise at this time;*
> - *conditions attached to the consent;*
> - *mitigators (bribes) to the local community to induce their acceptance of the development;[1]*
> - *delays as a result of redesigning the proposal to meet the planning requirements; lost commercial value of information disclosed to the public;*
> - *delayed return on investment from delay to the start of the revenue stream;*
> - *wasted effort if consent is refused.*

The life cycle perspective ensures that the true costs of production and/or service supply are taken into account when analysing the economic elements associated with potential environmental degradation and energy consumption, in addition to more familiar cost categories like capital outlays and operating expenditures. Examples of economic terms relevant from an environmental perspective are as follows:

- The traditional costing procedure – in this accounting procedure, only capital and operating (including environmental) costs are considered. This approach is rather simple and is applicable to studies involving comparisons of different alternatives.

- The comprehensive costing procedure – along with traditional capital and operating costs, additional cost elements derive from

---

1   Editor's note: this may obviously be a controversial element from an ethically plausible perspective.

liability, regulatory-related expenses, borrowing power and social considerations. This is a more realistic approach applicable to economic project analyses.

- Life Cycle Costing (LCC) – all the traditional cost elements of projects/products are considered until the final disposal of the end-result product.

As asserted in the *Handbook on Life Cycle Assessment* (Guinée et al. 2004: 9):

> *Where economic aspects are concerned, there is the Life Cycle Costing (LCC) approach for evaluating the economics of the life cycle of a product. LCC can be expected to become a standard addition to LCA applications.*

The Roles of Duration and Maintenance in the Environmental Assessment of the Life Cycle

The concepts of maintenance and sustainability are concurrent: the goal of maintenance is the extension of effectiveness and usability of assets. This is a specific objective for the built environment, as well as a design requirement (maintainability) for new constructions.

Extended durations for constructions, as a whole, through maintenance or replacement operations, alleviate widespread environmental consequences deriving from degradations or functional obsolescence that may otherwise dictate complete demolitions and reconstructions of buildings. More precisely, extended durations may lead to the reduction in resource utilization (materials and energy for material production) and in waste emissions.

Maintenance operations may range from simple repairs to replacements of parts to meet the required asset life extension. In extreme cases, when poor maintenance, degradation and/or loss of functionality take place, renovation of assets is preferable to demolitions or reconstructions in order to effectively extend the duration of the entire building or, at least, of its parts that are still in possession of residual performance capabilities. Actually, a building 'embodies' some energy that has been used in the material manufacturing process (from the extraction of raw materials to the final installation on-site): when demolitions take place, this amount of energy is lost and investment is necessary to provide energy for the new construction.

On the other hand, the continued asset functionality, enabled by maintenance operations, ensures that embodied energy is not wasted, especially for load-bearing structures which store the highest quantity of energy and therefore should not be subject to demolitions.

The Life Cycle of Constructions and the Life Cycle of Components

The notions of asset duration and maintenance are involved in the concept of construction life cycle. This may be longer or shorter, depending on utilization objectives.

If constructions are intended for temporary use, clearly the concepts of life cycle and, accordingly, of maintenance are not applicable, whereas certain re-usable components will have a longer useful life when disassembled.

Actually, most constructions have long lifetimes, longer than the service life of their components. As a result, it is required that both component life and requirements for maintenance be taken into account whenever performance degradations occur. With reference to the life expectancy of building components, relevant data provided by British and Swiss specialists account for a range between 20 years and more than 60 years, in the different component categories: outer and inner walls, roofs, windows and doors, linings and equipment.

The durability of materials, components or assemblies can be evaluated by comparing their useful service life with the period of time required by the ecosystem to incorporate the environmental impacts associated with their manufacture and their end-of-life disposal. A very similar approach is applicable to constructions in their entirety: in these instances, life cycles have to be related to the impacts deriving from the manufacture and disposal of their components.

A distinction should be made between the life cycle of constructions and the life cycle of their components, so as to avoid accounting only for the life cycle of whole constructions and merely identifying the concept of life cycle with their duration. Indeed, this concept should be extended to all accomplishments preceding and following the useful life of constructions, which are required for their completion and are related to the life of their components. The 'cradle-to-grave' cycle of constructions begins as soon as they are completed on-site and ends with their demolition; however, they are built from components that are manufactured in factories and, at their end-of-life, are disposed of or possibly recycled or re-used. Consequently, construction life cycles and component life cycles are different. As far as environmental assessment (and, specifically, LCA) is concerned, all resources involved are encompassed in the cradle-to-grave notion of the life cycle.

It should be noted that the definition of LCA takes into account the use of material, energy and water and the emissions into air, water and soil deriving from the different processes related to constructions: extraction of raw materials, transportation, component manufacture, building works and operational management, demolition and disposal.

The Influence of the Operation Stage on the Environmental Balance of Constructions

The operation stage generates the highest environmental (LCA) impact for constructions, taking into consideration their extended lifetime. Overall impacts can be reduced by convenient policies concerning energy management and maintenance programmes.

One of the main objectives of construction maintenance is to ensure performance levels for specified periods, so that degradation and obsolescence can be prevented and resources (especially energy) can be economized. Other benefits derive from extending the lifetime of constructions and their parts.

At the same time, however, maintenance operations – ranging from simple cleaning or painting works to complete replacement of parts – result in an increased environmental impact.

It has been asserted that LCA practices tend to neglect component lifetime scenarios in comparing the environmental impact of alternative solutions. This may lead to modifying the trend line of environmental assessment in the life cycle perspective and therefore should be reconsidered when reviewing project choices.

There are accordingly two possible options to be taken into account in construction processes. Option one is to adopt solutions that minimize maintenance requirements, while option two is to adopt flexible and reversible solutions, limiting the amount of component replacements whenever the effects of obsolescence and degradation are to be prevented.

Clearly, construction lifetime also affects provisions that should be environmentally consistent. This means, for example, that if a lifetime of 25 years is expected, lightweight and reversible solutions are more suitable. Conversely, for a life expectancy of 100 years (specifically, for residential use), even though the embodied energy content can be enormous, durable solutions with minor maintenance requirements are better.

Frequently, the issues related to the durability of materials and to maintenance and replacement programmes are somewhat neglected, so that the effectiveness and reasonableness of environmentally consistent provisions will be weakened.

In conclusion, environmental impacts require careful consideration during the operational stage as well as the construction stage and, later, whenever maintenance operations are concerned. The environmental design targets are energy savings in parallel with extended durations and reduced needs for maintenance operations and component replacements.

Scheduled Maintenance and Component Duration Scenarios

Lifetime environmental assessments and scheduled maintenance are likely to go hand in hand: if a programme of maintenance operations has been established, environmental assessments made during the design stage will include a definition of maintenance cycles associated with a certain technical solution and of the related environmental impacts across the life cycle. In addition, if a given degree of performance degradation is expected, a more accurate assessment of the environmental impact during the operation stage can be made for the technical solution that has been selected.

As mentioned above, a number of elements tend to be frequently neglected in environmental assessments. The role of component duration is one of these elements: durations are considered equal for components and constructions in which they are included. In addition, in many cases, there is an inaccurate treatment of the environmental impact from the maintenance operations and the replacements of various parts. Finally, the performance of components in use is often considered as constant, whereas the occurrence of performance degradations should always be accounted for in environmental assessments.

In most cases, the occurrence of these approximate approaches is caused by a lack of information on the duration of materials, on maintenance frequencies, on the variation of component performance with respect to time. Accordingly, valuable synergies between environmental assessments and maintenance programmes might be convenient.

Maintenance programmes are primary management tools for the execution of renovation activities at established intervals and for the allocation of stipulated resources. The preparation of a maintenance programme requires an enormous amount of data, especially concerning the life cycles of components and the expected use of the construction. Maintenance programmes efficiently support environmental assessments implementing an LCA approach.

In some cases, during the last few decades, there has been an increased occurrence of physical degradations in constructions, requiring comprehensive renovations when the constructions are 20–30 years old. Environmental sustainability cannot be discussed without emphasizing the drawbacks of reduced lifetime durations. Maintenance programmes provide the opportunity to prevent the risk of unexpected performance degradations and ensure appropriate quality levels throughout the lifetime of constructions, so as to reduce waste and diseconomies in the operational management of constructions and to accommodate technical/constructional solutions to variations in performance levels.

LCA in Support of Maintenance Programmes

So far, the concept of (life cycle) duration has been regarded as environmentally beneficial. On the other hand, environmental sustainability does not necessarily imply the concept of 'conservation': functional obsolescence and technological obsolescence might lead to operational diseconomies and higher environmental impacts deriving from inaccurate volume distribution or bad energy management.

Environmental sustainability factors essentially require that utilizations and environmental impacts be balanced throughout the whole life cycle (manufacture, operation and disposal). In turn, the environmentally harmful implications of both disposal processes for aged components and manufacturing processes for new components should be balanced against the environmental benefits deriving from improved component performance, improved energetic efficiency of utilities and optimized use of assets.

As a consequence of the above, LCA actions provide effective support to scheduled maintenance actions: the objectives of preventing degradations and reducing overall environmental impacts are likely to be achieved if a balance between performance losses and lesser impacts can be found, so that convenient replacement intervals are identified.

Certainly, the application of LCC principles will be helpful in identifying maintenance intervals as functions of costs to be incurred consequently. Awareness in formulating operational schedules might be improved by the combination of operational costs and environmental costs.

Product-Service Systems and Duration Assurance Scenarios

Component durability is certainly a key factor on account of increasing demands for performance enhancements. Extended durations can be effectively achieved by introducing product-service systems in the construction sector. Products are replaced by services that are carried out by these products in buildings so that manufacturers are required to provide the assurance of performance.

This is a critical issue, especially in the current climate of technological evolutions related to requirements for energy savings and demands for renewable energy sources. One example of the challenges to construction duration is insulation thickness in buildings for the purpose of reducing heat loss: insulation materials are in fact, broadly speaking, characterized by a limited lifetime (approximately 25 years) and – depending on the accuracy of the design effort – by some operational performance degradations. Whenever construction quality is poor, this may be affected by several factors: the poor quality of materials, the unknown time-dependent behaviour of new materials, the poor skill of certain operators, the ineffective management of subcontracted work, increased technological complexity and the lack of control regulations.

Applications of product-service systems should be extended to constructions in their entirety. Global service provisions for construction operation and maintenance may contribute to the improvement of management practices. The effectiveness of this integrated service may be greatly influenced by the current conditions of constructions and their components, and also by the accuracy of maintenance actions.

Environmental Certification of Constructions for Quality Assurance

Several existing mechanisms support environmental sustainability assessments for the purpose of environmental certification of constructions, while emphasizing benefits deriving from savings in the areas of energy, water, waste and pollution during the life cycle of constructions, including their disposal. These mechanisms (for example, BREEAM and LEED) have definite economic implications with reference to the profitability of investments, the cost-effectiveness of operational management, the better quality of the built (or the to-be-built) environment and the higher value of neighbouring areas.

The BREEAM approach (www.breeam.org) takes into consideration the criteria relating to materials, energy, water, pollution and operational and maintenance management.

The LEED approach (www.usgbc.com) covers the following areas: management planning for walls and floors, reduction of heat spots, improvement of energy efficiency, operational and maintenance planning and personnel training, Building Automation System component maintenance (both preventive and periodic), Heating, Ventilating and Air Conditioning (HVAC) systems maintenance, occupational safety and health provisions.

Comparatively, the elements taken into consideration in the Italian approach (www.itaca.org), as regards the assurance of performance level during the operational stage, include the following performance indicators:

- availability of construction documentation (provisions for documentation keeping and updating; construction logbook including information on construction variants and on maintenance programmes);

- the development and implementation of a maintenance plan focused on a multi-layered strategy – opportunity strategy, preventive/ scheduled strategy, predictive/condition-based strategy, failure-based strategy); and

- assurance of overall performance to ensure the durability and robustness of elements.

It is worth noting the standardization efforts led by international organizations, for example, ISO and CEN, in such areas as LCA, sustainability in building construction, service life planning of buildings and constructed assets, and sustainability of construction works.

References and Further Reading

Anderson, J., Shiers, D. and Steele, K. 2009. *The Green Guide to Specification*, 4th edn. Hoboken: Wiley-Blackwell.

BCIS, 2006. *Life Expectancy of Building Components: Surveyor Experiences of Building in Use*. London: Building Cost Information Service.

BRE Global Ltd., 2009. *BRE Environmental & Sustainability Standard*. Watford: BRE Global Ltd.

Chen, Z., Li, H. and Turner, J.R. 2007. 'Managing the Environment' in J.R. Turner (ed.), *Gower Handbook of Project Management*, 4th edn. Farnham: Gower Publishing, 483–521.

CIBSE, 2000. *Guide to Ownership, Operation and Maintenance of Building Services*. London: Chartered Institution of Building Services Engineers.

Edwards, S., Bartlett, E. and Dickie, I. 2000. *Whole Life Costing and Life-Cycle Assessment for Sustainable Building Design*. Watford: Building Research Establishment.

Guinée, J.B. et al. 2004. *Handbook on Life Cycle Assessment*. New York: Kluwer Academic Publishers.

ISO, 2006. *ISO 14040:2006 – Environmental Management – Life Cycle Assessment – Principles and Framework*. Geneva: International Organization for Standardization.

Chapter 19

Value for Money Assessment in Construction Projects: The Economic Effects of PPP/PFI in Projects

MASSIMO PICA

Introduction

In the twentieth century, Public–Private Partnerships (PPPs) – defined as agreements where public-sector organizations enter into long-term contractual agreements with private-sector entities for the construction or management of public-sector infrastructure facilities by the private-sector entity or the provision of services by the private-sector entities on behalf of a public-sector entity – became popular because of the possibility of using the instruments offered by project financing for the construction of facilities.

More precisely, PPPs are relationships between government-owned agencies and private firms aiming at providing services and infrastructures traditionally delivered by the public sector.

The participation of private partners in PPP projects guarantees a redistribution of project risks; moreover, the financial structure of such initiatives is another important aspect, both in terms of financing sources and in terms of balance among them. For example, under a PPP or Private Finance Initiative (PFI) scheme, it is not necessary to 'buy' an entire hospital, but what is actually needed is to make hospitalization services available so that risks will be shared with the private partner, who is to comply with the stipulated standards of safety, financial stability, dependability and quality.

The attention of specialists has been focused on the conditions under which governments should use PPP: with this aim in mind, the concept of Value for Money (VfM, introduced earlier in this book) is used and the approaches and techniques to evaluate it are analysed.

The Operational Practices of PPPs

PFI was introduced in 1992 in the UK, the first country in the world to adopt specific legislation for PPPs. Nowadays, PPPs are based on specific legislations in many countries, either members or non-members of the European Union (EU). The use of such an instrument to provide public services and infrastructures is becoming increasingly widespread.

The reason for the successful implementation of PPP/PFI in projects is due to a multiplicity of factors, which are – in their simplest form – related to particularly stringent national budget constraints, involving considerable limitations of public resources available for investments in projects, especially as a consequence of the financial crisis from the end of 2008 onwards.

Project financing is considered by a number of specialists as being undeniably advantageous with respect to the more traditional procurement practices. One of the main improvements is deemed to involve the correct apportionment of contract risks between the public and the private parties, especially after the transition to the operational stage, as dictated by Eurostat in its decision on the treatment of PPPs. This European 'best practice' for risk allocation is based on the analysis of those operations in which public authorities have the main funding responsibility for the services delivered.

Another chief advantage lies in the increased compliance with planned operations schedules and costs. This benefit can only be realized if contract terms are firmly agreed between the two parties before the awarding of the contract and cannot be changed at a later stage unilaterally. Past experience shows that this takes place only in certain cases. Sometimes, problems arise when project approval processes after the awarding of the contract entail massive modifications – or even a total rejection – of technical, contractual and financial conditions that had been mutually agreed.

Benefits also derive from the performance incentives of private parties. Project finance schemes assign direct responsibilities to private parties (in terms of their investments, costs and incomes) so that they are encouraged to develop good-quality projects which can be optimized in the long term.

Further advantages may arise from the interactions taking place between the two parties during the award process in order to attain a final formulation that will be the best in terms of the public interest and, at the same time, for the expected profitability of investors. Especially for complex projects, the optimum solution is defined as a result of stepwise negotiations leading to convenient refinements of possible solutions envisaged by the different parties.

The Approach to VfM Assessment

Public organizations are, basically, confronted with at least two basic questions that are relevant when having to choose between a PPP scheme and a more traditional procurement practice for construction projects in such areas as transportation, healthcare, detention and education.

The first question relates to whether a PPP scheme is possible; another relates to whether this scheme, if possible, is really more attractive than the traditional practices. VfM assessment can provide answers to the questions raised above through an appraisal of a number of elements, both quantitative – that is, determining the economic and financial viability for the public organization – and qualitative, leading to the identification of the most suitable procurement solution.

VfM methodologies tend, by their very nature, to identify objective solutions on the basis of both quantitative elements (such as those resulting from usual Outline Business Cases) and qualitative elements, the latter effectively contributing to a dependable and exhaustive selection process. In addition, qualitative assessments have grown in importance as *ex ante* appraisal mechanisms to ascertain the feasibility and viability of project financing schemes for the public sector and the ability of the private sector to effectively deliver services in response to common interests.

Elements of VfM Analysis

The starting point of a VfM analysis considers a set of specific elements responding to requirements stated at a project level or, upwards, at a programme level, including the following:

- An optimum project risk allocation to the different stakeholders, for example, as suggested by the Eurostat decision (dated 2004) on the treatment of PPPs.

- Analysis of project costs across the project life cycle, that is, Life Cycle Costs (LCCs) or, more generally, Whole Life Costs (WLCs), extending from mere construction costs and also implying a value-based criterion.

- Integration of planning and design efforts of facilities and services to be delivered throughout the lifetime of the project. This is of the greatest importance in determining the effective lifetime serviceability of the asset for the benefit of the user community.

- Implementation, by the public sector, of an output specification approach, describing in detail the community needs in terms of technical and contractual requirements, so that private entities are expected to formulate proposals in line with stated requirements, but possibly contributing with creative and technologically innovative solutions.

- Design flexibility, adapting the asset operational cycle to modifications that may be required throughout the lifetime of the project.

- The possibility of recovering project costs by appropriate planning of financial flows, on the basis of an asset market analysis or of the quantification of deliverable services and related pricing. This requires an accurate market risk allocation to the two parties, as a pre-requisite to the conditions under which sponsors and lenders may decide to participate in the effort.

- An investment rewarding system ensuring the highest performance incentive to private entities during the operational management stage.

- Accuracy in assessing contract terms, in order to consider all critical factors related to the serviceability of the asset, to the return on private investments and to other factors influencing the stability of financial flows.

- Assessment of project complexity and estimation of the project cost profile, especially in the operational stage.

- Appraisal of the supply side capacity, that is, the ability of the private sector to optimally implement the project and manage it in lieu of the public sector, on the basis of competence, know-how and higher competitiveness in terms of costs/benefits ratio.

The UK's Experiences in VfM Assessment

HM Treasury's Green Book provides a project life cycle perspective in distinguishing the three stages of VfM assessment:

- Stage 1 – Programme Level Assessment – is concerned with an arrangement of initiatives in a given area of public investments: hospitals, schools, offices, etc. Applications of PFI models are essentially appraised in these investment programmes through feasibility studies determining, from a comprehensive point of view, the existence (or absence) of conditions supporting a convenient PFI implementation.

- Stage 2 – Project Level Assessment – replicates the VfM assessment (and the qualitative analysis) on individual initiatives, again using a feasibility study implementation. As a consequence, conditions supporting the implementation of a PFI in each of these individual projects are identified, on the basis of the conclusions reached at the programme level, and any specific measure that is required is recognized.

- Stage 3 – Procurement Level Assessment – determines conclusively the degree of confidence and the quantitative level of VfM gained through PFI implementation from the selected proposal, in comparison to more 'traditional' appraisal systems.

The Objectives of Qualitative Analysis

While the assessment procedures are subject to changes across the three analysis levels that have been identified, there is no modification in the objectives of qualitative analysis, especially between Stage 1 and Stage 2. Viability, desirability and achievability are identified in qualitative analyses.

VIABILITY

The essence of PFI solution viability is the appraisal of effective contract requirements translating the objectives and the expectations of the public organization aiming at successful project outcomes.

While all public projects can be valuable to a certain degree, some of them may not be viable under project finance models, involving the contribution of private capital and an adequate level of investor profitability.

Viability analysis is based on the following elements:

- The ability to generate stipulated cash flows through *availability payments* or other forms of payments as appropriate (for example, tolls).

- Concessionaire performance measurements (especially when paid for by the public organization).

- A rough estimate of capital investments and of the stipulated levels and conditions of public contributions to expected capital expenditures.

- An assessment of the project operational flexibility, that is, its sensitivity to changing legislation, regulations and technical standards specific to the area of application envisaged.

- The definition of project boundaries and constraints in order to avoid potential conflicts interfering with planned scenarios and, for example, limiting the ability of private entities to deliver stipulated services.

DESIRABILITY

This part of the qualitative analysis is concerned with evaluating the benefits achievable by the public party in the implementation of PFI models, in comparison with potentially higher project development costs. Qualitative desirability verifications are accompanied, in principle, by quantitative analyses of VfM that define incomes or costs accrued as a consequence of expected advantages or disadvantages.

Broadly speaking, PFI mechanisms ensure better risk allocations and incentives for private parties to generate services of a better quality. On the other hand, public parties are expected to review costs arising from service specifications and service delivery procedures stated in PFI contracts, so these costs will be compared to the economic conditions for traditional procurement, taking into consideration the need of a more efficient public expenditure.

First, a detailed risk assessment is required. This is based on the following question: is the private party able to manage programme/project risks more efficiently than the public party, that is, at lower total costs? The context of this question is a qualitative risk analysis, which is essential in correctly identifying and allocating project risks, to be evaluated thereafter from a financial point of view in the quantitative analysis. Payment mechanisms and contract terms of PFI schemes are also investigated in order to determine if they are able to actually ensure the highest possible efficiency levels in risk transfer to the private party.

Second, a vital concept in PFI projects is innovation. The higher the degree of innovation in a project, the more – normally – the project will be in accordance with the contractual project finance strategy: in fact, private parties are allowed to invest in facilities and services having higher capabilities, so that expected returns from investments are ensured. On the other hand, excessive innovation levels would generate more prudential attitudes in investors and imbalances in debt pricing.

Another element to be explored in detail is the salvage value of investments, requiring that the service life of the facility be evaluated and that any salvage value, at the end of the concession period, be estimated. This is extremely important since public parties are interested in establishing a reasonable contract duration and an opportunity of acknowledging a final value without depreciation in order to avoid extended concessions.

Furthermore, the application of PFI schemes in projects implies that public parties provide concessionaires with payments based on the quality and quantity of services delivered, so that market risks will be entirely attributed to public entities. As a consequence, the selected payment system should consider efficient mechanisms for the assessment of services, under the direct responsibility of public parties for performance verifications (based on contract

Key Performance Indicators (KPIs)). Such mechanisms, for example, will consider risk rewarding conditions for the benefit of concessionaires and the application of specific penalties (when services do not meet satisfactory quality standards) and incentives (when public parties wish to encourage their private counterparts to achieve the defined objectives).

Finally, WLC are studied in the quantitative analysis, but Cost Breakdown Structures (CBSs) are actually considered and analysed in the qualitative analysis, especially with reference to costs for managing and delivering services, in the context of contract standards. Particularly noteworthy is the definition of maintenance programmes (both scheduled and unscheduled) that private parties are expected to comply with in order for facilities to be perfectly efficient when returning to public property at the end of the concession period.

ACHIEVABILITY

Assessments of feasibility and ensuing benefits cannot be sufficient to guarantee that the expectations of public parties will actually be achieved. Public objectives will be certainly met by PFI implementations under two additional conditions:

- the private market should be able to ensure an adequate expertise level; and

- the best proposal should be identified on the basis of the capability to undertake an efficient competition process.

The latter will in fact entail tender costs that are expected to be essentially higher in comparison to traditional procurement schemes.

Achievability will be primarily based on the ability of private parties to effectively respond to public demands, which means that these private counterparts are expected to demonstrate their interest in complying with the requirements in order to ensure that the PFI implementation in the project will actually be successful. Project success will be determined, essentially, by the existence of private markets having adequate familiarity with concession practices and willing to undertake lengthy and complex tender processes.

Prior market tests, conducted on a systematic basis, positively support project finance initiatives, ascertaining the interests and capabilities of private entities. Most specialists in project finance believe that this is a necessary 'best practice', which prevents inadequate proposals that will never be accepted by the market, while capturing constructive contributions for the benefit of the effective implementations of selected initiatives.

As regards tender procedures, public entities should have adequate capabilities to manage these procedures in order to ensure the highest level of unambiguity and competitiveness.

Competitive dialogue is the standard international practice for awarding PFI contracts, in which there is a strong interaction and cooperative negotiation between the parties, whether or not a preferred bidder is selected at a Best and Final Offer (BAFO) stage between the two surviving candidates. These procedures are usually highly sophisticated, requiring the existence of specific professional skills within public parties, and can also be lengthy in duration.

The following definition is provided by HM Treasury's *Value for Money Assessment Guidance*:

> *Competitive Dialogue is a procurement procedure introduced through the EU Public Sector Procurement Directive [204/18/EC] and incorporated into English law by the Public Contracts Regulations 2006, which came into force on 31 January 2006. It is considered that the Competitive Dialogue Procedure will be the relevant procurement procedure for the majority of PFI procurement.*

In itself, competitive dialogue has often been criticized because of high transaction costs placed on private entities, seemingly leading to limitations in competitiveness. Therefore, public organizations should ask themselves whether both contract value and project significance provide enough justifications to economic constraints encountered by tenderers, deriving in turn from acquisition procedures. The more effective the tender management, the less – potentially – will be the imbalance between tender participation costs and the actual project scope.

Frequently, even the best structured companies willing to tender to execute a project are constrained by the estimated amount of tender participation costs, including the resources to be engaged. Increased competitiveness and improved outcomes may be ensured through the application of incentives to tenderers, even considering the repayment of transaction costs.

Objectives of Quantitative Analysis

Quantitative assessments of the suitability of involving private funds in initiating and managing projects of interest to public parties can be simply made in comparison to similar initiatives if they were to be realized by public funding only. This comparison is to be made in monetary terms in order for the results to be directly and correctly interpreted.

For example, costs will be estimated for construction and related services entirely provided by private entities at the expense of the public party. Conversely, for comparative purposes, the estimate will be repeated for the partnership case, assuming that the concession contract covers both the construction and the life cycle management, and that the private party contributes to the expenditure.

It can be anticipated that, in most if not all cases, the cost of financing will be higher if the provision is entirely contracted to a private party by the public procurement agency, whereas it is most likely that the cost of procedures will be higher in the partnership case, due – as a minimum – to the complexities inherent in the contract awarding process.

It is assumed that, in each of the two aforementioned alternatives, costs include a monetary value for the risks integral to the initiative that could materialize and have an impact sooner or later throughout the project life cycle. While in the partnership case, risks and their costs will be shared between the two parties, along with any economic repercussions, in the other instance, risks and ensuing costs will be entirely charged to the public party.

In the construction stage, the monetary value of the cost risk is represented by an overspend in excess of the initial budget, whereas the risk of delayed completion can be measured, in monetary terms, by the income reduction caused by the delay in delivering the asset.

The identification of the risk owner will follow two different alternatives: in the case of public initiatives, the overspend will be entirely charged to the public party, while in the partnership case, the cost sharing formulation will be contractually agreed. Under these assumptions, the 'cost of risks' is the dominating element of the suitability of either contract implementation methodology.

Regardless of the amount of risk that is actually transferred to a private entity, its economic value will determine any VfM assessment involved in the initiation of a partnership, which in turn influences the added value earned by public entities as a result of risk transfer to private counterparts that will accept such risk transfer as long as they are in possession of a robust risk management system.

The notion of Public Sector Comparator (PSC) can be conveniently used to mean an estimated total cost under the assumption that a monetary value of all the risks inherent in the construction and life cycle management of the asset is also considered, when this is funded entirely by the public party.

In the partnership case, that is, in the PFI scheme, risks could (and actually *should*) be transferred to the private counterpart, so that the cost inclusive of risk can be compared with the foregoing case. The resulting difference between costs will be a measure of VfM, so that an excess of PFI costs would lead to rejecting the PFI alternative.

In this kind of comparison, the project life cycle perspective should be considered, on the basis of an estimate of costs to be incurred from the first idea of the initiative through the design phase and the subsequent period of operational management. For a usual life cycle duration of several decades, cost and risk estimates and also ROI estimates are required in a year-by-year cash flow representation for the two alternatives until the end of the life cycle. The Net Present Value (NPV) of cash flows will be used to compare the different cases for a given discount rate.

Essentially, a preliminary confirmation of the most suitable PPP model should consider the following areas of investigation (also deriving from the HM Treasury Guidelines):

- compatibility analysis with the relevant guidance and regulatory framework;

- the existence of risks that can be transferred to the private counterpart, defining the applicable contract requirements;

- organizational suitability and know-how of the public party for PPP initiatives;

- the viability of payment schemes connected to qualitative and quantitative levels of operational effectiveness;

- the public acceptability of requests to pay for the services on the basis of equitably acknowledged charges.

The Basic Costs and the Cost of Risks

There is a need for the calculations in the mathematical model to test the VfM (that is, the monetary worth of the quality-to-price ratio) of a PFI initiative against a more traditional PSC procurement, on the basis of costs charged to the public entity, in order to quantify the opportunity of pursuing either alternative and thoroughly considering the full range of costs for the investment (which is not always easily identifiable), the operational management, the finance costs and the risks, which are all included in LCCs and, as applicable, in WLCs.

LCC elements can be arranged into two main groups: basic costs and costs of risks. Basic costs are those charged to the public party for the project and for bringing the initiative to its completion, including design costs, construction costs, finance costs and operational management costs. Design costs encompass the entire design cycle, from the preliminary design stage to the detailed design stage. Construction costs are comprehensive of all phases leading to the final delivery of the asset. Finance costs are those charged by banks transferring money to either the public or the private partner. Operational management costs cover all functional needs for the delivery of services at the desired level (personnel, scheduled and unscheduled maintenance, technological upgrades, etc.).

In most cases, basic costs associated with PFI contracts are higher than those for PSC contracts. Typically, the largest differences occur for design costs and finance costs, whereas construction costs and operational management costs may be comparable.

Why are design costs significantly higher? PFI cases require particularly complex design processes, including the generation of early LCC estimates, covering the subsequent construction and operation stages which markedly influence the accuracy of such estimates.

As regards finance costs, the difference with respect to the PSC case may be due to more severe conditions typically imposed by banks on private partners compared to more favourable clauses generally applicable to public organizations.

Risk Transfer Mechanisms in PFI

Inherent in any planned and scheduled project initiative is the notion of risk, implying that the initial concept formulation for the initiative under consideration cannot take into account *ex ante* the future possible occurrence of events influencing the outcome of the initiative and, more precisely, inducing modifications in the initial assumptions for the project plan and schedule. Nevertheless, efficient risk management practices facilitate the anticipation of risks, their quantitative assessment and their allocation to each of the project stakeholders.

Actions to be taken by either party as a result of future events that may or may not actually occur require some degree of prefiguration during contract negotiations, for the purpose of identifying any risks that may materialize during the execution of the contract and of agreeing the risk share between parties. On the other hand, quite often, contracts and statements of work scarcely contemplate the quantification of these risks, that is, the extent of negative consequences for the party that agrees to the assumption of risks by accepting the contract and translated into additional resource consumption and higher expenditure.

While risk identification and risk allocation are usual – albeit not completely standard – practices, the implications of risk in the economic and financial framework of project finance initiatives are not typically treated with the same level of attention. This is particularly critical in VfM analyses, in which these implications are expressed in monetary terms, also taking into consideration assumptions for the management of potentially adverse events. Since the entire life cycle of PPP initiatives is considered as the period of analysis, from the planning stage through to the conclusion of the operational management stage, there will be some impact on the multiplicity and the increasing amount of risks in such initiatives.

If the notion of risk is examined from a pessimistic viewpoint, that is, with reference to unwanted events, this means that not only are there uncertainties as to whether any unfavourable event will in fact materialize, but that there are also more or less severe consequences to be expected from events of a certain magnitude.

In the case of the VfM approach, unwanted events are those causing cost increases in comparison to estimates and expectations stated during the planning stage: additional costs over the baseline of PSC/PFI express potential risks to be considered in the definition of total costs that will be charged to the public party.

How much risk is allocated to each party is a factor of specific relevance to the assessment of cost share. Certainly, the objective is not to maximize risk transfer to the private counterpart, but to ensure that risks are actually managed by the party which can do so to the best degree, so that the resulting cost will actually be reduced to a minimum. When an excessive number, or a convenient share, of risks is transferred to a private entity, the public organization could have to bear higher costs than would be expected if no transfer occurred: nevertheless, the cost of risk to be transferred – on the basis of relative risk management capability – will be included by the private counterpart in its project proposal. Instead, the more reasonable the risk allocation negotiated by the public organization, the more VfM will be obtained from a limitation of total initiative costs and from an optimum resource utilization.

In VfM methodologies, the assessment of various risk values cannot be separated from the concurrent risk allocation. Value is directly affected by risk allocation since, as mentioned above, the parties involved in managing a given risk have different abilities and attitudes in facing this effort.

Private entities are more capable of identifying and controlling construction cost overrun risks, while public organizations are better at challenging the dynamics of underlying services demands for partnership initiatives.

Additional and Concluding Remarks

Risk allocation and quantification are consequences of prior risk identification. Initially, all risks likely to be faced in the partnership initiative should be listed. This is a complex process, requiring consideration of similar earlier experiences as well as contributions of adequate skill and competence levels. While recognizing that each project has specific features, project risk identification can be supported by tools and methods suggesting the best allocation solution(s) for each partnership initiative. As a general rule, risk identification processes lead to distinguishing between transferable risks and retained risks, the former including project risks, construction risks and all those that can be more efficiently managed by the private party, and the latter to be allocated to the public organization.

It should be emphasized again that maximizing the risk transfer is not an objective; while it is required to reduce to the greatest possible extent the costs of uncertainties associated with the project, this cannot be resolved in a deterministic fashion during the planning stage.

PFI and PPP construction projects have been extensively discussed, from an economic point of view, by Boussabaine (2007), who states that his book:

> sets out to explain how PFI/PPP cost appraisal issues can be appreciated by means of the correct application of innovative costing methods, where the emphasis is on planning and control.

Specifically, Chapters 2 and 3 in Boussabaine's book are intended to:

> call for changes in the way that the whole life cycle value is perceived, created and exchanged.

References and Further Reading

Akintoye, A., Beck, C. and Hardcastle, C. 2003. *Public–Private Partnerships: Managing Risks and Opportunities*. Oxford: Blackwell.

Boussabaine, A.H. 2007. *Cost Planning of PFI and PPP Building Projects*. Abingdon: Taylor & Francis.

Boussabaine, A.H. and Kirkham, R.J. 2004. *Whole Life Cycle Costing: Risk and Risk Responses*. Oxford: Blackwell Science.

Fight, A. 2005. *Introduction to Project Finance*. London: Butterworth-Heinemann.

HM Treasury, 2003. *Supplementary Green Book: Guidance on the Treatment of Optimism Bias*. London: HM Treasury.

HM Treasury, 2004. *The Green Book: Appraisal and Evaluation in Central Government*, revised edn. London: HM Treasury.

HM Treasury, 2006. *Value for Money Assessment Guidance*. London: HM Treasury.

HM Treasury, 2007. *Quantitative Assessment User Guide*. London: HM Treasury.

Chapter 20

Driving Towards Successful Progress and Delivery of Construction Projects

MASSIMO PICA

Successful and Unsuccessful Construction Projects

As has been repeatedly pointed out, projects that are late and/or over-budget have significantly higher damage rates than projects that are on cost and on time. It is therefore worth studying what are the factors that contribute to projects being late and over-budget. For example, I have received from my British colleague Andrew Townsend[1] a statement noting that:

> UK construction is so introverted that it does not make the effort to learn from others.

This is followed by a list of reasons for project overruns and overcosts:

- *Clients who don't know what they want;*

- *Clients who are commercially naïve;*

- *Inappropriate contractual arrangements;*

- *Underfunding;*

- *Tendering based solely on price without capacity checks or quality checks on the bidders;*

---

1   Private correspondence.

- *Fragmented execution organisation with no continuity of management through the life of the project;*

- *Little or no incentive for pride in workmanship;*

- *Therefore little or no pride/ownership of the end product – no owner focus;*

- *Site execution controlled on cost with no regard for quality and its effect on the end product;*

- *Little or no schedule control expertise or management tools;*

- *Little or no quality assurance or quality control;*

- *Little or no understanding of handover and commissioning processes; and*

- *Much dispute often involving lawyers to clear snag lists and settle final invoices.*

Defining the Scope of Construction Projects – Preliminary Project Phases

One of the essential steps leading to successful construction projects is the development of a detailed definition of the project scope in accordance with stated business objectives. For decades, the increasing effectiveness of Project Management practices has become a business requirement for the purposes of minimizing capital costs and maximizing project profitability.

In the initial period of the project life cycle, the project profitability can be effectively influenced so that subsequent project authorization can be released to commit the majority of the project capital investment and contract. During this preliminary project timeframe, decision points are formally established to authorize the initiation of the project development effort. These recognized decision gates are also efficient mechanisms for ensuring the continuity of authorizations for further project funding when needed.

The conclusion of the early project effort takes place when the level of project definition is adequate to support a definitive estimate for the entire project cost and its projected rate of return in order for major project funding to be justified. The Engineering, Procurement and Construction (EPC) effort – which will be examined in more detail later – will ultimately focus on the final commissioning and delivery where the validation occurs for the earlier project effort.

The impact of scope changes on construction projects is heavily influenced by the time when those changes are incorporated. The earlier a change is considered and integrated into the project scope, the greater its prospective effect on the project profitability and the easier its incorporation. Conversely, later changes – specifically in the EPC timeframe – are far more expensive to implement and therefore are to be considered highly disadvantageous.

Late changes that can be potentially profitable are frequently not implemented when the benefits of such implementations are exceeded by the cost that will be incurred by doing so; on the other hand, the cost of implementing changes during the earlier phases of the project is much lower than if the same change is made after detailed engineering is underway.

In conclusion, whenever changes are sought proactively at an early stage, this will be greatly advantageous to the project profitability, far more so than would occur when the need for changes is recognized in later project phases. This also implies that potentially beneficial changes – and value improvements – are desirable as early as possible, whereas in the subsequent EPC timeframe, there is a good chance that they will not be cost-effective to implement. In addition, significant profitability may derive from applying expertise in construction, operations and maintenance early enough in the life cycle.

Within the scope of construction projects, financial and marketing opportunities are translated into the technical details of the project, after which project risks are identified and appropriately mitigated so that major funds can be authorized. As the work continues, the need for changes must be constantly considered, prior to entering EPC. The predictability of project life cycle costs must systematically be balanced against the requirement for the project to maintain its profitability or Return on Project.

Key issues of the preliminary project phases are the accuracy of cost estimates, the cumulative project hours and the contingency associated with cost estimates. In large projects, across the preliminary phases, the uncertainty of cost estimates may range from an initial ±40 per cent to a final ±10 per cent, while the contingency may correspondingly decrease from 15–20 per cent to around 10 per cent. The project hours spent in the preliminary timeframe can vary widely between small and large projects, including those projects where new or emerging technology is being applied.

Enhancements in the overall project performance are made possible by the early consideration of schedule and cost goals, to be agreed by customer and contractor representatives in an integrated business and technical project team.

The ultimate objective is to ensure both better cost performance and lower execution time of the preliminary project phases; in addition to influencing overall project costs and schedule and effective management, integrated project teams produce the lowest number of design changes throughout the project and, especially, fewer late changes. This implies lower investment costs, better and more predictable schedules, and better management with respect to projects where teams are not – or not properly – integrated: significant benefits may accrue whenever each project team member works closely with each other team member to produce the most profitable project outputs. However, once project teams are well integrated and individual roles and responsibilities are clearly identified, this advantage might be lost whenever key team members are changed.

Provisions for Best Project Performance in the Early Project Phases

The cost and schedule required for an optimum completion of the preliminary project phases are under constant pressure and have to be justified. This is especially true for 'fast-track' projects where time pressures might be significant. Higher levels of preliminary planning effort may lead to substantial cost and schedule savings.

The level of project definition along the preliminary phases has an immediate influence on the ultimate project output in terms of the number and consequences of changes in the subsequent EPC timeframe, especially after the beginning of the detailed engineering effort, when (late) project changes may have a major connotation, namely typical impacts greater than 0.5 per cent of the total project capital investment or one month in the critical path schedule. This confirms once again, as previously asserted, that better project performance should be pursued through proactive profit-improving changes at an early stage, along with the achievement of the best practical or highest level of project definition and with the limited need for changes during the EPC phase.

As regards the influence of the project size, frequently smaller projects benefit to a greater extent than larger projects from better project definition prior to initiating the EPC effort. Small projects typically also have a greater amount of late changes than larger projects.

Prior to the EPC timeframe, project teams should ensure that deliverables are released as stipulated in the various moments of the preliminary project phase. This typically begins with a strategic business assessment, an initial cost estimate and an initial project milestone schedule.

At a later stage, the emphasis is on refining previous cost and schedule estimates, as well as considering possible project alternatives.

In the subsequent project definition phase, further refinements of cost estimates and schedule details are expected to lead to project funding authorization, provided that the proposed project objectively shows the right combination of overall risk and projected economic performance. Finally, a detailed EPC phase master schedule and a detailed EPC phase execution plan are released as part of the typical project deliverables in this timeframe.

Engineering, Procurement and Construction

THE EPC TIMEFRAME AND SCOPE

The EPC effort generally begins with a preliminary engineering phase, which has a typical duration of less than a year. Preliminary drawings and technical specifications of varying levels of detail are prepared along with corresponding cost estimates in support of project proposals.

The subsequent detailed engineering phase usually has a duration of one to two years, during which contractors are expected to produce detailed estimates, detailed plans and detailed documentation.

Procurement and construction represent a multi-year effort involving activities to be performed concurrently by the purchaser and the contractor. The purchaser's emphasis will be on cost and schedule control, contractor control, contract planning and execution, quality control, health and safety requirements, and site management. The contractors' involvement will focus on cost and schedule control, supplier control, subcontractor control, contract planning and execution, quality control, health and safety provisions, and site management.

During the final start-up operations – and possibly in the commissioning phase (which, if included in the contract, will turn the EPC into the EPCC effort) – the owner and the contractor will be jointly involved in operational control, inspections and training if required.

THE TRADITIONAL EPC ARRANGEMENT

Traditionally, customers may assign engineering and construction management responsibilities to specialized professional organizations and contractors. This arrangement ensures that the procedure is simple and that costs are firmly established. In fact, all customer decisions are taken in the engineering phase and contractor selection in a fixed-contract price scenario generally ensures that the cost target is achieved.

On the other hand, longer execution times are to be expected, since the detailed engineering phase should be completed before proceeding with procurement.

Additional difficulties may arise when the engineering specialists do not take into sufficient consideration the site management perspective, since traditional procedures typically exclude contractors – that is, those who are more directly familiar with daily problems occurring in construction sites – from the engineering effort.

A lack of awareness of these problems might also lead to inaccurate estimates of construction costs by customers. When costs are overestimated, contractors will earn an unreasonably high profit, whereas when costs are underestimated, disputes or delays might result.

THE TURN-KEY SYSTEM

This arrangement basically follows the principle of maximum integration between the engineering and construction phases.

A key consideration is that sometimes these phases are so strongly connected that it would not be cost-effective to have the engineering effort completed before selecting a contractor. Therefore, both engineering and construction are assigned to the selected contractor and their integration leads to improved results in terms of the project life cycle schedule and cost. Moreover, the owner maintains exclusive inter-relationships with a single organization undertaking the engineering and construction efforts, instead of two separate entities.

The benefit of overcoming the difficulties inherent in the traditional method is counterbalanced by complications in the subcontracts arrangement. Frequently, when contractors do not possess certain stipulated engineering and construction skills, a number of specialist subcontractors must be involved in the project, causing subsequent coordination and control concerns.

THE OVERLAPPING PHASE MODEL

Unlike the turn-key system, this third solution enhances the connections between the engineering and construction phases, which become overlapped. The engineering effort is jointly managed by professional specialists and the owner through mutually agreed decisions resulting from top-down processes (that is, from the most general level to the most detailed); each set of decisions goes hand in hand with the construction effort, which is shared out among several specialized subcontractors.

While, apparently, construction timeframes can be shortened to some extent if this model is applied, the level of risk that the owner must accept can be increased by the multiplicity of organization and coordination efforts required in managing a host of subcontractors, along with the uncertainties inherent in construction cost estimates, which will be considered later in this chapter. The need for accuracy of construction control processes requires appropriate Project Management skills.

The Quantitative Performance of Construction Projects

Quantitative performance is measured by the ratio of the accomplished workload to the total workload.

This value corresponds to a 'useful' performance, expressing the actual effort expended in adherence to the statement of work/contract requirement.

In homogeneous units, for example: for a total excavation work of 5,000 cubic yards and an accomplished work of 1,200 cubic yards, we have 1,200/5,000 = 24 per cent.

The work done cannot, by and large, be measured using a single unit. There will be a combination of cubic yards of excavation, cubic yards of concrete, pounds of carpentry or piping, yards of cables, etc. – units that are not additive. Therefore, an appropriate single unit must be derived for comparison and calculation purposes, for example, workload, prices and parametric arrangement.

For each class of work elements, the ratio of the actual workload to the budgeted workload is calculated.

If no information on workloads is applicable, a similar calculation can be made using contract prices.

Conversely, calculations can be made to derive values for effectiveness (ratio) and variance (difference) from the actual output and the planned output, whereas efficiency is given by the ratio of the hours expended to the actual output.

The Financial Performance of Construction Projects

The financial performance is calculated as the ratio of the received cash to the contract value.

Supposing, for example, that an output F is expected when using an amount R of resources, whereas an actual output F' is produced using an amount R' of resources, the following (dimensionless) values can be defined:

- effectiveness as the ratio F'/F;

- productivity as the ratio $p' = F'/R'$;

- planned productivity as the ratio $p = F/R$;

- efficiency as the ratio p'/p.

Standard productivity, for a homogeneous class of work elements (that is, measurable with the same unit), is the average output per work hour to be statistically determined in standard conditions.

In real (non-standard) projects, an estimated efficiency is defined for the whole project or for individual WBS elements. The average value of efficiency is calculated as the ratio of the actual hours to the planned workload hours.

The Economic Performance of Construction Projects

The cost budgeting (sub)process is key to the successful progress of construction projects along their life cycle. Budgeting for construction projects is typically iterative and is arranged in various levels of analysis and – therefore – of accuracy, in common with (most) other categories of projects where cost management and schedule management are required. Schedule estimates are of major importance in construction projects, since costs are connected to quantities and to project characteristics as well as to project schedules, which sometimes have a significant influence. Therefore, taking a Bill of Quantities as the basis for the project budget – that is, multiplying quantities by unit prices – is not sufficient for an accurate budget, which implies considering that certain work may have different costs when performed in different times.

Construction cost as a function of the work duration shows a sequence of three distinct relationships. In the intermediate region, cost variations are limited and therefore negligible, so that the project budget more accurately reflects the Bill of Quantities. Beyond this region, the longer the work duration, the higher the cost due to increasing indirect costs; conversely, in the opposite region, where work duration tends to zero, the impact of higher direct costs generates a sharp increase of construction costs, as the project crash time – that is, the minimum work duration allowed by the current technology – is approached.

More precisely, it is required that the relationship between the level of detail of the engineering effort and the process of cost and schedule analysis be defined, along with the relationship between, again, the level of detail of the engineering effort and the final cost control.

While the Bill of Quantities is typically an integral part of the scope of construction engineering, it should not be – as asserted earlier – the only output of the budgeting effort. Project budgets should take into account, as accurately as possible, project schedules, indirect costs and other time-related costs, in addition to a well-conceived risk analysis.

Budgets derive from early cost estimates made during the preliminary engineering effort, in conjunction with adequate information on historical costs and on accounting data concerning the common costs at the corporate level. Whenever projects are new and no historical cost data are available, consideration might be given to using average costs for the class of the specific project, costs estimated by analogy or analytical procedures.

Detailed budgets are prepared on the basis of quantity estimates and work hour estimates for individual engineering work elements, such as the following: general plans and functional sketches, structures, pre-fabrication, mechanical, electrical, thermal, the Bill of Quantities, the Bill of Materials and material specifications, manuals and catalogues.

Buildings are Not Repeatable

There may be similarities in building design, but the complete repeatability is prevented by differences in the characteristics of foundation soils, the combination of construction materials and/or the arrangement of facilities. As a consequence, it is impossible to standardize or industrialize – beyond a certain limit – the production processes, which on a case-by-case basis have to be tailored to the peculiarities of the individual projects. Different soils or different materials (in terms of classes, quantities and qualities) provide for some degree of unpredictability in the finished products, in comparison with series production as is typical in manufacturing companies. Another example of the peculiarity of construction projects is provided by the duration and uncertainty of the project execution cycle. Actually, before the project is completed, several problems may be likely to manifest themselves so that the project will be delayed; this is only partially due to management deficiencies, because other factors have to be typically considered, such as the approval of design variants – in the case of public works – or breaks caused by atmospheric events, or any other circumstance that was not accounted for in the project feasibility study. Project planning is complicated by these unpredictable situations; complications are caused, on the one hand, by planning difficulties induced by the presence of some works (for example, soil drillings, earthmoving and foundations) that are connected to the characteristics of the project site and, on the other hand, by the high levels of uncertainty frequently characterizing both the planned schedule and the cost of executing the project.

The peculiarities of production cycles for construction companies create constraints on both the economic cycle and the financial cycle. Prior to the beginning of the project execution, expenditures and other charges connected to the construction site have to be accounted for, along with costs for final site disposal; as regards the span of financial cycle, its extended duration may be caused by unexpected payment delays. Taken together, these reasons lead to negative project cash flows for extended periods, to the extent that the company may have to contribute to project costs across the contract duration. In the event that this circumstance is reproduced in all ongoing projects, negative cash flow impacts will show synergies, especially in bad economic conditions as a result of higher interest rates. Passive interests will therefore become more significant so that the financial health of the company and the profitability of individual projects can be seriously endangered or even overturned.

The combination of all these peculiarities contributes to a higher uncertainty of construction business in comparison with other production areas. This uncertainty leads to an increased corporate level risk, requiring appropriate attention and expenditure of resources in planning and control processes, including individual company projects.

New Ideas for Construction Projects in Evolving and Complex Environments

Project investments in the current construction practice are often developed and realized in extremely dynamic and unpredictable contexts. In many cases, project objectives, priorities and resource allocations are reviewed. Deterministic metrics, methodologies and best practices characterizing traditional project environments are no longer applicable to these situations.

Large construction projects are by their nature inherently complex and are frequently 'too big to fail', otherwise leading to the economic disruption of the construction company itself. Especially in this case, and to some extent for smaller-size projects, it is impossible to manage the uncertainty and unpredictability of changes induced by the project operational environment.

Appropriate management and control of project complexity, along with new methodologies for project performance measurement, represent a critical success factor in the cost-effective development and implementation of projects and, as deemed relevant, programmes of any nature and purpose. Complexity is, in itself, an invisible entity; it acts silently and therefore it is an enabler for unexpected situations in such a way that the troubles produced cannot be anticipated. This requires that a proper measurement mechanism be made available to constantly supervise projects while assessing project complexity through the adoption of a dynamic approach. In turn, project metrics of this kind could assist Project Managers and relevant stakeholders in supporting their institutional duties.

Broadly speaking, different practices to deal with project complexity can be identified.

One of the more frequently used and expeditious methods is to confuse the concepts of complexity and complicatedness and adopt a sort of 'come hell or high water' strategy on the basis of pre-determined patterns.

Project Managers in complex contexts should adopt a 'diplomatic', albeit up-to-the-minute and dynamic, behaviour on their battlefields, using their negotiation skills when interfacing with project stakeholders, while maintaining a pragmatic attitude in terms of managing project inter-relationships.

It should also be emphasized that the Project Management capability of construction companies essentially depends on three basic factors: planning proficiency at the company level, project planning and control proficiency, and the experience level of Project Managers.

In the first place, it is appropriate to point out that the profit margins of individual projects contribute to a company's achievement of economic and financial goals. If these goals are not clearly, pre-emptively and realistically established, then no reference 'target' will subsist to drive company's projects and to empower Project Managers' efforts.

Several elements actually contribute to the planning and control proficiency of construction companies. One of these is the arrangement of management planning and control processes, along with the definition of centres of economic accountability in charge of projects. Another significant element is represented by the emphasis given to the arrangement of economic objectives in an appropriate and consistent hierarchical structure:

Long-term economic objectives
⇩
Annual corporate economic objectives
⇩

Economic objectives of projects in progress
⇩
Economic objectives of work packages of each project

Specific project economic objectives should be shared among corporate management and Project Managers. Effective communication and reporting mechanisms should be put in place among Project Managers, management control authorities and high-level management in order to:

1.   analyse variances between planned and actual results;

2.   identify required corrective actions;

3.   finally ascertain the effectiveness of envisaged actions.

In addition, Project Managers should commit themselves to proper economic responsibilities and to the achievement of stipulated outcomes in the presence of advantageous incentives.

All of the contributing elements mentioned above are assessed by means of quantitative indicators, for example, using a simple scoring scale of 1 to 5 to represent increasing planning and control capabilities at the corporate level. High scores may have leveraging effects both on individual project planning and control capabilities and on Project Managers' professional skills and competencies.

As regards project planning and control proficiency, this is monitored throughout the entire life cycle of construction projects, typically during conceptual design, project planning, project execution and project closure. Project planning considers the following elements:

1.   project scope;

2.   methodologies adopted;

3.   resource allocation and activity duration;

4.   commitment of corporate management and technical management;

5.   IT platforms;

6.   interactions with other project life cycle stages and with other entities, both within the company and outside.

The elements listed below, in turn, are considered during the execution of the project:

1.   quantity and types of project monitoring actions;

2.   frequency of controls;

3.   standardization of procedures;

4.   communication management;

5.   commitment of corporate management and technical management;

6.   IT platforms;

7.   interactions with other project life cycle stages and with other entities, both within the company and outside.

Again, all contributing elements are assessed by means of quantitative indicators, for example, using a classification scale of 1 to 5 to represent growing levels of Project Management proficiency.

The experience level of construction Project Managers may be assessed in two broad separate areas:

1.   Familiarity with Project Management techniques:

    •   hierarchical project structures (WBS, ABS, etc.);

    •   Responsibility Assignment Matrices;

    •   risk management techniques;

    •   project cost management techniques;

    •   project scheduling and control techniques (PERT, CPM, CCM);

- project monitoring and control techniques (Earned Value Management).

2. Familiarity with basic management techniques correlated to Project Management:

- quality system;

- health, safety and the environment;

- economic, financial and legal matters;

- organizational structures and processes;

- change process management;

- standards and regulations.

Indicative classifications range from a moderate skill level, achieved on an individual basis (which is ranked 1), to the possession of accredited certifications (which is ranked 5).

References and Further Reading

AIA 2007. *Integrated Project Delivery: A Guide.* Washington, DC: American Institute of Architects.

BIS 2010. *Guidelines for Managing Projects.* London: Department for Business, Innovation and Skills.

Cabinet Office 2011. *Government Construction Strategy.* London: Cabinet Office.

CMAA 2003. *Capstone: The History of CM Practice and Procedures.* McLean, VA: Construction Management Association of America.

Ecorys 2011. *Sustainable Competitiveness of the Construction Sector.* Rotterdam: Ecorys SCS Group.

McNally, C., Smith, H. and Morrison, P. 2011. *Improving Portfolio, Programme and Project Financial Control.* London: The Stationery Office.

Chapter 21

Construction Project Monitoring in Complex Contexts

MASSIMO PICA

The Scope of Project Control

While managing a project involves taking care of all project actions from its conception until its complete realization, project control is deemed to be complete when the works have been finished. In addition, at the design stage, it is certainly advisable to consider, in a proactive way, the whole life cycle duration, that is, until the asset is disposed of. This is the final stage of the asset life cycle and, specifically, is the end point of the scope of total cost and schedule management falling within the Project Manager's responsibilities as a professional in charge of the project life cycle – however simple or complex the project may be – including assessment and control of costs, time and quality.

It is commonly understood that Project Management follows a multi-disciplinary approach in optimizing the response to cost, time and quality constraints while effectively managing the project scope and maintaining proper oversight of competencies and skills, the performance of human resources, risk control, communication arrangements and procurement source selection.

This approach, largely based on deterministic practices, is no longer sufficient to deal with uncertainties and complexities that are frequently inherent in current projects. Actually, traditional approaches have, in a number of cases, failed to give the right emphasis to the appraisal of project complexity, which is essentially based on the response to the following questions:

- How complex and critical is the project (sometimes in the context of a programme/portfolio of projects)?

- What are the more complex projects in a programme/portfolio and what is their impact on the complexity of the whole programme/ portfolio?

- Which elements are likely to generate the highest degree of complexity in individual projects or in programmes including these projects?

- Which projects in the programme/portfolio are likely to be more subject to change?

- What are the most significant criticalities (resources, etc.) influencing the success or failure of the project?

Indeed, project mechanisms cannot always be easily represented by pre-defined models describing in a deterministic fashion the life cycle of the project and, hence, its possible range of behaviours. It is possible to conceive more and more stringent project reviews in order to prevent and alleviate the occurrence of critical and emergency situations, but there are no means to foresee how the project will react and change in the presence of internal or external stimuli that cannot be definitely predicted.

On the other hand, any project should take into account an enormous amount (in some specialists' view, a real plethora) of methodologies, information management practices and operational procedures in order for its management to be effective. This suggests that only in a very limited number of cases is it possible or wise to deploy the complete collection of available instruments.

The selected approach should therefore be clearly tailored to the specifics of the project. First, it is essential to adopt different approaches for different projects because:

- if simple projects are managed using complex methodologies, there will be a risk of inefficiencies both in terms of the schedule and in cost management due to time-consuming project formalities;

- conversely, if complex projects are managed using simple methodologies, a lack of coordination in Project Management will lead to the risk of errors, duplications and reworks.

Another specific question is the following: under which conditions does a particular project require a different approach with respect to other projects?

A trap is concealed behind this question. Actually, it is not the project output that makes the real difference; between two projects with similar outputs, differences could involve the variables influencing the project complexity, which in turn require different Project Management approaches.

Most approaches are based on a small set of variables identified during the early project stages, thus avoiding delays in allocating correct project categories.

Project estimated schedule and budget are not per se reliable complexity indicators. A project involving 500 team members for a month is certainly much more complex than a project with two team members working for a year. In the same way, the individual value of a project budget does not give a full picture of the project complexity.

In several cases, therefore, the variables to be investigated (beginning, with an inevitable degree of approximation, before the project is initiated) are, for example:

- project effort;

- number of team members;

- number of heterogeneous (internal or external) specialists involved;

- the geographical distribution of team members.

While the variables mentioned above exist in every project, additional variables can be involved in specific cases.

The project effort represents the amount of work needed to bring the project to its completion. The greater the effort, the more significant the actions to be undertaken, the outputs to be checked and the costs of reworks required when the presence of errors becomes evident too late.

The number of team members provides an indication of the extent of coordination required in the project and therefore of the most appropriate organizational arrangements for managing the project, for example, appointing team leaders if the coordination among team members becomes more demanding for an individual Project Manager.

The number of heterogeneous specialists is related to the heterogeneity of a company's functionalities that are involved in the project (including those interfacing with customers and suppliers). This is a primary variable since different functions often have different targets, different approaches and heterogeneous operating practices. Therefore, the amount of coordination that is necessary becomes greater and requires a much higher level of attention in communication management.

The last item in the list of variables refers to the difference between co-located teams and distributed (or maybe virtual) teams. The latter intrinsically require additional planning of communication arrangements in order to make all of the vital project information regularly available.

Moreover, the list as shown is certainly incomplete. It does not mention, for example, the degree of project innovation. Projects that are minimally based on existing know-how will be more complex than projects that are familiar in terms of most of their details, all other conditions being equal.

The primary objective of this project appraisal system is, essentially, to adapt management provisions to the project characteristics so that the co-existence of the project and Project Management can be harmonious. The different arrangements between macro-processes in Project Management contexts having dissimilar levels of complexity relates to at least two factors:

- the number of Project Management processes (in simpler cases a detailed planning can be omitted);

- the changes in the formal process steps (control is minimized in simpler cases and there are also minor differences in high-level planning and in the project transfer and closure stage).

Construction project monitoring will be effective if the following provisions have been followed from the beginning:

- identify the entire project scope, on the basis of a Work Breakdown Structure (WBS) and of a subsequent detailed project activity list;

- define achievable objectives, to be quantified in terms of activity durations, costs and resources;

- draft activity bar charts to ensure that delivery dates are met using available resources;

- develop project budgets, cash flows, cumulative costs, incomes and profits;

- review and record project performances, comparing planned achievements with actual achievements and forecasting future trends, as well as promptly adopting corrective measures when required;

- identify areas of responsibility for each contract lot or activity;

- develop proper project communication mechanisms;

- reduce project risk and uncertainty while focusing on critical activities;

- consider contract constraints (on the project schedule, cost and resources);

- establish an efficient basis for a project cost/benefit analysis when relevant.

Review of the Basic Elements of Project Cost and Schedule Management

The main objective of cost and schedule management in construction projects is the proper utilization of human resources, facilities, materials and funds to achieve a successful completion of the project with respect to the specific cost, time and technical performance constraints.

Accordingly, project costs and schedules are systematically planned and controlled, focusing especially on the identification of potentially critical occurrences that might lead to higher costs and extended durations, so that the relevant recovery provisions can be envisaged. Among the major challenges that construction Project Managers mostly face – largely in common with other categories of projects – there may be change resistance, a lack of resources, skill gaps or merely basic problems with unrealistic timescales.

Cost and schedule management is a major effectiveness factor in providing a common baseline for project planning and expenditures in order to enable proactive project control.

Cost management encompasses all activities employed to bring the project to completion within the approved budget, typically including cost planning and estimating, cost control and cost reporting.

Schedule management covers all activities leading to the timely accomplishment of the project:

- schedule definition (activity description and sequencing, activity duration estimates and schedule baseline establishment);

- schedule control, comparing the current working schedule and the baseline schedule;

- schedule reporting.

Cost Management and Control in Construction Projects

THE PURPOSE OF PROJECT COST MANAGEMENT

The purpose of cost management in construction projects – as is applicable in most project contexts – is to ensure an effective appraisal of planned payment profiles, of actual cash outflows and of potential deviations. Cost management therefore includes the definition and implementation of corrective measures against deficiencies in cost streamlining.

Furthermore, provisions are made to forecast future incomes and expenses in support of budget preparation and cash flow planning. Concurrent cost and schedule management allows the accurate time phasing of costs and resources. Concurrent cost and change management provides for the evaluation of cost impacts from project changes.

Overestimating and underestimating project costs can be equally detrimental to the successful performance of a project. While overestimating can prevent fund allocation to the project or lead to the choice of a different alternative in a comparative exercise, underestimating can preclude sufficient financial support and can therefore lead to a higher risk of project failure.

Accurate and systematic cost estimates effectively support project funding and budgeting processes and, during the execution of the project, cost control processes.

PROJECT COST CONTROL

A project Baseline Cost Plan (BCP) is used to collect mutually agreed financial data – as part of an initial business agreement – and is subject to agreed changes in accordance with a specific formal procedure.

An Estimate at Completion (EAC) and an Estimate to Complete (ETC) are regularly delivered to the customer at specified dates in order to provide an appraisal of the total expenditure of the project upon its completion (EAC) and of the total expenditure for the work to be performed from the specified date until the project is completed (ETC).

The EAC and the ETC, in the case of Cost Reimbursement contracts, are based on all incurred costs up to the specified date and on the estimated cost of all the remaining project work up to completion and including the approved business agreement changes.

For fixed-price contracts, the EAC is based on the agreed milestone payment plans, including all payments made, all future planned payments and their dates, along with the approved contract changes.

Fundamentals of Project Schedule Management

SCHEDULE DEFINITION

As part of proactive Project Management strategies, project planning is extended to the appropriate level of detail for the project stage considered. Networks of activities, milestones and their interconnections provide for effective schedule management, in addition to risk assessment and mitigation.

The project WBS defines the network of project activities and the logical dependencies among them. In addition, for this network, activity durations are estimated and schedule contingencies are defined.

On this basis, and taking into account customer schedule requirements and available resources, the project schedule can be completely defined.

Project managers have to be particularly careful when monitoring their projects and looking closely at project performance. Network schedules, kept current as required throughout the project life cycle, are primary critical tools in monitoring project performance. The definition of the critical path leads to devising the corrective provisions for critical activities in accordance with the established project schedule.

Schedule reporting from the contractor to the customer, incorporating the critical path, supports the required overall visibility of the project status at any time, focusing especially on warning signs that may indicate that the project is severely going off-schedule and – even worse – that it is unlikely to recover, that schedule margins have been decreased and that project milestones will not be achieved.

Project Performance Reports

GENERAL CONSIDERATIONS

Performance reports are essential tools for the purpose of monitoring project performance. Project managers are provided with information on performance against the baseline plan, costs actually incurred, variances deriving from lack of compliance with plans and estimates of projected final costs, along with impact analyses for project cost, schedule and technical performance.

The following definition is provided by the PMBOK® Guide for the concept of Performance Measurement Baseline (PMB):

> The Performance Measurement Baseline is an approved plan for the project work to which the project execution is compared, and deviations are measured for management control.

Whenever scope, schedule and cost baselines are integrated in a PMB, this is regularly reviewed in a process called an Integrated Baseline Review (IBR).

COST INDICATORS: NON-CONFORMANCE COSTS

The following findings of a project review may be indicative of the need for corrective measures concerning project cost:

- A significant difference between the estimate of cost to complete and the budgeted cost for the project work remaining.

- A significant difference between the cumulative Cost Performance Index (CPI), that is, the ratio of the current authorized budget for a completed work element (Budgeted Cost of Work Performed (BCWP)) to the costs actually incurred up to the review date (Actual Cost of Work Performed (ACWP)) and the To-Complete Cost Performance Index (TCPI = Work remaining/Cost remaining).

- A significant lack of confidence in the project EAC (EAC = ACWP + Estimate for remaining work) or ETC (ETC = EAC – Actual Cost).

- Inadequate control account budgets for work remaining.

- An inability to explain the rationale for the EAC.

- Optimistic Estimates at Completion, not considering risks.

Whenever a project review is held, most attention should be addressed to the level reached by the Non-conformance Costs (NCCs), namely all costs incurred in excess of estimated values to comply with contractual requirements and costs incurred to manage non-conformities revealed in project execution.

Most frequent challenges in estimating baseline costs may include human errors leading to underestimations (these may also derive from too hasty estimating processes dictated by senior management). In addition, there are other root causes for the occurrence of NCCs, as mentioned below. For example, an inaccurate product/service design may lead to a lack of compliance with requirements.

NCCs may also arise if the project scope has not been clearly and exhaustively defined and communicated in the preparatory stage of the project; in this case, some project elements could not be provided for in the baseline and could therefore be missing, or conversely could be supplied despite not being within the scope of the project.

Both internal and external project activities may contribute to the growth of NCCs. Internally, potential cost increases derive from qualitative or quantitative causes: lower project performance, unpredicted personnel re-skilling needs, overall organizational inefficiencies, unit costs higher than those estimated in the baseline, and an excess of skilled and expensive resources. Externally, potential causes of higher costs are: poor performance of subcontractors, delayed delivery of subcontracted work, internal reworks on subcontractor deliveries and/or reworks by additional external suppliers, unpredicted tests and controls, and inaccurately low subcontractor cost estimates.

SCHEDULE INDICATORS

The following findings of a project review may be indicative of the need for corrective measures concerning project schedule:

- unrealistic activity durations;

- an unrealistic relationship logic between tasks;

- a significant number of fixed start or finish dates for activities;

- unjustified schedule reserve reductions;

- a baseline schedule that is uncorrelated to the budget timeline;

- the current schedule being uncorrelated to the ETC timeline.

Monitoring and Control of Construction Projects

GENERAL REMARKS

Project control is an essential management function in bringing construction projects to successful completion during their life cycle. As reported in the PMBOK® Guide, project control processes are undertaken to compare the actual performance to the planned performance of projects, to analyse variations, to evaluate possible alternatives and to implement the most appropriate corrective measures when required.

In project monitoring, before the actual project control, the project performance is measured, analysed and reported at a specified date ('time now') to represent the current project situation, whereas in the subsequent project control (Pilcher 1985), five phases are involved:

- planning to achieve project objectives;

- scheduling of inputs and outputs of construction processes;

- definition of resource organization and quantities to convert inputs into outputs;

- feedback process comparing actual processes to planned processes;

- evaluation of variations and decision support system to implement the required corrective actions.

Accordingly, project teams and site managers are enabled to identify most challenging areas, especially with reference to project performance, costs and schedule. In the usual management practice of construction sites, resources (personnel, materials, equipment and indirect resources) are evaluated using a cost/schedule control system to measure their productivity, that is, the efficient and effective use of operating workforces, machinery and manufacturing equipment. Therefore, one of the mandatory requirements for construction project success is represented by the integration of information from the construction site concerning the project schedule, cost and performance.

SCHEDULE CONTROL METHODS AND METRICS FOR CONSTRUCTION PROJECTS: THE PERCENTAGE OF COMPLETION

Traditional models for construction plan definition and progress measurements include bar charts, the Precedence Diagramming Method (PDM) and schedule control diagrams derived from the Line of Balance (LOB) technique. While bar charts and LOB diagrams are typically used as graphical illustrations of simpler projects or parts of complex projects, the PDM can be effectively used in support of larger projects.

The application of these methods is based on the management data listed in Table 21.1.

Table 21.1   Schedule control methods

Management data	Bar chart	PDM	LOB
Activity list	Yes	Yes	Yes
Activity start date, finish date, duration	Yes	Yes	Yes
Milestones, control dates	Yes	Yes	Yes
Percentage of completion	Yes	Yes	Yes
Logical relationships		Yes	
Floats/critical activities		Yes	
Activity location/Operator's arrangement			Yes
Resource productivity			Yes

The percentage of completion (PoC) is a widely used project control metric providing an expeditious and efficient parameter to monitor the project progress. In the Cost-to-Cost approach, the PoC is given by the ratio of the actual project cost to the EAC at 'time now' (see also Chapter 10 of this volume).

THE LOCATION-BASED MANAGEMENT SYSTEM (LBMS)

Referring to Table 21.1, it has been found that by integrating the three methods, it is possible to obtain an extremely flexible mechanism, called the Location-Based Management System (Kenley and Seppänen 2010).

This integration of models is particularly effective for complex construction projects, requiring more detailed models for resource flow across project activities. LBMS-based planning and scheduling define project macro-activities aggregating groups of homogeneous activities that are carried out repetitively in the different places of the construction (for example, the levels of a building or the work areas of an infrastructure) in accordance with a 'Location Breakdown Structure' (LBS). An LBS is a hierarchical representation of construction locations permitting the classification, aggregation and disaggregation of construction work areas.

Alerts are generated by the system when a delayed predecessor causes an expected delay in the execution of a successor. By and large, LBMS models provide basic information for project schedule, resource and cost control.

References and Further Reading

Demeulemeester, E.L. and Herroelen, W.S. 2001. *Project Scheduling: A Research Handbook*. Dordrecht: Kluwer Academic Publishers.

Kenley, R. and Seppänen, O. 2010. *Location-Based Management for Construction*. Abingdon: Spon Press.

Klein, R. 1999. *Scheduling of Resource-Constrained Projects*. Dordrecht: Kluwer Academic Publishers.

Pilcher, R. 1985. *Project Cost Control in Construction*. London: Collins Professional and Technical Books.

PMI® 2013. *The Guide to the Project Management Body of Knowledge*, 5th edn. Newtown Square: Project Management Institute.

References and Further Reading

Conclusions

Value Management and Value Improving Practices (VIPs) in the Life Cycle of Construction Projects

MASSIMO PICA

The Concept and Practice of Value Management

Stephen Simister, in his chapter on managing value in the *Gower Handbook of Project Management*, takes into consideration:

> the concept of value and how it is produced by the functionality of the facility delivered by the project.

Simister also identifies Value Management as:

> primarily concerned with ensuring that the client's needs are clearly defined and that a true scope of work is produced for the project such that the value a project will provide is defined.

These assertions provide an excellent introduction to the subject of Value Management in the life cycle of construction projects.

Due to the characteristics of construction projects – such as only one time establishment, big investment scale, complicated structure and high energy consumption in operation processes – the cost management theories and methods of construction projects are different from other general products. Value management can be efficiently applied to the total life cycle of construction projects, as well as considering function analyses in investment decision stages and combining cost management methods such as supply chain management and Kaizen costing based on objective cost management in implementation stages, in order to realize the value of construction projects while minimizing life cycle costs.

Value management aims to add value to projects in terms of time, cost and quality. It maximizes the functional value of a project by managing its life cycle until the beginning of the utilization stage, balancing all decisions against a value system determined by the client. Value engineering is, in turn, a part of value management which considers specific aspects of design, construction, operation and management. It is useful in reducing wasteful processes and inefficiency in specific aspects of design, construction and maintenance. Workshops are organized to enable stakeholders to participate in defining and achieving their needs. Clearly defined objectives of the project, the various alternatives and the choice of the correct one, health and safety, sustainability, design quality, buildability, operation/maintenance and disposal should all be considered during value management reviews and evaluation of options.

Value management – and, whenever relevant, value engineering – should be practised at regular stages during the project life cycle with the following purposes in mind:

- establishing what value means to the customer in terms of business benefits and priorities;

- identifying and agreeing upon business needs;

- identifying and evaluating options (including Private Finance Initiative options) for meeting business needs;

- selecting and agreeing the best option to meet business needs (that is, confirming whether or not a project is required);

- defining clearly and agreeing upon the project objectives (through stakeholder buy-in);

- selecting and agreeing upon the best project option;

- setting and weighing the selection and award criteria for the appointment of the integrated supply team;

- evaluating the bids against the selection and award evaluation criteria;

- refining the design to maximize value and eliminate waste and those aspects not directly related to meeting the project objectives.

Value engineering, per se, usually follows a job plan, which involves a series of steps that need to be followed in order to determine the most promising options or proposals.

Traditionally, the initial step is the identification of the business problem, the customer needs and priorities. After information/data regarding values, costs, risks and other project constraints are collected, ideas may be generated to meet the needs and priorities previously identified. This is usually best undertaken via a workshop with all the stakeholders and project team members. The principle is that ideas are generated in a 'criticism-free' atmosphere, which promotes free thinking and creative ideas.

The next step is the identification of the most promising options from the last stage, which are then developed and appraised. The results from this last stage are presented to the workshop group and a decision is made on which proposal to pursue. An action plan is prepared to take the proposal forward; at the final feedback stage, the success of the options implemented is assessed to provide lessons learned and inform future projects.

Such an approach provides the following benefits:

- a simple, clear definition of stakeholders' needs;

- identification and analysis of all alternatives and the correct option to be considered;

- proposing how value for money can be achieved;

- proposing means to reduce waste and inefficiency and therefore prevent unnecessary expense; and

- improved teamworking with joint ownership of solutions.

Risk Implications in Value Management

The general concept of risk in Project Management has already been introduced and explored in earlier chapters of this book. Risk involves uncertain outcomes, whether positive opportunity or negative impact. Some amount of risk taking is inevitable, whatever the project. A deliberate acceptance of some degree of risk is implied because the value to the business makes it worthwhile.

Risk management includes all activities required to identify and control the risks relating to the preferred project option. Risk management for construction projects encompasses the activities listed below:

- identifying and assessing the risks in terms of impact and probability;

- establishing and maintaining a joint risk register, agreed upon by the integrated project team;

- establishing procedures for actively managing and monitoring risks throughout the project and during occupation on completion, ensuring that members of the team have the opportunity to engage in a dialogue that will promote agreement of an appropriate allocation of risk;

- updating risk information throughout the life of the project;

- ensuring control of risks by planning how risks are to be managed during the life of the project in order to contain them within acceptable limits;

- allocating responsibility for managing each risk with the party that is best able to do so.

Risk management plans should be in place early enough to control risks quickly and effectively if they arise.

Risks should be allocated to individual risk owners within the integrated project team, who should fully understand the specific risks for which they are responsible. The risks should be managed actively throughout the life of the project in accordance with a risk management plan, which should deal with all risks, whether retained by the client or transferred to others in the integrated project team. The business case should include a time element and the risks of this changing should be kept constantly under review.

In addition, in the case of construction projects, the risk register is the typical document used to record the above information. It should be maintained collectively by the integrated project team and regularly updated throughout the project life cycle, as risks will be constantly changing. Risk management plans may be recorded on the risk register.

The key intentions of risk management are to ensure that risks are identified at project inception, that their potential impacts allowed for and, where possible, that the risks or their impacts are minimized. Risk management involves several stages, namely:

- risk identification in order to determine what the risks are;

- assessment of risks to determine the probability of occurrence and potential impact or severity;

- taking appropriate remedial action;

- monitoring, updating and controlling risks;

- feedback on how well risks were managed and lessons learned.

After possible causes for risks and effects from their occurrence have been considered and fully understood, a risk response should be decided upon. The management actions that may be taken include the following:

- Avoidance – where risks have such serious consequences on the project outcome that make them totally unacceptable, measures might include a review of the project objectives and a re-appraisal of the project, which may lead to the replacement of the project or its cancellation.

- Reduction (including elimination) – typical action to reduce risk that can take the form of redesign, more detailed design or further site investigation to improve the information on which estimates and programmes are based. Different methods of construction can also be envisaged to contribute to risk reduction.

- Transfer – involving a different member of the integrated project team, who would be responsible for the consequences should the risk arise. The object of transferring risk is to pass the responsibility to another party that would better able to manage it.

- Retention/acceptance – risks that are not transferred or avoided are retained by the client, although they may have been reduced or shared. These risks must continue to be managed by the client to minimize their likelihood and potential impact. A 'do-nothing' approach is unacceptable. Even when risks have been transferred, the customer still needs to track the management of the risk to ensure that the aims of the project continue to be delivered satisfactorily.

Value Improving Practices in the Life Cycle of Construction Projects

VALUE IMPROVING PRACTICES IN LIFE CYCLE COST AND VALUE MANAGEMENT

The value, or profitability, of construction projects – and, by and large, capital projects – can be enhanced by applying structured solutions collectively referred to as Value Improving Practices (VIPs), in comparison to the application of less profitable, more traditional engineering and Project Management practices. VIPs analyse project characteristics and features that are achieved at recognized optimum times during the life cycles of capital projects.

The AACEI's publication *Total Cost Management Framework* states that:

> *Generally, VIPs should consider cost over the life cycle of the asset and project ... because the ultimate goal of most enterprises is long term profitability. VIPs must also be used in the early design and planning phases because the ability to influence value diminishes rapidly as scope definition and design progress.*

The publication quotes the sentence written in 1989 by the authoritative founder of the correlated disciplines of Value Analysis and Value Engineering, Lawrence D. Miles, who stated in his *Techniques of Value Analysis and Engineering* that the:

> *best value is determined by two considerations: performance and cost.*

Correspondingly, the *Total Cost Management Framework* asserts the following:

> *This statement recognizes that owners rarely are willing to pay any cost for performance and if owners can get the performance at no cost,*

*they will almost certainly be most satisfied. However, very little is free,
and in a competitive environment, the goal is usually to obtain equal or
better performance at a lower cost than before and at a lower cost than
the competition in consideration of risk.*

Applications of VIPs to capital projects have been statistically demonstrated
to markedly enhance project profitability. The term 'Best Practical' or 'Best
in Class' identifies the highest-performing (upper 20 per cent) projects,
where capital costs are reduced by implementing efficient work processes (as
discussed in Chapter 21 of this volume).

When process efficiency is combined with rigorous applications of VIPs,
project cost performance improvements can be expected in terms of capital cost
reductions, allegedly up to 20 per cent. These achievements may derive from
continual adaptation and enhancement of the VIPs themselves to ensure their
extended relevance and capability to improve project performance in parallel
to efforts that can be accomplished by project teams.

There are several classes of VIPs that can affect capital project profitability
above the level that can be reached by the project team on its own. Each VIP
may have a different purpose and focus, which are primarily as follows: facility
quality, technology selection, project process simplification, constructability,
predictive maintenance and waste minimization.

The most appropriate VIPs to be applied to a specific project are selected
during a VIP planning session, taking place right after the start of the project
for the purpose of accommodating the VIP schedule to the overall schedule of
life cycle stages prior to entering the detailed design, tailored to the features of
each individual project.

The cost, schedule and/or performance elements of capital projects are
improved, as reflected in VIPs, using specific non-traditional practices. VIPs
are essential during the preliminary project stages. Formal and documented
practices involve repeatable work processes. Performing VIPs requires enabling
experts who do not belong to the project team.

On the other hand, VIPs are none of the following: merely 'good engineering
practices'; simple brainstorming sessions or strategy sessions; 'business as
usual'; cost reduction/scope reduction exercises; or project readiness/design
reviews.

FACILITY QUALITY VIP

In this class of VIPs, the highest value or profitability is determined (not exclusively) in terms of: capital investment; planned facility life; expandability; operating costs; and environmental controls.

This VIP is used to confirm the best overall project philosophy and to incorporate overall risk concepts in the facility design and operation. The outputs of this VIP assist the Project Management team in updating the project execution plan for each of the preliminary project stages mentioned above. In order to best achieve this purpose, this VIP should be preferably performed in advance of any further VIP effort in the early stages of the project.

TECHNOLOGY SELECTION VIP

The purpose of this VIP is to apply evaluation criteria in accordance with the business objectives of the project in order to identify more effective technologies compared to the current ones in use and consequently to select the most competitive technological solution.

This VIP will eventually produce documents stating which technological assessment criteria are appropriate and to release a prioritized list of technology options for each selected project specification.

The technology selection VIP provides the best results when conducted during the initial phase of the project.

PROCESS SIMPLIFICATION VIP

The primary objective of this VIP is to optimize the construction process so as to ensure the right balance of schedule constraints against the expected facility operability and overall life cycle costs, mainly resulting in the reduction of both investment and operating costs.

Expectations and requirements related to the project processes are systematically differentiated for the purpose of process simplification; expectations are evaluated for their possible elimination, in accordance with stated constraints and priorities.

In more detail, the objectives of this VIP are as follows:

- reduction of capital costs;

- improvement in the project critical path schedule;

- higher process effectiveness;

- reduction of follow-up lifetime costs (specifically, operating and maintenance costs);

- an increase in overall project productivity;

- reduction of waste generation.

Formal workshops are planned to execute process simplification VIPs. They take place at least once in the project preliminary phases, whereas for larger and more complex projects, an earlier process simplification workshop can be appropriately added.

CONSTRUCTABILITY VIP

This VIP is determined by the opportunity of implementing the newest Engineering, Procurement and Construction principles and the associated lessons learned, in accordance with the facility operations and maintenance requirements and for the purpose of improving the scope, cost, schedule, quality and safety of the construction.

In order to specifically recognize this practice as an actual VIP – thus, consistent with the comparison to less profitable, more traditional engineering and Project Management practices, as pointed out previously – profitability improvements are sought above those which the project team will have identified in the course of its ordinary work.

The constructability VIP extends from the beginning of the preliminary project phases through to the completion of the commissioning stage. Its main objective is to optimize the joint utilization of operations, maintenance, engineering, procurement and construction expertise – both on-project and off-project – while adding the following characteristics to the more traditional approach:

- execution of one or more formal facilitated constructability VIP workshops;

- focus on the pertinent aspects of each engineering stage of the project;

- detailed functions review of planning, design, procurement, fabrication and installation to ensure that the aims of lowest capital expenses and the shortest reasonable schedule are safely and successfully achieved;

- appropriate consideration of operability and maintainability with reference to operations and maintenance requirements and available expertise.

Early constructability VIP workshops should be focused on the overall construction project strategies, especially regarding site layout and accessibility in addition to coordination with any existing or nearby facilities.

Constructability VIP workshops in a subsequent project phase should be focused on more detailed arrangements of the site layout and further analyses of schedule constraints and the influence of fabrication processes and available expertise on the expected completion of later construction stages.

Finally, constructability VIP workshops held towards the conclusion of the preliminary phases of the project should be focused on additional provisions for effectively completing a preliminary approach to the detailed EPC stage, in which prior lessons learned will be reviewed and considered for convenient implementation.

PREDICTIVE MAINTENANCE VIP

This VIP is related to the following basic definitions:

- Reliability – the ability of an element to accomplish its stipulated function under fixed conditions or to maintain its quality without perceivable variations under stated conditions of use.

- Durability – the ability of an element to maintain a stated performance level in a specified period of time.

- Duration – a defined period of time in which an element is able to maintain its physical, performance and aesthetical characteristics (this period usually begins when the element is installed or assembled).

Predictive maintenance (from the Latin expression *manu tenere*, that is, 'keeping or putting aside an asset in safe conditions') is a class of preventive maintenance that follows the identification and the measurement of one or more parameters, and the extrapolation of the residual time to failure in accordance with the appropriate models.

The predictive (or condition-based) strategy consists of periodic and pre-planned inspections and assessments to identify the moment in which a remedial action is absolutely required. This action may fall into one of four categories:

- *Time-directed* – when the prevention of a failure is envisaged.

- *Condition-directed* – in order to identify the occurrence of a failure.

- *Failure-finding* – in order to recognize hidden inefficiencies.

- *Run-to-failure* – deliberately deciding not to undertake maintenance until a failure occurs.

Predictive maintenance is different from – and newer than – preventive maintenance, which is limited to periodic inspections and repairs to avoid unplanned breakdowns.

Predictive maintenance has the following benefits:

- it reduces maintenance costs;

- it improves the confidence of extending time intervals between consecutive maintenance actions;

- it improves reliability;

- it provides a more predictable maintenance schedule.

This VIP, if not dictated otherwise by contractor's standards, should preferably be implemented in the feasibility phase of the project.

WASTE MINIMIZATION VIP

This VIP incorporates environmental requirements into the facility design and combines life cycle environmental benefits and positive economic returns by:

- removing or reducing the generation of waste through source reduction;

- recycling by use, re-use or recuperation those potential waste materials/components that cannot be removed or reduced;

- treating all waste that is still generated to reduce volume, toxicity or other harmful effects before storage or disposal.

This VIP, if not dictated otherwise by contractor's standards, should be executed in a formal workshop and preferably implemented in the feasibility phase of the project.

VIP PLANNING AND IMPLEMENTATION

Each VIP has its own unique connotations and should be performed at a certain time and in accordance with a certain procedure in order to produce the best results for the project. VIPs are powerful mechanisms to improve the overall (life cycle) economics of projects.

VIP specialists report that the return on investment (ROI or, more precisely, return on project (ROP), as already mentioned in this text) for the cost of implementing each VIP is usually much greater than for the overall proposed project, even as great as at least an order of magnitude above.

It is essential to reiterate that the benefits achievable from VIPs cannot be realized by merely executing 'good engineering'. The application and implementation of VIPs to a certain project must be intentionally and carefully planned in the initial period of the project; in all cases, this VIP planning meeting should take place immediately after the start of the project.

Before the beginning of a VIP, the goals, objectives and scheduled time for the formal workshop must be agreed upon by the (integrated) project team. The formal workshop is always structured to make the best use of the multi-disciplinary team's time and effort.

Appendix 1

The New ISO Standard 21500 Guidance on Project Management

CARMINE RUSSO

Introduction

We all certainly know of the existence of standards (national and international) and that these have initiated the manifestation of Project Management certifications that mostly target individual professionals rather than organizations. The following are but a few examples: PMP, ISIPM (Italian Institute of Project Management) Basic, PRINCE2®, IPMA and A+.

ISO has published guidance on Project Management, ISO 21500:2012, which was released in September 2012.

Regardless of this orientation, most Project Management standards are process-oriented. For this reason, many companies have developed in-house methodologies that are fundamentally inspired by these standards.

One of the major process-oriented certification bodies that have a considerable influence around the world is the Project Management Institute (PMI®) and its Project Management Body of Knowledge (PMBOK®) Guide. There are other process-oriented certifications in Europe (namely ISIPM and its Guide to Project Management Knowledge). Another well-known European certification is the IPMA Competence Baseline certification (ICB rel.3).

The purpose of this appendix is to emphasize the major similarities and differences between the ANSI and ISO standards, namely between the PMBOK® Guide and ISO 21500:2012 standard.

This appendix will cover the latest (fifth) edition of the PMBOK® Guide.

Summary

The first thing that can be observed is that the issues of the PMBOK® Guide and ISO 21500 standard are very close. In fact, they present a set of processes that have actually been organized in the same way.

By taking a look at the ISO standard, it can be seen that in its 47 pages, it is limited to the introduction of the processes, their inputs and their outputs.

On the other hand, the PMBOK® Guide describes, over more than 450 pages, Project Management processes, their inputs, their outputs and their associated tools and techniques.

If we put it all together in a chronological order, we can see that the ANSI standard appeared earlier than the PMBOK® Guide. The ISO standard has been approved by national committees and was issued in September 2012. The new edition of the PMBOK® Guide was issued at the end of 2012.

Another thing that we realize is that ISO uses most of the PMBOK® Guide processes, but it has introduced minor adaptations: the risk knowledge area has been repositioned, as has human resource management.

A major change is related to stakeholder management; the subject group (knowledge area) has been introduced by ISO and it also appears in the new edition of the PMBOK® Guide. The two processes introduced by ISO in this subject group were two processes of the communication knowledge area of the fourth edition of the PMBOK® Guide.

ISO processes do not make use of the iterative approach of the scope definition, but they are more likely to be oriented towards a cascade approach. Therefore, the ISO standard is perhaps less attractive for organizations that use an agile approach.

Process Organization

The Process Organization of both standards (ANSI and ISO) is structured into Project Management stages and topics.

Table A1.1   The Process Organization (ANSI and ISO)

	ISO 21500	PMBOK® Guide (5th edition)
Topics	10 subject groups	10 knowledge areas
Stages	5 process groups	5 process groups
Processes	39 processes	47 processes

By taking a look at the following scheme, the first noticeable aspect is the introduction of a new knowledge area both in the ISO standard and the fifth edition of the PMBOK® Guide: stakeholder management.

Table A1.2   Comparison of the ISO standard and the PMBOK® Guide

	ISO 21500	PMBOK® Guide (5th edition)
Process Groups	Initiating	Initiating
	Planning	Planning
	Implementing	Executing
	Controlling	Monitoring and controlling
	Closing	Closing

	ISO 21500 subjects	PMBOK® Guide (5th edition) Knowledge Areas
Areas	Integration	Integration
	Stakeholder	—
	Scope	Scope
	Resource	Resource
	Time	Time
	Cost	Cost
	Risk	Risk
	Quality	Quality
	Procurement	Procurement

INTEGRATION

4.3.2	Develop Project Charter	Initiating
4.3.3	Develop Project Plans	Planning

4.3.4	Direct Project Work	Implementing
4.3.5	Control Project Work	Control
4.3.6	Control Changes	Control
4.3.7	Close Project Phase or Project	Closing
4.3.8	Collect Lessons Learned	Closing

STAKEHOLDERS

| 4.3.9 | Identify Stakeholder | Initiating |
| 4.3.10 | Manage Stakeholders | Implementing |

SCOPE

4.3.11	Define Scope	Initiating
4.3.12	Create WBS	Initiating
4.3.13	Define Activities	Initiating
4.3.14	Control Scope	Control

RESOURCE

4.3.15	Establish Project Team	Initiating
4.3.16	Estimate Resources	Planning
4.3.17	Define Project Organization	Planning
4.3.18	Develop Project Team	Implementing
4.3.19	Control Resources	Control
4.3.20	Manage Project Team	Control

TIME

4.3.21	Sequence Activities	Planning
4.3.22	Estimate Activity Durations	Planning
4.3.23	Develop Schedule	Planning
4.3.24	Control Schedule	Control

COST

4.3.25	Estimate Costs	Planning
4.3.26	Develop Budget	Planning
4.3.27	Control Costs	Control

RISK

4.3.28	Identify Risks	Planning
4.3.29	Assess Risks	Planning
4.3.30	Treat Risks	Implementing
4.3.31	Control Risks	Control

QUALITY

4.3.32	Plan Quality	Planning
4.3.33	Perform Quality Assurance	Implementing
4.3.34	Perform Quality Control	Control

PROCUREMENT

4.3.35	Plan Procurements	Planning
4.3.36	Select Suppliers	Implementing
4.3.37	Administer Contracts	Control

COMMUNICATION

4.3.38	Plan Communications	Planning
4.3.39	Distribute Information	Implementing
4.3.40	Manage Communication	Control

ISO 21500:2012 provides guidelines for the management of the project and can be used by any type of organization, including public organizations, armed forces and private communities, or for any type of project, regardless of its complexity, size or duration.

ISO 21500:2012 also provides a high-level description of the concepts and processes that are considered to constitute good practice in Project Management. Projects are placed in the context of programs and portfolios of projects. The standard refers to the project and does not provide detailed guidance on the management of programs and project portfolios: these issues are addressed only in the context of Project Management.

ISO 21500:2012 was published on 4 September 2012 as output from the ISO/PC236 Project Management Committee, which involves more than 50 countries

Table A1.3 ISO 21500 standard knowledge areas vs. processes

Knowledge Areas	Initiating	Planning	Implementing	Controlling	Closing
Integration	4.3.2 Develop Project Charter	4.3.3 Develop Project Plans	4.3.4 Direct Project Work	4.3.5 Control Project Work 4.3.6 Control Changes	4.3.7 Close Project Phase or Project 4.3.8 Collect Lessons Learned
Stakeholders	4.3.9 Identify Stakeholder		4.3.10 Manage Stakeholders		
Scope	4.3.11 Define Scope 4.3.12 Create WBS 4.3.13 Define Activities			4.3.14 Control Scope	
Resource	4.3.15 Establish Project Team	4.3.16 Estimate Resources 4.3.17 Define Project Organization	4.3.18 Develop Project Team	4.3.19 Control Resources 4.3.20 Manage Project Team	
Time		4.3.21 Sequence Activities 4.3.22 Estimate Activity Durations 4.3.23 Develop Schedule		4.3.24 Control Schedule	
Cost		4.3.25 Estimate Costs 4.3.26 Develop Budget		4.3.27 Control Costs	
Risk		4.3.28 Identify Risks 4.3.29 Assess Risks	4.3.30 Treat Risks	4.3.31 Control Risks	
Quality		4.3.32 Plan Quality	4.3.33 Perform Quality Assurance	4.3.34 Perform Quality Control	
Procurement		4.3.35 Plan Procurements	4.3.36 Select Suppliers	4.3.37 Administer Contracts	
Communication		4.3.38 Plan Communications	4.3.39 Distribute Information	4.3.40 Manage Communication	

(including participants and observers). Since 2006, the Committee has had the task of working on the long-awaited standard.

The PMI® has been a major sponsor of the standard. The Committee had been chaired by the British Standards Institute through the ANSI, while the PMI had acted as a secretary. Recalling that the ANSI itself adopted the PMBOK® Guide as a standard for Project Management in 1999, nobody should be surprised to know that the new ISO standard looks very like the PMBOK® Guide. The ANSI represents the interests of 125,000 American companies (including IBM, Microsoft, Apple, Adobe, Cisco, Google, HP, Xerox, Verizon, etc.) and 3.5 million professionals. It is also a founding member of ISO.

The recipients of this standard are:

- managers and sponsors of the project so that they can better understand the principles and practice of Project Management to facilitate the provision of adequate support and guidance for their Project Managers and project teams;

- project managers and project team members so they can have a common basis of comparison for their design standards and practices with those of others;

- organization managers.

Chapter 2 of ISO 21500

The following terms are defined in Chapter 2 of ISO 21500:

- Activity.

- Application area.

- Baseline.

- Change Request.

- Configuration Management.

- Control.

- Corrective Action.

- Critical path.

- Lag.

- Lead.

- Preventive Action.

- Project life cycle.

- Risk register.

- Stakeholder.

- Tender.

- Work Breakdown Structure Dictionary.

Paragraph 3.2 of ISO 21500: 'Project'

A project is a unique set of processes consisting of coordinated and controlled activities with start and finish dates, which are undertaken to achieve an objective.

This definition is an improvement over the corresponding one that is provided by the PMBOK® Guide, which was the last definition stating that a project is executed with the goal of producing 'deliverables'. In particular, the products are not mentioned in the definition of ISO 21500.

However, the definition retains the term 'unique' in relation to the series of project processes, which in fact causes the same problems as those caused by the PMBOK® Guide. When a project begins, all of the project processes are not defined. According to ISO 21500, the set of project processes is defined as a result of the execution of process 4.3.3.

It follows that it is not known whether this set of processes is unique when a project is started. Therefore, strictly speaking, something can be started that is not a project according to this definition.

A Brief Observation on the Conceptual Vision of the ISO 21500 Standard

In the real world, there are generally two types of projects: investments and commercial. From Figure 1 of the standard, referring to the project environment in an organization, it seems that ISO 21500 retains an interest for investment projects.

It seems that deliverables are passed from the organization to operation: only these operations generate benefits! This is not the case in commercial projects, which generate benefits producing directly requested deliverables. This is the main reason for the project execution in an organization (see Section 3.4.3 of ISO 21500).

The Italian (European) Standard UNI EN ISO 9001:2008

Figure A1.1 below reproduces Figure 1 on page 5 of this standard (System of Quality Management Model based on the processes). It shows that customers play a significant role in defining requirements as input elements.

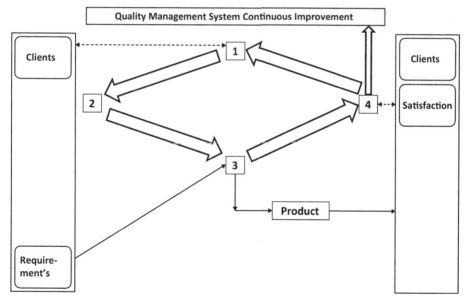

Figure A1.1   ISO 9001:2008

Note: ⟶ Activity with added value
       - - -► Information flow

Monitoring of customer satisfaction requires the evaluation of information relating to customer perceptions as to whether the organization has or has not complied with its requirements.

The model shown covers all the requirements of this International Standard, but does not show processes in a detailed manner.

Management's Responsibility[1] – Resource Management[2] – Product Realization[3] – Measurement, Analysis and Improvement[4] all contribute to continuous improvement of the quality management system.

It is also possible to apply to all processes the methodology known as 'Plan-Do-Check-Act' (PDCA). This methodology can be briefly described as follows:

- Plan: establish the objectives and processes necessary to deliver results in accordance with customer requirements and the policies of the organization.

- Do: implement the processes.

- Check: monitor the processes and product against the policies, objectives and requirements for the product and report the results.

- Act: take action to continually improve process performance.

Table A1.4   ISO 21500 and PMBOK: Comparison between process groups

	ISO 21500	PMBOK® Guide (5th edition)
Process groups	1. Initiating	1. Initiating
	2. Planning	2. Planning
	3. Implementing	3. Executing
	4. Controlling	4. Monitoring and controlling
	5. Closing	5. Closing

As can be seen, both standards divide project processes into five groups. The only difference is in the names.

Table A1.5   ISO 21500 and PMBOK: Comparison between knowledge areas

ISO 21500 subjects	PMBOK® Guide Knowledge Areas
Integration	Integration
Stakeholder	—
Scope	Scope
Resource	Resource
Time	Time
Cost	Cost
Risk	Risk
Quality	Quality
Procurement	Procurement
Communications	Communications

It can also be seen that:

- the ISO standard is based on the PMBOK® Guide;

- ISO 21500 adds 'Stakeholder' to the nine knowledge areas of PMBOK®;

- the Human Resource Area has been renamed 'Resource' in order to cover both types: human and others;

- the knowledge areas are called 'subjects'.

ISO 21500 and PMBOK: Comparison between Processes

The structure of the description of processes in ISO 21500 differs from that in the PMBOK® Guide. The main difference is that ISO 21500 does not provide the description of the tools and techniques.

The description of each process in ISO 21500 consists of a simple general description and a table containing the primary inputs and outputs.

The descriptions are substantially shorter than those of the PMBOK®Guide: in practice, for two ISO processes, you only need one page, while the PMBOK® Guide takes several pages to describe a process.

Table A1.6   Integration – stakeholder

ISO 21500	PMBOK® Guide
4.3.2 Develop Project Charter	4.1 Develop Project Charter
4.3.3 Develop Project Plans	4.2 Develop Project Management Plan
4.3.4 Direct Project Work	4.3 Direct and Manage Project Execution
4.3.5 Control Project Work	4.4 Monitor and Control Project Work
4.3.6 Control Changes	4.5 Perform Integrated Change Control
4.3.7 Close Project Phase or Project	4.6 Close Project or Phase
4.3.8 Collect Lessons Learned	

ISO 21500	PMBOK® Guide
4.3.9 Identify Stakeholders	10.1 Identify Stakeholders (taken from Communication Knowledge Area)
4.3.10 Manage Stakeholders	10.4 Manage Stakeholder Expectations (taken from Communication Knowledge Area)

Table A1.7   Scope – resource

ISO 21500	PMBOK® Guide
4.3.11 Define Scope	5.1 Collect Requirements
	5.2 Define Scope
4.3.12 Create Work Breakdown Structure	5.3 Create WBS
4.3.13 Define Activities	6.1 Define Activities (taken from Time Management Knowledge Area)
	5.4 Verify Scope
4.3.14 Control Scope	5.5 Control Scope

ISO 21500	PMBOK® Guide
	9.1 Develop Human Resource Plan
4.3.15 Establish Project Team	9.2 Acquire Project Team
4.3.16 Estimate Resources	6.3 Estimate Activity Resources (taken from Time Management Knowledge Area)

Table A1.7   Continued

ISO 21500	PMBOK® Guide
4.3.17 Define Project Organization	
4.3.18 Develop Project Team	9.3 Develop Project Team
4.3.19 Control Resources	
4.3.20 Manage Project Team	9.4 Manage Project Team

Table A1.8   Time – cost

ISO 21500	PMBOK® Guide
Moved to Scope subject	6.1 Define Activities
4.3.21 Sequence Activities	6.2 Sequence Activities
Moved to Resource subject	6.3 Estimate Activity Resources
4.3.22 Estimate Activity Durations	6.4 Estimate Activity Durations
4.3.23 Develop Schedule	6.5 Develop Schedule
4.3.24 Control Schedule	6.6 Control Schedule

ISO 21500	PMBOK® Guide
4.3.25 Estimate	7.1 Estimate Costs
4.3.26 Develop Budget	7.2 Determine Budget
4.3.27 Control Costs	7.3 Control Costs

Table A1.9   Risk – quality

ISO 21500	PMBOK® Guide
	12.1 Plan Risk Management
4.3.28 Identify Risks	12.2 Identify Risks
4.3.29 Assess Risks	12.3 Perform Qualitative Risk Analysis
	12.4 Perform Quantitative Risk Analysis
4.3.30 Treat Risks	12.5 Plan Risk Responses
4.3.31 Control Risks	12.6 Monitor and Control Risks

ISO 21500	PMBOK® Guide
4.3.32 Plan Quality	8.1 Plan Quality

Table A1.9   Continued

ISO 21500	PMBOK® Guide
4.3.33 Perform Quality Assurance	8.2 Perform Quality Assurance
4.3.34 Perform Quality Control	8.3 Perform Quality Control

Table A1.10   Procurement – communication

ISO 21500	PMBOK® Guide
4.3.35 Plan Procurement	12.1 Plan Procurements
4.3.36 Select Suppliers	12.2 Conduct Procurements
4.3.37 Administer Contracts	12.3 Administer Procurements
	12.4 Close Procurements

ISO 21500	PMBOK® Guide
Moved to Stakeholder subject	10.1 Identify Stakeholders
4.3.38 Plan Communications	10.2 Plan Communications
4.3.39 Distribute Information	10.3 Distribute Information
	10.5 Report Performance
Moved to Stakeholder subject	10.4 Manage Stakeholder Expectations
4.3.40 Manage Communication	

Conclusions

Without going into the details of each process, one thing that seems to be emphasized in ISO 21500 is the collection of lessons learned, which is a dedicated process.

This is a very important innovation because the logic of giving importance to the 'past' is finally recognized and standardized.

Particular attention is given to the stakeholders that make up a separate knowledge area. This is because the Project Manager's job is essentially a matter of communication and relationships.

ISO 21500 provides 39 processes, while there are 42 processes in the PMBOK® Guide. The 39 ISO 21500 processes have their direct equivalents in the PMBOK® Guide. Four processes were moved between subjects. Four pairs of processes in the PMBOK® Guide have been merged into four individual processes in ISO 21500. Two PMBOK® Guide processes were not placed in ISO 21500. Four new processes have been introduced in ISO 21500. They are:

- 4.3.8   Collect Lessons Learned.

- 4.3.17   Define Project Organization.

- 4.3.19   Control Resources.

- 4.3.40   Manage Communication.

Appendix 2

Project Optimization through AHP Decision Support Methods

BARBARA BOCCASINI

Introduction to Decision Support Methods

The decision-making field presents two main branches. The first one uses complete transitive aggregation methods defined as compensatory, while the second one is based on a finite discrimination capability of the decision maker and uses methods defined as non-compensatory. In particular, the compensatory methods:

- are based on the assumption that the decision maker has a perfect discrimination capability;

- present a preferences system that is completely transitive (if a>b and b>c, then a>c);

- have a resulting order defined as complete.

Conversely, the non-compensatory methods:

- are based on a finite discrimination capability of the decision maker;

- present a preferences system that is intransitive (even though a>b and b>c, you cannot affirm that a>c).

This appendix deals with Multi-Attribute or Multi-Criteria Decision Methods (MADM) and, in particular, with the Analytic Hierarchy Process (AHP) method, which is very adaptable and can be used in different fields such as the determination of the cost/benefit ratio, intervention strategies, Project Management scheduling, etc. A limitation of this method is due to the arbitrary choice of the numerical scale used and to the large number of pairwise comparisons to manage.

The Semantic Saaty Scale

The main principle of MADM methods is a scalar approach for qualitative attributes: each attribute will be associated with a list of arbitrary intervals that are able to preserve the attribute order. In general, MADM methods are based on three macro-steps:

- the identification of criteria and attributes;

- the selection of a series of possible alternatives;

- the evaluation of attribute values for the different alternatives.

The importance of the AHP method is due to the introduction of a new value scale that is able to translate comparative qualitative appreciation into quantitative terms: the Semantic Saaty Scale created by Thomas Lorie Saaty in the late 1970s. In order to explain the principle behind this scale, we will

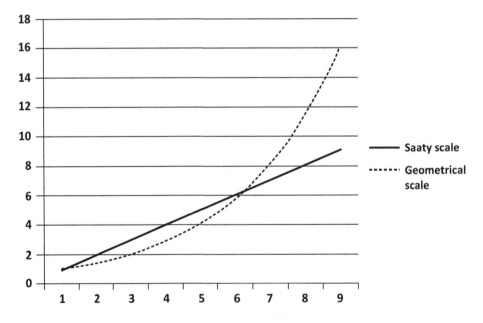

Figure A2.1   The Saaty scale and the geometrical scale

first compare it with the geometrical scale. Figure A2.1 on the previous page provides a graphical comparison between these two scales.

To perform a sort of translation from qualitative terms to numerical values, Saaty established a finite set of numerical values composed by integers from one to nine. Table A2.1 below shows the correspondences among the semantic scale, the Saaty scale and the geometrical scale.

Semantic evaluation	Numerical Saaty values	Numerical geometrical values
equal	1	1
	2	$1*\sqrt{2}$
low	3	2
	4	$2*\sqrt{2}$
significant	5	4
	6	$4*\sqrt{2}$
strong	7	8
	8	$8*\sqrt{2}$
absolute	9	16

Table A2.1   Correspondences among scales

Introduction to the AHP Method

Justifying the AHP acronym, the AHP method:

- is analytic because it breaks down the problem into its constitutive elements;

- is a hierarchy method because it structures these constitutive elements in a hierarchical manner referring to the arrangement of the main objective and sub-objectives;

- will process judgements and data in order to reach the final result.

This method makes it possible to manage a certain amount of incoherence due to an acceptable degree of incorrect evaluations made by the decision maker; this objective is achieved by the decomposition of macro-problems into different micro-problems that will as a result be simpler to manage. The three main axioms for this approach are:

- reciprocity: it is possible to affirm that if A = 2*B, then B = ½*A;

- homogeneity: elements to be compared will not be too dissimilar;

- interdependence: at each level of the hierarchy, judgements about objectives will be independent from judgements about objectives or alternatives pertaining to lower levels.

The goal of the AHP is to achieve the macro-objective by rational decisions about a large number of micro-objectives: this method provides the decision maker with the opportunity to measure and synthesize the large number of factors contributing to the solution of a complex problem and, as such, enables the identification of the result which best meets the multitude of objectives by taking charge of a series of factors/criteria or sub-criteria.

The AHP decision-making approach combines several existing tools, such as consistency evaluation, pairwise comparison and the eigenvectors method, and uses qualitative judgements expressed by numbers. After having defined the problem and identified a list of factors to be considered, the AHP method contemplates the following steps:

1. organization of the problem into a hierarchical structure (dominance hierarchy);

2. execution of a pairwise comparison related to the importance of each factor for each level and group of the hierarchy;

3. insertion of dominance coefficients in a pairwise comparison matrix;

4. determination of a consistency ratio;

5. calculation of local and global weights representing the priorities.

The Dominance Hierarchies

Through a decomposition of the problem, starting from the reciprocal relationship among all the variables involved in the decision-making process, we will be able to build a structure in which the information can be represented in an orderly way that defines a dominance hierarchy. This process can be executed by either following a bottom-up approach or a top-down approach, but the latter is the most commonly used approach. The decomposition structure is obtained by specifying:

- the global objective (super-criterion);

- the evaluation criteria;

- the sub-criteria (each criterion has some);

- the possible alternatives (different solutions identified for the problem we are dealing with).

Assuming 'i' and 'j' as two indexes indicating two possible alternatives and 'a' as the value of the comparison, a_{ij} will be the ratio of the relative value of one alternative ('i' alternative) with respect to another ('j' alternative).

The pairwise comparison provides a priority scale defined by compiling a matrix composed by $n*(n-1)/2$ elements with:

$$a_{jk} = a_{ik}/a_{ij}$$

where a_{jk} represents the ratio of the relative value of a certain property of the elements to be compared two by two (pairwise comparison).

Table A2.2 below provides the meaning of the matrix elements.

Table A2.2   Relative importance scale (semantic Saaty scale)

Importance intensity a_{ij}	Definition	Explication
1	Same importance	Activities that equally contribute to the objective
3	Weak importance of one over the other	One activity slightly preferred to the other
5	Essential or strong importance	Experience and judgment strongly prefer one activity to the other
7	Proved importance	One activity is strongly preferred and its supremacy can be demonstrated in practice

Table A2.2   Continued

Importance intensity a_{ij}	Definition	Explication
9	Absolute importance	Evidence of the importance of one activity over the other is as high as possible
2, 4, 6, 8	Intermediate values of judgements between two adjacent judgements	Compromise is needed
Inverse of non-zero values	If the i activity has a non-zero value when compared with j activity, then j activity has the reciprocal value when compared to i activity	N/A

Normalization

After calculating the priority vectors, we will apply a normalization to the matrices: each element in the matrices will be divided by the sum of all of them, which means dividing each column element by the sum of all elements in the same column.

In this way, the priority vectors will be obtained. The fundamental scale is then established by taking the lower measure as a unit of measurement and by comparing all other measures to it.

In order to perform a correct comparison, the set of elements to be compared will be homogeneous:

- the dominance of the largest element will not be more than nine times greater than the dominance of the smallest one (if this requirement is not satisfied, the group will be split into two or more groups);

- on the other hand, elements of a group will not be too similar in terms of dominances (if this requirement is not satisfied, other elements will be introduced into the same group).

This step is achieved by calculating a vector representing the order of the alternatives for each possible criterion of comparison and leads to a set of K sorting vectors. Each single scale enables the determination of an order of the alternative importance referred to every single criterion. These scales are usually not sufficient to define a global order among possible alternatives:

therefore, the criteria will be ordered by relative importance with respect to the super-criterion (the final objective called 'goal') by another vector which is called the criteria order vector; this criteria order vector is defined starting from the square matrix of their pairwise comparison. Figure A2.2 represents an illustration of possible decision-making options.

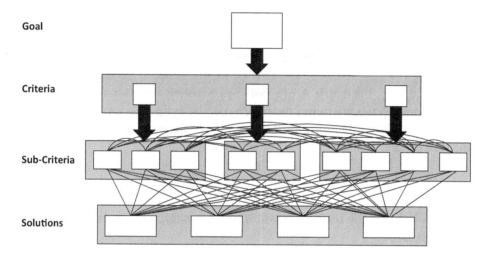

Figure A2.2   Illustration of decision-making options

This decomposition aims at preparing the following analysis founded on the pairwise comparison.

The Pairwise Comparison

The Saaty theory is based on the assumption that the decision maker normally concentrates on the solution of many partial problems instead of deducing the final solution, taking into account all of the problem aspects.

This approach provides the opportunity to define a set of K square positive and reciprocal matrices **A** in which, for a defined k, a certain matrix element (a_{ij}) is a number representing the decision-maker's preference of the i alternative over the j alternative.

These matrices will be derived from the pairwise comparison between all the K criteria and indicates the relative importance of criteria in terms of achieving the global objective (super-criterion or goal). These matrixes, in order to grant the symmetry of importance judgments, will be squared, positive and reciprocal.

In fact, the elements which fill these matrixes will be the dominance coefficients a_{ij} to ensure that:

- if $i = j$, then $a_{ij} = 1$;

- for each value of i and j, $a_{ji} = 1/a_{ij}$.

In case $a_{ji} \cdot a_{jk} = a_{ik}$, the matrix $\mathbf{A} = (a_{ij})$ will be consistent and its main eigenvector will be equal to n. Otherwise, the matrix will be simply reciprocal. The ratio scale comes from the reciprocal pairwise comparison matrix by solving the following:

$$\sum_{j=1}^{n} a_{ij} w_f = \lambda_{max} w_i$$

whose solution is the main eigenvector; the normalization, in this case, is not needed because:

$$\sum_{i=1}^{n} w_i = 1$$

The generic eigenvector of the equation can be found by the perturbation of the following consistence formulation:

$$AW = \begin{array}{c} \begin{array}{ccc} A_1 & \cdots \cdots & A_n \end{array} \\ \begin{array}{c} A_1 \\ \cdots \\ \cdots \\ A_n \end{array} \begin{bmatrix} W_1/W_2 & \cdots & \cdots & W_1/W_n \\ \cdots & \cdots & \cdots & \cdots \\ \cdots & \cdots & \cdots & \cdots \\ W_n/W_1 & \cdots & \cdots & W_n/W_n \end{bmatrix} \begin{bmatrix} W_1 \\ \cdots \\ \cdots \\ W_n \end{bmatrix} = n \begin{bmatrix} W_1 \\ \cdots \\ \cdots \\ W_n \end{bmatrix} = nW \end{array}$$

in which $\mathbf{A}$ has been multiplied on the right by the weight transposed vector:

$$w = (w_1, w_2, \ldots, w_n),$$

and the result of this multiplication is:

$$\mathbf{A}w = nw$$

As a consequence, in order to recover the ratio scale, we will solve the following homogeneous system of linear equations:

$$(\mathbf{A} - n\mathbf{I})\, w = 0$$

This homogeneous system has a non-trivial solution if and only if the determinant of $(\mathbf{A}\text{-}n\mathbf{I})$ is null, which means that n is an eigenvalue of matrix **A**. As **A** has unitary rank, because every line is a constant multiple of first line, all eigenvalues will be null except one. Moreover, as the sum of the eigenvalues of a matrix is equal to the sum of the diagonal elements, in our case, n is an eigenvalue for **A** and there is only one non-trivial solution.

Local Weights Evaluation

If the matrix **A** is not consistent, the system of linear equations defined above is not to be applied and two important mathematics results coming from the matrix theory will be used:

- If $\lambda_1, \lambda_2, \ldots, \lambda_n$ satisfy the equation $Ax = \lambda x$ (which means that $\lambda_1, \lambda_2, \ldots, \lambda_n$ are the n eigenvalues of A) and for each value of i, we have $a_{ii} = 1$, then:

$$\sum_{i=1}^{N} \lambda_i = n \ (i = 1, \ldots, n)$$

- If we slightly modify the a_{ij} values of a positive and reciprocal matrix, the corresponding values of eigenvalues will slightly and continually vary.

As a consequence, we can affirm that when all elements on the main diagonal of **A** are equal to 1, the matrix is consistent; so, slightly modifying a_{ij} values, the main eigenvalue λ_{max} of **A** has a value which is very close to n while the other eigenvalues are close to zero.

To solve our problem, we will then identify a vector w which satisfies the equation:

$$\mathbf{A}w = \lambda_{max}\, w.$$

There are three possible methods to determine the local weights:

- The absolute method – a scale made by a sorted set of levels (for example, excellent, good, satisfactory, not satisfactory, poor, very bad) representing the degree of satisfaction of the decision maker assigned to each final objective. This scale may be different depending on the objectives to be reached. First, the local weights of final objectives are to be determined with the main eigenvector technique. Then, we will evaluate the weights of the levels associated with each final objective using the same technique (through the pairwise comparison of these levels and applying the main eigenvector technique). The local weights of the actions (representing the possible alternatives) will not be evaluated by comparing the actions pairwise, but assigning to each action the weight of the level that best represents the action performance related to the considered objective. With this method, the degree of acceptability of an action will be judged using the standards (levels).

- The distributive method – the actions are compared pairwise with reference to the final objectives. Their local weights, evaluated with the main eigenvector technique, will be normalized so that their sum will be equal to 1. This method makes it possible to establish the action priority in case the co-presence of similar actions (or copies of the same action) structurally modifies the preference.

- The ideal method – the local weights of the actions, once evaluated, will be normalized by dividing by the weight of the highest value action (therefore, for each final objective, the best action weight is 1). This method will be used when we decide to choose the best action independently of the number of existing copies of the same action (for example, in the event of the purchase of a computer or a car).

Global Weights Evaluation

This is the final step common to all the three different techniques used to calculate the above-mentioned local weights, that is, to calculate the global weights or the priorities of the actions applying the principle of the hierarchical composition in order to evaluate the importance of each element with reference to the goal. Each element local weight is multiplied by those of the corresponding higher-level elements and the resulting products are to be summed. Proceeding top-down, local weights of each element of the hierarchy will be progressively transformed into global weights. The global weights of the elements situated at the basis of the hierarchy, at the level following that of the final objectives, represent the main result of our evaluation.

As the final elements are actions to be taken, global weights make it possible to establish an order of preference: an action, a plan or a project will be preferred to another when its global weight is higher than the other.

Now, we need to make a distinction between the intrinsic weight and the specific weight:

- The intrinsic weight – this weight is a constant value in a scale which reflects the importance that the decision maker assigns to an objective with reference to the higher-level objective (the goal) on the basis of a system of values. In order to assess the intrinsic weights of the objectives, the decision maker has to take into account the context of the environmental characteristics and the specific decisional situation (different environmental component vulnerability, economic or political problems, etc.), but should not consider the performances and the properties of the actions to be evaluated.

- The specific weight – in the distributive and the ideal methods, the value and the meaning of the specific weight depend on the type of normalization chosen for the identification of the local weights of the actions. When the sum of the local weights of the actions is equal to 1 (distributive mode), the objective specific weights reflect the importance of action performances, considered altogether and with respect to the objectives. When the weight of the best action for every single objective is 1 (ideal mode), the specific weights reflect the importance of best performances of the actions on the different objectives. In both cases, the specific weights only depend on the full set of actions to evaluate and on their performances. When this set changes, the objective specific weights can also change.

In the distributive and the ideal modes, the normalization cancels out the differences of the discrimination between the objectives; in other words, the differences of the performances of the action referred to the objectives, once measured with their normalized values, lose their discrimination capacity. In order to correctly evaluate the local weights of the objectives (w) and to avoid the problem of the normalization of the local weights of the actions, we will multiply the objectives local intrinsic weights by their corresponding specific weights and will then normalize the resulting products. The intrinsic weights of the objectives will be calculated by defining the pairwise comparison matrix and then applying the main eigenvector technique. In order to determine the dominance coefficients, the decision maker will answer the following questions: which of the two objectives is the most important to follow in order to achieve the goal? To what extent? In order to calculate the specific weights, the technique is the same, but the questions to be answered are: given these two objectives, for which of them are the overall performances of the actions better? To what extent? If the weights of the actions have been normalized so that the value of the best performance is equal to 1 for each objective (ideal mode), the questions to be answered are: between the higher performances of actions that are referred to in these two objectives, which one is the best? To what extent? If the weights of the actions have been normalized in such a way that the value of the best performance, for every objective, is equal to 1 (ideal mode), the question to be answered is: which is the best among the higher performances of the actions referring to in the two objectives? To what extent?

The Consistency Index

It is now appropriate to establish whether the weights obtained actually reflect the evaluation of the person who made the comparison – in other words, if and to what extent the values of the ratios w_i / w_j, calculated after having determined the main eigenvector w, are consistent with the a_{ij} expert estimations. For this purpose, the AHP method uses the following consistency index (CI), which is useful to measure the gap between these two values:

$$CI = \frac{\lambda_{max} - n}{n - 1}$$

The AHP method assumes that CI has to be compared with the Random Index (RI); the latter is obtained by calculating the average of the values of CI of several reciprocal matrixes of the same order, the coefficients of which are generated in a random manner by a computer.

If the CI value exceeds the threshold conventionally established at 10 per cent of the RI value, the deviation from the condition of perfect consistency cannot be accepted and decision makers will modify their judgements, trying to increase the consistency, partially or totally modifying its a_{ij} values. This procedure is to be reiterated.

There is a simplified way to calculate the Consistency Ratio (CR) which uses the Random Consistency Index (RCI): the method simply consists of dividing the CI values by the RCI values shown below:

n	1	2	3	4	5	6	7	8	9
RCI	0	0	0.58	0.90	1.12	1.24	1.32	1.41	1.45

Conclusions

The AHP method suggests two different ways to reach the conclusion:

- The distributive synthesis – in the event of normalized weights of the alternatives for each of the objectives, the AHP method structures all alternatives into a priority scale based on their relative value. This kind of synthesis is recommended in planning, in resource allocation in case of scarcity of resources or, more generally, in case the alternatives to be considered present a unique value for many objectives and there are no similar actions or copies of actions to be compared.

- The ideal synthesis – in the event that the most preferred alternatives in a group receive their priority from the node immediately above it, this synthesis method is to be preferred as it is used to choose a single best alternative. We will use ideal synthesis when the interest is addressed to higher-range alternatives or when there are different alternatives with the same weight (some alternatives can also virtually be copies of other existing alternatives).

The distributive AHP mode produces preference scores by normalizing the performance scores: this method consists of taking the performance score from each possible alternative and dividing it by the sum of the performances of all the alternatives under the same criterion. This means that the preference of each alternative may increase when the score of another alternative is reduced or that some other alternatives have to be deleted.

The ideal mode compares each performance score to a benchmark such as the performance of the best alternative under the considered criterion. In this way, the preference for the alternative taken into consideration is independent of the performances of other alternatives (obviously with the exception of the one taken as the benchmark).

Finally, the distributive mode should be used when the decision maker is interested in the gap between the importance of the different alternatives with reference to the criterion. The ideal synthesis mode should be preferred when interested in how each alternative behaves towards a fixed reference (benchmark). For example, the distributive mode is recommended when the decision maker estimates that the preference for an alternative which has a superior rank for a criterion increases when the performances of all other alternatives of lower rank decrease.

Appendix 3

The PILOT Method and Software Tools for Decision Making

BARBARA BOCCASINI

Introduction to the PILOT Method

In this appendix we will illustrate an example of Decision Support analysis. The method that will be illustrated is called PILOT (Product Investigation, Learning and Optimization Tool); among the improvement methods, this one belongs to the family of the optimal design solution choice methods. This method has been designed by W. Wimmer of the University of Vienna and was introduced for the first time at an international conference in Glasgow in August 2001.

Wimmer presented his method with the intention of using it for development sustainability and ecodesign, but the PILOT method is a versatile method which can be used for any project optimization. In fact, this method allows decision makers to use qualitative information as a numerical and mathematical support.

The PILOT method represents a development of the Ecodesign Checklist Method (ECM). Compared to the ECM, this new method provides a wide number of focal points, different work approaches and a detailed description aimed at exhaustively explaining each identified focal point.

The PILOT project has been developed by the Australian Government and has been successfully tested by some companies before being sold as a CD-ROM. This CD-ROM, along with the associated book, contains different guidelines, each of which presents:

- specific information about the goal to be achieved;

- interdependences with other guidelines;

- an example explaining the meaning of the guideline;

- a useful question supporting the assignment of the preferences;

- a general question aimed to help realize the project draft.

The PILOT method can be divided into three principal sub-methods:

- The Product/Project Life Cycle (PLC) – this is normally used during the learning phase in order to analyse the whole life cycle of a product or a project (typically in the post-project phase or in the revision phase). Of the three sub-methods, this is the most frequently used because it takes into consideration every aspect of the entire project life cycle; however, if the intention is to focus on a particular aspect of the problem, this method would not be the best to employ compared to the other methods because it normally emphasizes all possible problems. In addition, deep competences about all PLC aspects are needed in order for individual experts to use this sub-method so that, in most cases, it requires a team to deal with the detailed procedures (checklists).

- The Product/Project Development Process (PDP) – this sub-method focuses on aspects relevant to specific development phases. Before using this sub-method, the product or project nature will be identified. This method is mainly used to establish a strategy for project or product optimization.

- Product/Project Development Strategies (PDS) – this sub-method is used to classify products or projects by selecting some characteristics and then suggesting possible optimization strategies. It can be used for new projects because it makes it possible to consider all the aspects and is recommended when quick and final decisions are needed.

From the ECM method, the PILOT method inherited the checklists which might be used in the industrial field by working teams or interdisciplinary groups and can be used to make an estimation of a project as well as to provide new considerations on how to optimize projects.

As well as for other decision support methods, in the PILOT method, the first step consists of creating a precise structure in which all the information about the project has to be organized. In the next step, the decision maker has to choose a value representing the preference of each criterion; for this activity, the PILOT method uses checklists.

The checklists represent a mechanism used to identify project characteristics by compiling a matrix which is presented as a questionnaire allowing experts to numerically evaluate different aspects by simply answering questions. Optimization strategies, along with the associated guidelines, are related to individual project characteristics.

There are different kinds of checklists depending on the knowledge of the decision maker: there are specific checklists for engineers, designers, managers, etc.

Working with checklists means performing the following five steps:

1. assigning an importance rate (W = weight) to every single estimate question (10 if very relevant, 5 if not very relevant and 0 if not influential);

2. assigning an estimate (E) by answering the questions (yes = 1; enough = 2; not much = 3; no = 4);

3. prioritizing assignment by multiplying the importance rate of the estimate (P = priority = W*E);

4. realizing a risk evaluation: approximate estimation of time, costs, technological problems in measurements, etc.;

5. assigning responsibilities and deadlines: for each value, a realization progress owner and a deadline should be identified.

Higher priority values will result from a high importance rate (W) and a low estimate (E). Figure A3.1 on the next page shows an example of a possible problem-solving situation with given values for W and E.

Only higher priority measures will be considered and only risk involved in their realization will be taken into consideration. Therefore, starting from the

Criterion	Sub criterion	W		E		P = W * E	
A	A1	W_{A1}	10	E_{A1}	4	P_{A1}	40
	A2	W_{A2}	5	E_{A2}	2	P_{A2}	10
	A3	W_{A3}	10	E_{A3}	3	P_{A3}	30
	A4	W_{A4}	5	E_{A4}	4	P_{A4}	20
	A5	W_{A5}	0	E_{A5}	4	P_{A5}	0
	A6	W_{A6}	5	E_{A6}	3	P_{A6}	15
B	B1	W_{B1}	5	E_{B1}	4	P_{B1}	20
	B2	W_{B2}	5	E_{B2}	3	P_{B2}	15
	B3	W_{B3}	0	E_{B3}	3	P_{B3}	0
	B4	W_{B4}	5	E_{B4}	2	P_{B4}	10
	B5	W_{B5}	10	E_{B5}	2	P_{B5}	20
C	C1	W_{C1}	5	E_{C1}	4	P_{C1}	20
	C2	W_{C2}	10	E_{C2}	3	P_{C2}	30
	C3	W_{C3}	10	E_{C3}	1	P_{C3}	10
	C4	W_{C4}	5	E_{C4}	1	P_{C4}	5
	C5	W_{C5}	10	E_{C5}	3	P_{C5}	30
	C6	W_{C6}	5	E_{C6}	2	P_{C6}	10
	C7	W_{C7}	10	E_{C7}	4	P_{C7}	40
D	D1	W_{D1}	5	E_{D1}	1	P_{D1}	5
	D2	W_{D2}	10	E_{D2}	3	P_{D2}	30
	D3	W_{D3}	5	E_{D3}	2	P_{D3}	10
	D4	W_{D4}	0	E_{D4}	3	P_{D4}	0
E	E1	W_{E1}	10	E_{E1}	2	P_{E1}	20
	E2	W_{E2}	5	E_{E2}	2	P_{E2}	10
	E3	W_{E3}	10	E_{E3}	3	P_{E3}	30
	E4	W_{E4}	5	E_{E4}	4	P_{E4}	20
	E5	W_{E5}	10	E_{E5}	4	P_{E5}	40

Figure A3.1   Calculation of priority values

situation illustrated in Figure A3.2, we will reach a smaller set of sub-criteria (questions) to take into consideration, as shown in Figure A3.3 opposite. The purpose of this approach is to identify, as early as possible, those measures that represent a substantial improvement and, at the same time, those measures that can be implemented with an affordable risk. The correlation of high-priority measures to the possible improvement actions will enable us to realize a list of the possible improvements ordered by importance; after having evaluated the risks, the possible actions will be realized in the order given by this result.

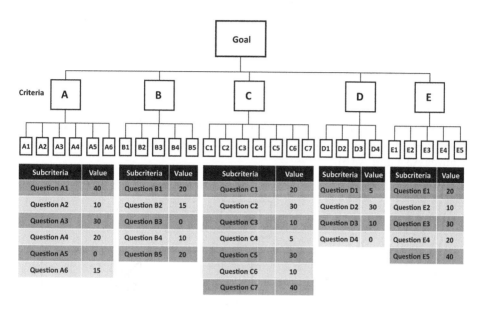

Figure A3.2   Arrangement of criteria and sub-criteria – step 1

From Figure A3.2, deleting all measures which have P < 20, we will obtain Figure A3.3.

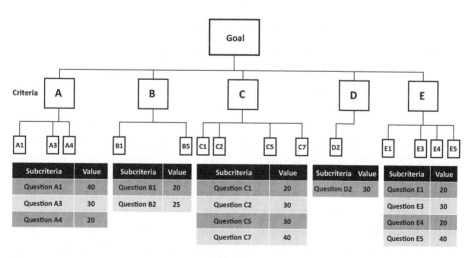

Figure A3.3   Arrangement of criteria and sub-criteria – step 2

The Dominance Hierarchy

By performing a Life Cycle Analysis for a project, we will be able to find out a group of criteria to be considered in our decision-making problem (for example, if we need to identify which project phase has the main impact with reference to a known criterion, the project phases can represent the criteria).

Starting from the whole set of criteria and sub-criteria, in order to create a dominance hierarchy, we will start from the answered checklist and will consider only the sub-criteria (questions) which have reached a high evaluation (answers); this will be done by choosing a minimum value for the answers (see Figures A3.4 and A3.5).

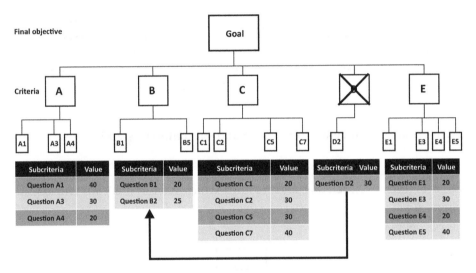

Figure A3.4   Arrangement of criteria and sub-criteria – step 3

Using some precautions, we may homogenize the number of sub-criteria making up the different criteria. The basic idea is to identify those criteria which have a very small number of sub-criteria and to move these sub-criteria under other criteria: in our example, we will merge together criteria B and D so that the all remaining criteria will have three or four sub-criteria each (Figure A3.4).

As will be seen later, this step is important to allow the assumption that each criterion has the same weight with reference to the main objective (the goal). We will now analyse the following situation in order to draft a correlation table.

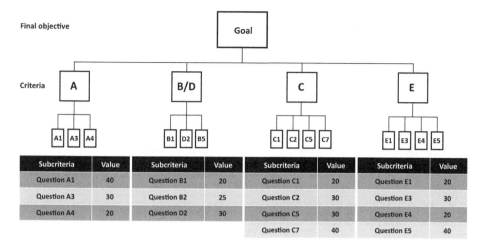

Figure A3.5   Arrangement of criteria and sub-criteria – step 4

The Correlation Table

The table we are going to fill will be a correlation table that considers all possible design modifications we can apply influencing every PLC phase of a generic project; the proposed modifications are shown in the headings of the columns, while the rows contain a high-priority measure. In this correlation table, each box contains a value representing the correlation index between the measures

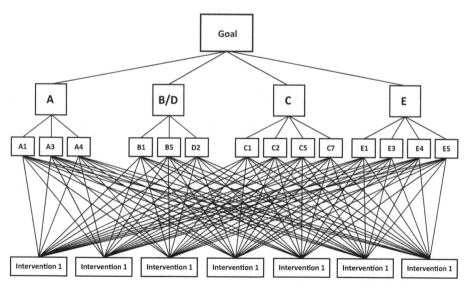

Figure A3.6   Arrangement of criteria and sub-criteria – step 5

(sub-criteria corresponding to the row) and possible interventions (actions to take corresponding to the column).

The realization of this measure can be related in different ways to the possible modifications to apply: a higher correlation between measures indicates a higher level of interest to apply to the specified modification. In our example, adding to the graph seven possible interventions to be compared with all the sub-criteria defined, the situation will be as follows. As we can see in Figure A3.7, the correlation index can assume three possible values:

- 1 if there is a strong correlation between the measure and the intervention;

- 0.5 if there is a medium correlation between the measure and the intervention;

- 0 if there is no correlation between the measure and the intervention or the correlation is very low.

Sub criteria	W	1	2	3	4	5	6	7
A1	40							
A3	30							
A4	20							
B1	20							
B5	20							
D2	20							
C1	30							
C2	30							
C5	40							
C7	30							
E1	20							
E3	30							
E4	20							
E5	40							
TOTAL W	—	170	165	235	185	145	200	125

Figure A3.7   Correlation index

Key: 1 ▮ 2 ▮ 3

The last row of the figure summarizes the global value of each intervention which is obtained, for each column, by summing the products of every index I_x by the corresponding measure importance rate W_x; for each intervention, we will obtain, if n is the number of the sub-criteria:

$$W_{TOT} = \sum_{x=1}^{n} = (I_x * W_x)$$

The Comparison Matrix

In order to fill the comparison matrix, we can start from the simplified correlation table containing only the resulting data relevant to the specific application. This table will be normalized in such a way that the sum of every row is equal to 1. Note that if a sub-criterion has correlation indexes equal to zero for each possible intervention, these measures will be deleted from the table and will not appear in the comparison matrix. In Figure A3.8 below, we can see, for our example, the corresponding matrix that contains consistency index values calculated by dividing each index by the sum of every index in the same row.

Sub criteria	Int. 1	Int. 2	Int. 3	Int. 4	Int. 5	Int. 6	Int. 7
A1	0,29	0,14	0,29	0	0,14	0,14	0
A3	0	0	0,2	0,2	0	0,4	0,2
A4	0	0,4	0	0	0,4	0,2	0
B1	0,11	0,11	0,22	0,22	0	0,11	0,22
B5	0	0,25	0,25	0,25	0	0	0,25
D2	0	0	0	0	0,33	0,33	0,33
C1	0,33	0	0,17	0,33	0	0,17	0
C2	0,29	0,14	0,29	0,29	0	0	0
C5	0,11	0,22	0,11	0,11	0,22	0	0,22
C7	0	0	0,4	0	0,2	0,4	0
E3	0,25	0,25	0,16	0,25	0	0,13	0
E4	0,17	0	0	0,17	0,17	0,17	0,33
E5	0	0,14	0,29	0,14	0,14	0,29	0

Figure A3.8 Intervention values for each sub-criterion

In our example, starting from Figure A3.8, where: $W_1 = 40$, $W_2 = 40$, $W_3 = 30$, $W_4 = 30$ and $W_{TOT} = (W_1 + W_2 + W_3 + W_4) = 140$, we obtain the normalized weights of Figure A3.9:

$W_{1N} = W_1/(W_{TOT}) = 40/140 = 0.29$; $W_{2N} = W_2/(W_{TOT}) = 0.29$

... and so on.

Measures are characterized by a priority and each possible intervention can be related in different ways to the different measures. If a linear combination is deemed acceptable, we will assign a priority to each intervention (global values calculated in the last row of correlation table).

INTERVENTION	Total W
Intervention 3	72,07
Intervention 6	66,12
Intervention 4	55,01
Intervention I	47,5
Intervention 2	47,33
Intervention 5	44,38
Intervention 7	37,67

Figure A3.9   Total values for interventions

This is how, starting from a checklist, it is possible to build a dominance hierarchy and a priority matrix. The next step will be the elaboration of these values using decision software.

Super Decision Software Data Elaboration

In Figure A3.10, we can see an example of the super decision software clusters used for an industrial application.

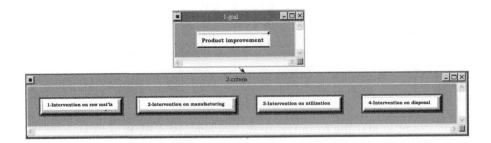

Figure A3.10 Example of super decision software clusters

The first thing to do when using the super decision software is to realize the scheme by building the clusters that make up the programme structure. The highest cluster will be the one containing the main objective and the bottom cluster will be the one containing the possible alternatives:

- first cluster for the goal;

- second cluster for the criteria;

- third cluster for the sub-criteria;

- fourth cluster for the possible alternatives.

When all the nodes have been created, the next step will be to connect them to each other:

- the goal will be connected with all the first level criteria, as represented in Figure A3.10;

- each criterion will be connected only to its related sub-criteria:

    - use of materials considering their performance;
    - prefer materials made from renewable raw materials;
    - prefer recyclable materials;
    - avoid inseparable composite materials.

- each sub-criterion will be connected to all possible alternatives.

Once the scheme has been completed with every connection, it will be possible to introduce the data into the software tool. Using the function 'node comparisons' of the super decision software, a dialogue window will appear in which we can insert values taken from the comparison matrix (Figure A3.11).

Another possible way to insert values is to directly answer the questionnaire corresponding to the matrix using the function illustrated in Figure A3.12.

In the event that all we have is represented by a checklist in which the values do not express a comparison between two alternatives, but only a weight related to each possibility, the software provides us with the option of introducing data by direct data entry.

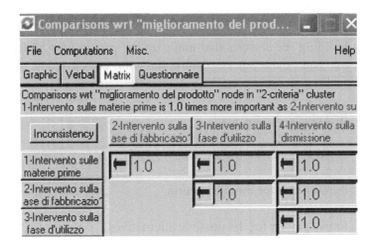

Figure A3.11 Comparison matrix

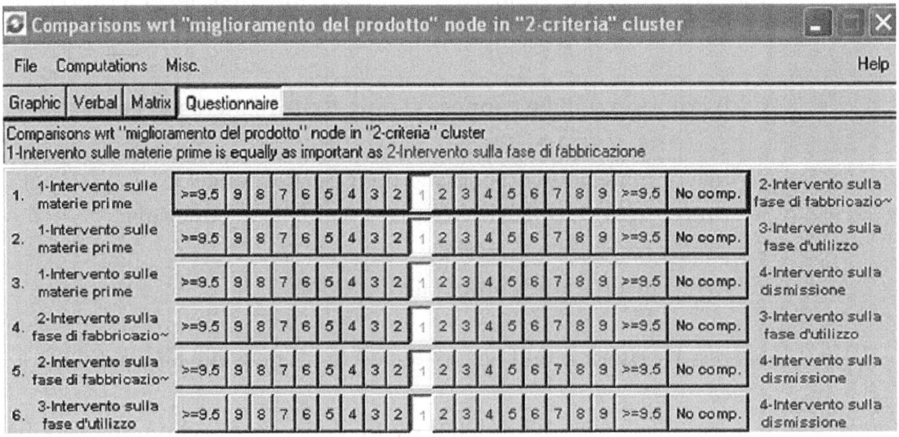

Figure A3.12 Comparison questionnaire

First, we need to set each criterion at the same weight: for a total weight equal to 1, we will set first level criteria weight at 1/(number of criteria). In Figure A3.14 below, an example with four criteria is shown: the weight of each criterion is equal to 0.25.

Then, we need to normalize the weights of the sub-criteria: the weight obtained from the checklist for each sub criterion will be divided by the sum of all sub-criteria connected to the same criterion.

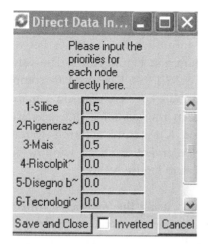

Figure A3.13 Direct data entry

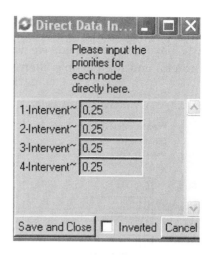

Figure A3.14 Direct data entry with four criteria

Measure	Alternative						
	1	2	3	4	5	6	7
1	0.5	0	0.5	0	0	0	0
2	0.25	0.25	0.5	0	0	0	0
3	0.17	0.33	0.33	0	0	0	0.17
4	0.5	0	0.5	0	0	0	0
5	0	0	0	0	0	1	0
6	0.25	0.13	0	0.13	0.25	0.13	0.13
7	0	0.5	0	0.5	0	0	0
8	0.14	0.14	0.14	0.14	0.14	0.14	0.14
9	0	0.2	0	0.4	0.2	0.2	0
10	0.14	0.14	0.14	0.14	0.14	0.14	0.14
11	1	0	0	0	0	0	0
12	0.4	0	0.2	0	0.2	0.2	0
13	0	0.5	0	0	0	0	0.5
14	0	1	0	0	0	0	0
15	0	0.25	0	0.5	0.25	0	0
16	0.14	0.14	0.14	0.14	0.14	0.14	0.14
17	0.25	0.25	0.5	0	0	0	0
18	0	0.5	0	0	0	0	0.5

Figure A3.15 Correlation index

Once the normalized weights calculated for each criterion and related sub-criteria have been obtained, we will now introduce the priorities between sub-criteria and the possible alternatives shown in Figure A3.13. The values in Figure A3.15 will be used to compile the normalized comparison matrix, where each row contains the correlation index for a measure referred to each possible intervention. Each window will be filled as in Figure A3.16.

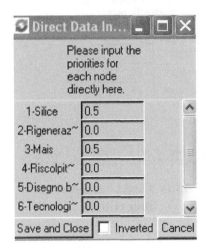

Figure A3.16 Data input in windows

Finally, using the 'synthesis' function of the super decision software, the result will appear in a few minutes: the software processes all the data we have introduced and is able to make the choice in accordance with the decision maker's evaluations. The solution will appear as shown in Figure A3.17.

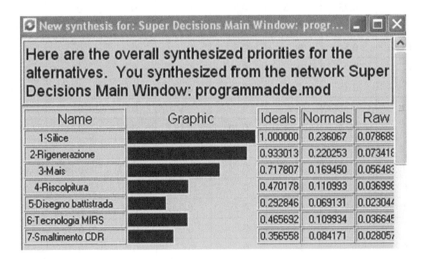

Here are the overall synthesized priorities for the alternatives. You synthesized from the network Super Decisions Main Window: programmadde.mod

Name	Graphic	Ideals	Normals	Raw
1-Silice		1.000000	0.236067	0.078689
2-Rigenerazione		0.933013	0.220253	0.073418
3-Mais		0.717807	0.169450	0.056483
4-Riscolpitura		0.470178	0.110993	0.036998
5-Disegno battistrada		0.292846	0.069131	0.023044
6-Tecnologia MIRS		0.465692	0.109934	0.036645
7-Smaltimento CDR		0.356558	0.084171	0.028057

Figure A3.17 Solution

Conclusion: Sensitivity Analysis

As the dominance hierarchy of possible interventions resulting from the super decision software has been calculated assuming that each criterion has the same weight referred to the goal, an interesting sensitivity analysis may be performed.

This kind of analysis makes it possible to study how these results vary when modifying the priorities of the alternatives. In the graph obtained from this analysis, each line represents the variation of priorities for each intervention and a straight vertical line represents the priority of the criterion we are evaluating (see Figure A3.18): when displacing this straight vertical line, the super decision software calculates the new resulting intervention priority values.

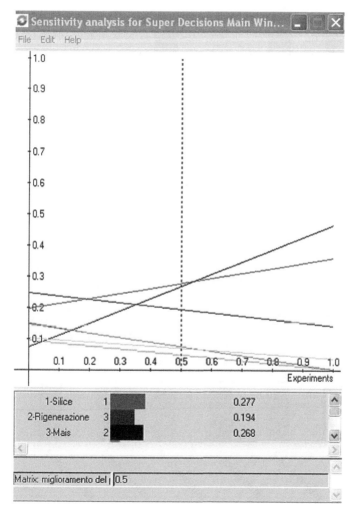

Figure A3.18 Sensitivity analysis

In the following, we will apply sensitivity analysis to our first criterion. The first criterion weight W_1 has been 0.25 up to now as there are four criteria, each with the same priority rate; Figure A3.18 represents what we obtain by applying sensitivity analysis to this criterion. The intervention ratings as calculated by the software are represented in Figures A3.19–A3.26 for different ranges of W_1.

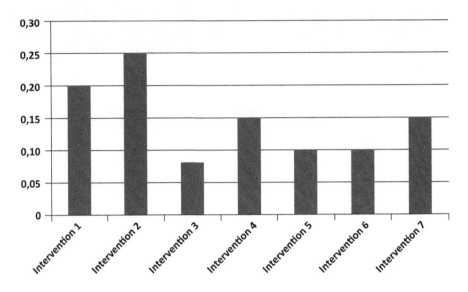

Figure A3.19 Intervention ratings for $0<W_1<0.05$

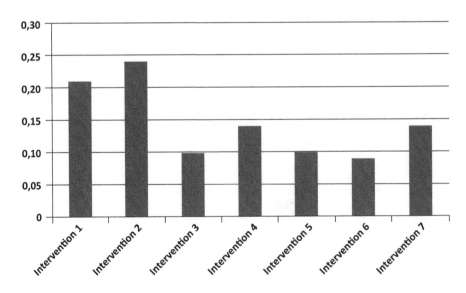

Figure A3.20 Intervention ratings for $0.05<W_1<0.07$

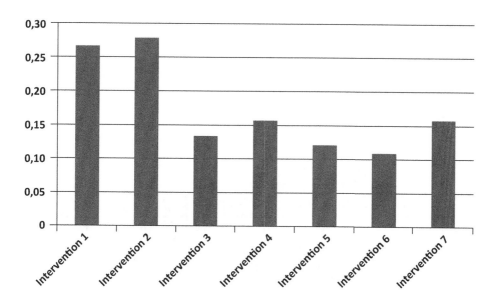

Figure A3.21 Intervention ratings for 0.07<W_1<0.15

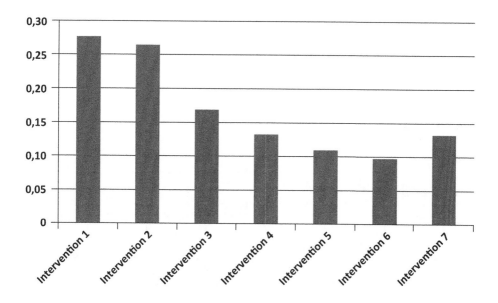

Figure A3.22 Intervention ratings for 0.15<W_1<0.19

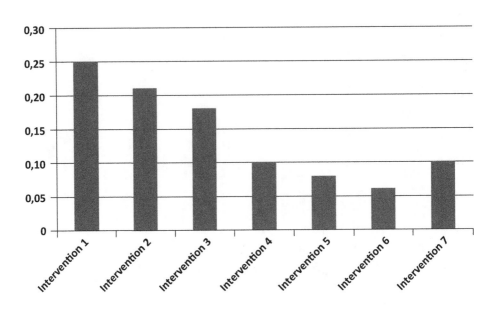

Figure A3.23 Intervention ratings for $0.19 < W_1 < 0.36$

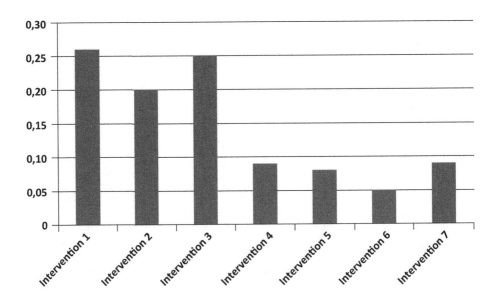

Figure A3.24 Intervention ratings for $0.36 < W_1 < 0.54$

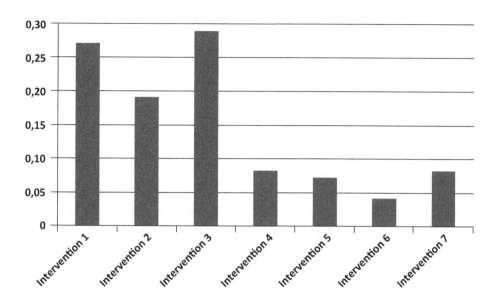

Figure A3.25 Intervention ratings for 0.54<W₁<0.57

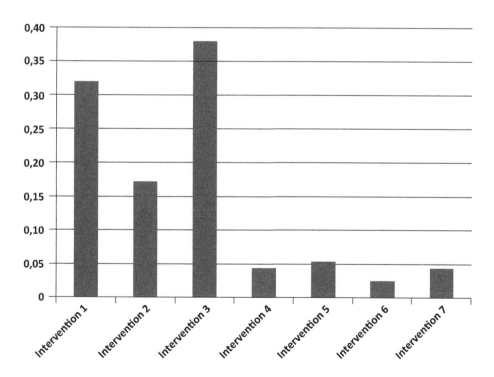

Figure A3.26 Intervention ratings for 0.57<W₁<1

These graphs show how the choice of the intervention to be applied may vary when the priority of a criterion is modified: in our example, the best choices can be:

- intervention 1 if $0.15 < W_1 < 0.54$;

- intervention 2 if $0.07 < W_1 < 0.15$;

- intervention 3 if $0.54 < W_1 < 1$.

Note that when W_1 varies, W_2, W_3 and W_4 will also vary, with the sum $W_1 + W_2 + W_3 + W_4$ remaining equal to 1.

This application of super decision software makes it possible to very easily adapt our results to situations that can vary: this is very important as a continuous study of a specific case often leads to new considerations that imply a variation of some variables or some values in the application.

Appendix 4

Project Evaluation through Impact Analysis Methods: An Example

FEDERICO MINELLE and FRANCO STOLFI

Introduction

In the project evaluation environment, the estimate and measurement of the overall impact (that is, the project outcome) is becoming an increasingly important matter. This means that the full set of benefits yielded by the deployment of each project deliverable, throughout the whole project and product life cycle, is considered.

It is worthwhile to start sharing some basic definitions used frequently in this appendix:

- Project life cycle – this is the time span (for example, months or years) between project start-up and closing, certified by the release of all the (tested and accepted) deliverables contractually identified.

- Project and product life cycle – this is the time span (for example, months or years) from the time that the project final result (output) starts to operate until its revamping/decommissioning or replacement.

Usually, the project evaluation first encompasses economic and financial features. It is performed considering investment cash flow (for example, by month or year), calculated as the differential cash flow in the alternative hypothesis of doing or not doing the project: namely the 'time-framed vector' balance between revenues and expenses accounted for the project from its start-up until the end of its product life cycle. To be more specific, the time-phased overall balance between financial benefits (revenues) and related costs (expenses) is the project net benefit, which will be considered in order to justify the investment to be implemented (see also the section on 'Project Schedule and Cash Flows' in Chapter 15).

The two cash flow components (revenues and expenses), analysed in broad terms, include the following:

- Outflow – expenses/costs required to implement the project (input) until its product deployment (output), costs required to operate the project product (as a difference +/-) compared to not implementing the project. Among these are project implementation costs (more specifically, contractor/supplier, Commercial Off the Shelf (COTS) purchases) and/or operating costs (more specifically, product maintenance, personnel/ICT systems operation, direct/indirect manufacturing materials).

- Inflow – revenues/savings or any other benefit generated by the project result which can be reasonably expressed in monetary terms. Among these are organization savings (for example, personnel displacement/cut-off, internal/external reduction in costs) and/or increased revenues (that is, wider range and volume of billable product/services), which are all made possible by the implementation of the project.

Very often, the evaluation of the project success goes far beyond monetary benefits, expecially for government projects. In order to achieve a comprehensive evaluation, other benefit categories must be included, which are not easily definable in monetary terms, but in any case have to be quantitatively measurable values. Often these other benefits are generated by quality improvements, but, provided they are translated in quantitative terms, are the true success indicators of the project. Examples of other benefits generated are efficiency factors on rendered services/products (for example, the waiting/processing time of a certain case, the number of delayed/incorrectly processed cases, the delivery time of a service/product or the number of customer complaints) and effectiveness factors related to the service/production activity (for example, the scope/volume of free and billable services/products, the volume/range of users or the response time that is suitable to customer needs) or to the organization institutional role (for example, the number of processed cases, the number of issued norms, the number of inspections or prevention/repression initiatives).

The following pages of this appendix will outline a comprehensive model for the 'impact evaluation' of a project developed according to a multidimensional approach which includes as project success indicators, in addition to traditional financial analysis for investment evaluation, non-monetary (but necessarily measurable) benefits. These are specifically emphasized hereafter.

Model Description

The 'impact analysis' model[1] was developed and applied, as an experimental approach to evaluate the 'outcome' of about 50 ICT projects within the monitoring process[2] of 134 e-Government projects, implemented by local government institutions (especially municipalities, provinces/regions, public health structures, education authorities), but co-financed by the Italian Department for Innovation and Technology (central government).

The method source is the *e-GEP* (e-Government Economics Project) framework,[3] an extensive model composed by 92 base indicators, which are hierarchically layered to be grouped according to three main value drivers or evaluation areas: efficiency, effectiveness and democracy (social participation):

> *in such a way as to produce a multidimensional assessment of the public value potentially generated by eGovernment, not limited to just the strictly quantitative financial impact, but also fully including more qualitative impacts.*

The main issue faced by the aforementioned model, and pragmatically solved by the monitoring team, was to 'quantify the qualitative impact'!

The 'impact analysis' model, while retaining the same conceptual framework and structure of the original framework, is significantly simplified and related to the context, reducing the model complexity in order to operationally define each indicator (that is, the data source, computation algorithms and the normalized value range).

---

1   See AgID (Italian Agency for ICT): Guidelines for ICT Quality – *Manual 8: Feasibility Analysis for ICT Procurement*, February 2009 (in Italian). Available at: www.agid.gov.it/agenzia/valutazione-e-monitoraggio/manuali-ict.

2   Performed by a joint venture of specialized consulting firms (Ambrosetti, PRS, Between) under the supervision of CNIPA (now AgID) for the '1st Announcement for e-Government Project Selection', March 2002.

3   A study performed by the consortium of RSO (Italian consulting firm) and LUISS Management (research department of LUISS University of Rome), on a mandate of the e-Government Unit of European Commission: Measurement Framework Final Version, May 2006.

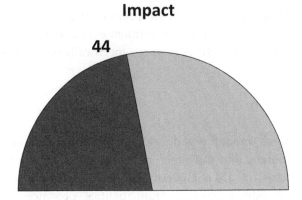

Figure A4.1   Impact overall indicator

The final model is composed of 23 base indicators, hierarchically layered and grouped in the three above-mentioned value drivers (efficiency, effectiveness and e-democracy); each base indicator has a 0–100 range and a relative weight (up to 100 per cent for each layer/group), in order to contribute to the weighted average at the upper layer. At the top of the 'pyramid', an overall impact indicator can therefore be calculated (see the example in Figure A4.1 above),

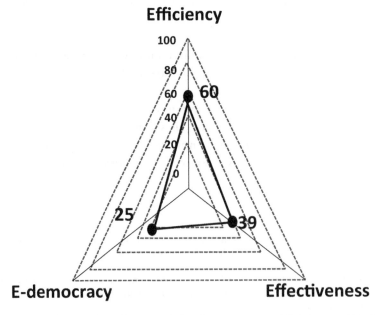

Figure A4.2   Measure of value-drivers indicators: Efficiency, effectiveness and e-democracy

always defined on a 0–100 range. The example shown is a real case for one of the e-Government projects monitored within the above-mentioned assignment.

This overall value was composed of three second-layer indicators, also based on the same value drivers (efficiency, effectiveness and e-democracy). An example of their measurement can be seen in Figure A4.2 on the previous page, together with a short description of their main characteristics and a list of the third-layer indicators upon which they are built.

EFFICIENCY

The main assumption is that better efficiency of e-Government services can be reached only if they are supported by innovation action on organization and their processes. The associated main indicator is composed of three third-level indicators:

- Cashable financial gains – this is a measure of cost saving benefits(or an increase in revenues) generated through the organizational efficiency improvement yielded by the implementation of the project. It includes cost reductions both for personnel (that is, the saved time/effort, valued according to standard unit cost) and for purchased goods/services (that is, the savings on direct/indirect purchased goods/services required for process operations, valued according to historical unit prices).

- Better empowered employees – this is a measure of the number of employees who received formal/informal training in order to operate in the re-engineered – new or innovated – processes (that is, the number of trained employees compared to the total number of individuals involved in the re-engineered processes) and the number of employees assigned to other processes (that is, the number of re-assigned personnel due to a reduction in the personnel needs of the re-engineered process).

- Better organisational and IT architectures – this is a measure of the number of 'transactions' completed by individuals/businesses on the new/re-engineered processes (that is, the number of transactions via the new ICT implemented channels for any single process compared to the previous total number of transactions); the number of re-engineered processes (that is, the number of reengineered processes as a result of the implementation of the project compared to the previous total number of traditional processes); the number of digitized documents managed in the re-engineered processes (that is, the number of digitized and authenticated documents generated/accepted in the re-engineered processes implemented by the project compared to the previous total number of traditional processed documents).

An example of how to represent efficiency area indicators is represented in Figure A4.3 opposite.

EFFECTIVENESS

This measures the increased benefits for the main stakeholders (individuals or businesses) as a direct consequence of better local government activity, provided that they are driven by e-Government policies/operations based on ICT solutions. The associated main indicator is composed of two third-level indicators:

- Reduced administrative burden – this indicator is composed of the time and costs saved by the main stakeholders (individuals and businesses) due to new services utilized.

- Customer satisfaction – this indicator is composed of certified limits on process malfunctions (that is, the number of claimed malfunctions on re-engineered processes of the project), the average reduction in case processing time (that is, the average time to process a case, end-to-end, compared to the previous average time), the usage of online services on extended time (that is, the number of transactions during unattended service hours) and the average services usability (that is, the control of online functions usability, according to relevant quality ICT metrics).

An example of how to represent effectiveness area indicators is given in Figure A4.4 opposite.

E-DEMOCRACY

The main assumption is that an increased access to better (that is, more accurate, updated and easy to understand) information is a driving factor for the increased and proactive participation of individuals and business representatives in local government policy definition and control, in order to

Value drivers	After op's time		Sub-areas	After op's time		Indicators	After op's time
A	Efficiency	60	A1	Cashable financial gains	50	A1.1	Personnel cost reductions	100
						A1.2	Purchases cost reductions	0
			A2	Better empowered employees	100	A2.1	Trained employees	100
						A2.2	Employees assigned to other processes	100
			A3	Better organisational and IT architecture	40	A3.1	Transactions completed on the new channels (citizens)	16
						A3.2	Transactions completed on the new channels (enterprises)	20
						A3.3	Reengineered processes	50
						A3.4	Digitalized documents in the reengineered processes	94

Figure A4.3 Efficiency area indicators

Value drivers	After op's time		Sub-areas	After op's time		Indicators	After op's time
B	Effectiveness	39	B1	Reduced administrative burden	12	B1.1	Time saved for citizens	10
						B1.2	Time saved for businesses	13
						B1.3	Costs saved for citizens	11
						B1.4	Costs saved for businesses	12
			B2	User satisfaction and service level	65	B2.1	Limits on process mal-functions	99
						B2.2	Average reduction of file processing time (end-to-end)	64
						B2.3	Usage of online services on extended time (off teller hours)	60
						B2.4	Average services usability	49

Figure A4.4 Effectiveness area indicators

improve the democratic process of the social community. The associated main indicator is composed of two third-level indicators:

- Transparency and accountability – this indicator is calculated by the number of services enabling online case tracking (individuals and businesses) for the re-engineered services.

- Participation – this indicator is composed of the user shift on new channels both by individuals and businesses (that is, the number of transactions on new channels compared to the total number of transactions for the same process), service coverage on the district area for both individuals and businesses (that is, the proportion of district citizens/businesses potentially reached by the online services) and digital authentication/registration for services used both by citizens and businesses (that is, the number of authentications/registrations compared to the total district citizens/ businesses actually reachable by the online services).

An example of how to represent e-democracy area indicators is given in Figure A4.5 opposite.

In order to ensure that the financial side of the project is not overlooked, the same example shows how the 'impact analysis' model represents cash flow values in the following tables (see Table A4.1 for inflow and outflow detailed values and Table A4.2 for the cash flow balance), which consider the governmental institution 'value for money', as well as the 'public value', including the whole set of stakeholders (citizens and businesses).

According to accounting conventions, brackets mean a negative cash flow, while bold figures represent:

- in the time period cash flow: the first time period when the balance turns into a positive value (hopefully, the end of main project expenditures and the start-up of product/service operations);

- in the cumulative cash flow: the first time period when the cumulative balance turns into a positive value (the widely used Payback Period (PBP) financial indicator). In the example, the inclusion of stakeholders' benefits moves the PBP more than two time periods earlier.

Value drivers	After op's time	Sub-areas	After op's time		Indicators	After op's time
C Democracy	25	C1 Transparency and accountability	52	C1.1	Services enabling online case tracking	52
		C2 Participation	10	C2.1	User shift (citizens) on new channels	10
				C2.2	User shift (businesses) on new channels	10
				C2.3	Services coverage on the district area (citizens)	32
				C2.4	Services coverage on the district area (businesses)	6
				C2.5	Digital authentication for services use (citizens)	0
				C2.6	Digital authentication/ registration for services use (businesses)	0

Figure A4.5   E-democracy area indicators

Table A4.1   Cash flow array

Cash flow – inflow and outflow (values in k€)

Time period		1	2	3	4	5	6	7	8
Outflow	Implementation project costs	249	2,266	1,016	0	0	0	0	0
	Operations product costs	40	66	364	186	279	270	257	244
	Total outflow	*289*	*2,332*	*1,380*	*186*	*279*	*270*	*257*	*244*
Inflow	Gov't personnel (equivalent) savings	270	752	911	956	1,003	1,053	1,104	1,051
	Gov't purchases cost reduction	0	0	0	0	8	22	21	20
	Citizens' time (equivalent) savings	163	231	616	614	641	677	718	696
	Businesses' time (tantamount) Savings	0	5	143	132	129	186	203	219
	Citizens' purchases cost reduction	38	54	116	117	124	133	143	138
	Businesses purchases cost reduction	0	1	14	13	13	20	23	25
	Total inflow	*471*	*1,043*	*1,800*	*1,832*	*1,918*	*2,091*	*2,212*	*2,149*

Table A4.2   Cash flow balance

Cash flow – inflow and outflow balance, by time period and cumulative (values in k€)									
Time period		1	2	3	4	5	6	7	8
Cash flow (by time period)	Total (overall)	183	(1,288)	420	1,647	1,640	1,822	1,955	1,904
	Total (gov't)	(18)	(1,579)	(469)	771	732	805	868	826
Cash flow (cum.)	Total (overall)	183	(1,104)	(685)	962	2,602	4,424	6,379	8,284
	Total (gov't)	(18)	(1,597)	(2,066)	(1,295)	(563)	242	1,110	1,937

Impact Analysis at the Project Closeout and during the Product Life Cycle

In the project closeout process (unless the project has been prematurely terminated), an impact analysis should be performed, applying usual approaches as detailed in Chapter 9. At that point, all the relevant indicators based on project performance are calculated from actual data: time, cost and product quality (the latter, in the worst case, can be reliably estimated) and therefore an 'almost definitive' project business case evaluation can be performed (definitive benefits will be evaluated only after the project closeout). It is suggested that this evaluation be an item of the 'closeout meeting' to be held during the closing process (as defined by the PMBOK® Guide), by the Project Manager, together with the project team and, subsequently, with the Project Management Steering Committee (the Project Board, to use the terminology of PRINCE2®).

Any deviation from the current (and initial) baseline may support an eventual action plan to select a more suitable path for the product (for example, by an ad hoc maintenance programme, an increased user/customer support initiative).

In the meantime, just because project business justification has to consider the whole product life cycle timespan, in the project closeout process, the Project Management Steering Committee (or otherwise the Project Manager personally) has the specific task of planning a post-project impact review, assigning appropriate responsibility and accountability within the organization (for example, Operation Manager, Programme Manager, PMO).

This final evaluation, to be done after a suitable time (usually after 6–12 months, allowing for the transition to a 'steady state') in order for the whole impact of project/product to be detected, has the purpose of reaching an after-the-fact view of the actual value of the project and its product, in accordance with the PRINCE2® criteria.

The argument that could arise is if any project/product pitfall is evidenced only at that time, it is probably too late to recover it! This is not always true (that is, in case of a patch or improved product release), but, in any case, it will constitute a 'lesson learned' for the project knowledge base of the same organization. We are always able to learn from previous errors!

In summary, for every project closeout event, the impact analysis should include the following actions, which are all related to the business case justification:

- to verify if the project output (product) is still aligned with the assumptions of the initial cost/benefit analysis;

- to analyse any cause which eventually drove the project and its output (product) away from the planned impact profile;

- to register the 'lessons learned' about adherence (or not) to the planned (and eventually updated) impact profile;

- to prepare (and then perform at the proper time) the 'post-project cost/benefit review', which should include:

  - project and operational process organization'
  - the timing and approach of the post-project review'
  - metrics/indicators to be measured and their relevant sources'
  - the impact profile (planned/updated baseline) to be matched with actual metrics/indicator values.

Summary of Operational Mode and Advantages

In the operational mode, the following evaluation process can be adopted:

- Costs and benefit reasonably expressed in *monetary terms*, applying the proper financial concepts (see the sections on 'Project Schedule and Cash Flows' and 'The Economic Evaluation of Construction Projects' in Chapter 15).

- The part of the benefit that cannot (easily) be expressed in monetary terms, but that must be expressed in 'quantitatively measurable' values: first the description of the affected matter (for example, the average time of case processing or the percentage of claims in processed cases) and then an adequate metric must be selected (even a proxy one or more) to measure and consequently evaluate the planned/actual effect.

In a timewise perspective, the impact evaluation must be performed by adopting the same approach/model in order to ensure uniformity and consistency across the whole evaluation process, and must be performed throughout the project life cycle, but also considering the project and product life cycle, at least in its first period after deployment (for example, after 6–12 months in operation).

More specifically, the impact evaluation should be performed:

- before the project start-up, during the feasibility study, in order to contribute to take the decision on whether to proceed or not to proceed with the project investment (*ex ante* evaluation);

- during the implementation of the project, in pre-defined milestones of the project life cycle or at ad hoc points (that is, triggered by significant changes to the project baseline or product outcome) in order to verify if the project business justification is still valid and the expected outcomes of the project are reasonably feasible (*in itinere* evaluation).

- after project closeout, namely during the first operations period (for example, 6–12 months) in order to evaluate how many expected benefits were actually yielded (*ex post* evaluation).

Provided that the model is consistently applied, it makes it possible to obtain uniform project and product performances evaluations, based on a solid ground of measurable metrics, using comparable indicators along the time for the whole project and product life cycle.

Should this approach be applied to a set of many comparable projects, it would make it possible to gain a sound benchmarking tool for portfolio management.

In addition, the *ex post* evaluation is a powerful tool to analyse root causes which might have affected the project so that it failed to deliver the expected cost/benefit output. If still feasible, it could point out corrective actions that could eventually recover the target benefits.

Index

For Product Safety Concerns and Information please contact our EU
representative GPSR@taylorandfrancis.com Taylor & Francis Verlag GmbH,
Kaufingerstraße 24, 80331 München, Germany

Printed and bound by CPI Group (UK) Ltd, Croydon, CR0 4YY

01/05/2025

01858363-0003